Public Bureaucracy

Values and Perspectives

James A. Medeiros

David E. Schmitt

Northeastern Universit

DUXBURY PRESS *North Scituate, Massachusetts*

Duxbury Press

A DIVISION OF WADSWORTH PUBLISHING COMPANY, INC.

Public Bureaucracy: Values and Perspectives was edited and prepared
for composition by Sara Hill. Interior design was provided by Dorothy
Thompson, and the cover was designed by Oliver Kline.

L.C. Cat. Card No.: 76-9927
ISBN 0-87872-118-5
PRINTED IN THE UNITED STATES OF AMERICA
2 3 4 5 6 7 8 9 — 81 80 79 78

To
Jamie, Kerry Ann
and
Alana, Michael, and Kara

Contents

Preface

Today, government touches virtually every facet of our lives. It supports, regulates, and promotes private business. It monitors our environment, seeks to promote our health, and attempts to encourage sexual equality. Public agencies even operate some of our key services, such as subway transportation and the production of electrical energy.

The scope and complexity of these tasks have left legislatures and elected executives increasingly displaced by the public bureaucracy. Government agencies not only administer programs and deliver services, they make policy decisions in all areas of government activity. Yet government bureaucrats are not elected, nor are the nature and role of public bureaucracy carefully defined by the Constitution.

Also, public bureaucracy confronts contemporary demands and pressures of vital consequence. Growing budgetary restrictions and scarcer resources require greater effectiveness and efficiency. Continuing concern for racial and sexual equality as well as growing demands for the protection of individuality require modified management strategies, and the growing policy-making role of public bureaucracy requires the strengthening of political controls. What approaches and techniques will enable public bureaucracy to meet contemporary pressures? What values and goals should government agencies pursue in meeting today's challenges? These issues will provide the focus of this book. We shall first describe the role and functions of public bureaucracy in the context of its internal and external environment. Then we shall explore three major avenues to the study, operation and improvement of public bureaucracy, namely, the machine, humane, and political.

The machine focus deals with the technical and structural facets of public administration and concerns itself with such values as productivity and efficiency. Humane bureaucracy centers on people within organizations and concentrates on such human values as self-fulfillment and individuality. The political approach analyzes techniques for increasing democratic controls over government agencies and has as its principal value the notion that public bureaucracy should be servant and not master.

Each of these values — machine, humane, and political — has a necessary and legitimate place in a democratic society. In view of contemporary budgetary and economic pressures, machine values have become increasingly important. In light of contemporary demands for equality and individuality, humane bureaucracy approaches are an important element in determining the degree of equality and stability in American society. Because of the increased size, complexity, and scope of public bureaucracy, techniques and strategies aimed at greater political control help determine the very ability of our political system to be democratic.

Thus, public bureaucracy must develop capacities for the achievement of all three values. Contemporary problems demand more than an emphasis on any one approach. Similarly, today's students should have a familiarity with specific tools and techniques, not merely an understanding of concepts for measuring the performance of public bureaucracy. This book, then, seeks to provide a balanced introduction to the study of public bureaucracy, with consideration of its environment, its intellectual heritage, and its contemporary techniques. We believe that the development of multidimensional capacities reflecting machine, humane, and political values to be an urgent necessity for public bureaucracy in America.

Many people contributed to the development of this book. We appreciate especially the advice and suggestions of the following professors at Northeastern University: David W. Barkley (retired), George E. Berkley, Robert E. Gilbert, Seth I. Hirshorn, Edward M. Humberger, Chester A. Janiak, and Wendell C. Lawther. James A. Medeiros wishes to thank the National Association of Schools of Public Affairs and Administration (NASPAA) for a fellowship that resulted in assignment to an agency characterized by sensitivity to the values noted above. Particular thanks are extended to Maxim Dem'chak, Dr. Gertrude T. Hunter, Andrew Johnston, and Edward Montminy, all of the U.S. Public Health Service. The suggestions of Walter W. Mode and the research assistance of Howard E. Landau are greatly appreciated.

The editorial assistance of Sara Hill is appreciated as is the advice of reviewers and students on various drafts. Above all, the support of our wives, Joan and Gabrielle, and the inspiration derived from our children, to whom this book is dedicated, have been a vital factor in the book's development. Any remaining limitations are, of course, the responsibility of the authors.

The Roles, Scope, and Values of Public Bureaucracy

1

Modern society is organized society. Factories, business concerns, government agencies, and private social clubs operate by means of a complex series of rules and regulations. Even communes, which emerged in part as a reaction against the organizational confines of contemporary social systems, establish organizational frameworks and frequently adhere to strict systems of informal rules. But it is formal groups that constitute the dominant organizational structure in contemporary Western nations.

Nearly all organizations in modern society are structured as bureaucracies, and bureaucracies influence every facet of American life. Anyone who has ever collected unemployment or welfare checks, veterans' benefits or social security, has come into contact with a bureaucracy. The air we breathe, the water we drink, the food we eat is regulated or inspected by a government bureaucracy; so are the medicines we take, the houses we live in, and the cars we drive. Even our family, social, and sex lives are influenced by government operating through a bureaucracy. Parents may lose their children if government agencies, with court approval, view them as unfit. State inspectors attempt to enforce age limits on liquor consumption. Abortion, contraceptives, and sexual practices are all the subject of public law, administered by public employees. Just what is this bureaucracy whose activities so pervade our lives? And where did it come from?

The word "bureaucracy" denotes a way of structuring a group of people to achieve specified goals. It is characterized by specific organizing principles, namely specialization of function, action according to fixed rules, and a hierarchical, or chain of command, authority structure, with power concentrated at the top of the pyramid. In a simple hierarchy, people are organized into ranks, with each rank superior to the one below it. A bureaucracy is typically divided into subunits based on the division-of-labor principle in which people hired for their specialized skills accomplish specific tasks or functions. Coordination and control of subunits and employees are based largely on the orders of superiors within the hierarchy.[1]

The Constitution makes no mention of the word "bureaucracy," yet today it lies at the core of the American political-social system, a result of the size and complexity of modern life. Public bureaucracy — the growing, interconnected system of government agencies and offices — is the administrative arm of the legislative, executive, and judicial branches of government. Many of these agencies perform economic or social functions for society. For example, as a result of presidential and congressional concern in the 1930s that it was the government's duty to provide a retirement and certain "welfare" income for citizens, an agency was established to create and enforce a system of mandatory saving called social security. And this agency, the Social Security Administration, is now embedded in American life, its programs affecting nearly everyone who holds a job (and many who do not).

Now, in the late twentieth century, the Social Security Administration is just one of over a hundred federal, or national, departments and agencies — bureaucracies — employing nearly 3 million people. And over 10 million people are employed by state and local government bureaucracies, making about 13 million people, or about 1 in 6 of all employed Americans, who work at all levels of government. Thus, public, or government, bureaucracy is the largest employer in the United States, and it continues to grow. This rise in public employment causes an inevitable increase in government expenditures; in salaries alone the federal government spends over 37 billion dollars a year, with state and local governments spending over 100 billion dollars annually.

Largely because of its size and complexity, public bureaucracy today is often associated with terms like "red tape," "inefficiency," even "corruption." News stories of welfare and Medicare fraud perpetrated by the public are common, as are tales about lengthy delays in receiving needed aid because of "bureaucratic inaction." Yet, "bureaucracy" is more than a synonym for "heartless," more than a cliché for the Kafka-esque horrors of modern government. It remains, for example, a method by which beneficial change is attempted. The instinctive reaction of most people who perceive a problem is to form an organization to oversee its solution.

This book will review the role played by public bureaucracy in modern society; it will examine the scope of public administration and review the problems it faces. "Public administration" refers to the managerial activities of government officials and workers designed to achieve public policy objectives by means of the bureaucratic structure. Of course, such activities are often misdirected, and they may fail. Our underlying premise, however, is that public bureaucracy has the potential for substantial flexibility and the capacity to carry out its tasks in a responsible and responsive manner — responding with efficiency and sensitivity not only to its own managers and employees but to the citizens it serves and to the elected officials whose duty it is to exercise control over it.

THE ROLES OF PUBLIC BUREAUCRACY

Making Public Policy

Followers of public affairs recognize the importance of legislative, judicial, and executive decisions in shaping the quality of contemporary life. Some citizens believe that any fundamental government policy is determined in the Oval Office of the White House, in the august (but often empty) chambers of Congress, or in the reasoned, deliberative sessions of the Supreme Court. It is often further presumed that this pattern of formal policy making is replicated at the state or local governmental levels. But this view of public policy making is only partially correct, since it fails to recognize the critical role performed by public bureaucracies in shaping public policy.[2]

Public bureaucracy, in fact, lies at the very core of the American political-constitutional system. If we define politics as the process of determining "who gets what, when, and how," then public bureaucracies are by any standard firmly entrenched in the midst of this "resource allocation" process.[3] Although bureaucracies ordinarily are officially subservient to elected executives, legislatures, and courts, their size, their expert staffs, and their linkage with interest groups give them a power potentially unmatched by other coordinate branches of government. While it is comforting to believe that bureaucracies are closely regulated by law and watched carefully by judges, legislators, and chief executives, their political and technical resources often preclude such oversight.

To understand the role played by American bureaucracy, one needs to recognize that it is born out of the interplay of competing political interests and values. The longevity and health of public bureaucracies depend on the nature of the political interactions they foster and maintain. Public bureaucracy and politics are, therefore, inseparable.[4] Although the creative and independent impulses among public agencies may vary, most are quite aggressive in protecting or expanding their role. To defend the legitimacy of their actions they will lobby in Congress, court favor and sympathy with executives (or challenge them as well), marshal strong legal defenses in test court cases, and recruit new supporters. By carefully cultivating alliances with kindred supporters within government or within society, bureaucracies can develop into powerful arsenals of influence.[5] An environmental agency, for example, may consciously elicit the cooperation of conservation groups, garner the support of legislators, and challenge the decisions of other government agencies — all for the purpose of enhancing its own capacity to survive and to achieve its objectives.

This political aspect of public bureaucracy, however, does not come without a price. Alliances can be beneficial or they can be damaging. An alliance with an interest group may help foster public representation for that interest, but it may also force an agency to become the captive of an external, narrow group.

Equally important, the political nature of bureaucracies complicates our ability to determine what their role should be. Since the American political system is one of competing values and interests, bureaucratic action can always be "justified" according to one or more of the conflicting values. We ask bureaucracy to perform public tasks, to be representative, to be efficient, to be subservient to political leaders, to be sympathetic toward citizens with whom they deal, and to be generous to their employees. With such a broad political value spectrum from which to choose, bureaucracies can defend almost any action by claiming responsiveness to one or more of the above standards.

Public bureaucracy is important because politics is important. Perhaps the paramount role performed by public bureaucracy is involvement in public policy making. This role is fulfilled by bureaucracy for several reasons, as we have already indicated. It has the skills, legitimate authority, and clientele contact. But its role in policy making is also enlarged because of the constraints on the more formal branches of government. Legislators, for example, often are unable to resolve many of the practical aspects of legislation; they simply cannot anticipate all of the specific cases or circumstances that might arise in implementing a law. Furthermore, tying the hands of administrators with needless restrictions would lead to inefficiency and inaction. A dam needed for flood control, for example, might have to be built unnecessarily large, thus wasting money and possibly damaging the local environment. Or it might not get built at all. Also, on sensitive political issues, elected officials sometimes deliberately pass on to administrators decision-making authority to save themselves from the embarrassment of taking a stand or to facilitate achieving a compromise where it might not otherwise be possible to reach agreement.

The policy statements of courts, executives, and legislators, then, are often characterized by mixed objectives, broad generalities, and unclear commands, so public bureaucracies contribute to the making and formulation of public policy by interpreting law and reconstructing it into more operational dimensions. Indeed, political conflict often arises when groups or other formal participants challenge the manner in which that interpretation or restructuring is undertaken.[6] Interpretations of civil rights legislation by government agencies such as the Department of Health, Education, and Welfare or the Department of Justice have been particularly subject to controversy and challenge.

An indirect consequence of public bureaucracy's political role is the stability and continuity it provides to the political system. No matter what changes occur among the elected legislators and executives, radical and sudden changes in policy are unlikely in most domestic areas. The political system tends to respond sluggishly to changes mandated by elected politicians, in large part because of the major role played by public administrators in the making and implementation of policy. Bureaucrats may, for example, resist outright directives they believe to be erroneous or immoral. More typically, they may reinterpret directives in a way consistent with past policy. Public bureaucracy provides an ongoing instrumentality for carrying out and moderating the political functions of society. Of course, this role benefits the status quo and limits the power of voters to alter public policy through their elected representatives.

Delivering Services

By managing and implementing public policies, public bureaucracies serve an instrumental function. They provide public health programs, monitor the purity of the air, attempt to control crime, maintain the safety of our drinking water and food, and provide a host of other services. But these programs are not self-achieving. Public services require organization. Skills have to be meshed, employees have to be trained, an operational structure has to be perfected, and the final output evaluated. Even where services are contracted out to private business, as in refuse collection, a public organizational capacity must exist for control purposes.

Representing

Generally, people think of representation only in terms of the executive or legislative branch of government. While these centers of power represent many interests, public organizations also reflect and represent diverse constituencies. Their alliance patterns with certain groups external to the organization are useful as a channel for group demands. Local medical associations representing physicians may exert considerable influence over health agencies, which need the cooperation of health personnel. Similarly, organized labor tends to have a significant voice in the Department of Labor, which implements policies of importance not only for union members but also for the entire country. Thus, medical groups and organized labor have influence on public policy not only through elected legislators and executives; they also help shape public policy by their interactions with government agencies. Of course, the pressures of private groups upon public bureaucracy may seriously reduce its responsiveness to broader interests or to elected public officials.

The heterogeneous but nonelected internal composition of organizations may also provide an opportunity for the representation of a wide variety of ideas and values. Some have argued that because of its membership mix, bureaucracy is far more representative of the broad spectrum of American ideas and values than the House or Senate.[7] While Caucasian male lawyers predominate in many legislatures, public agencies typically have a more diverse socioeconomic composition. Bureaucracy, therefore, is a supplementary source of political representation. We shall later see, however, that such representation may not necessarily result in policies of benefit to broad interests.

Educating

Not only do agencies administer public programs, they also help create expectations about public policy. While they participate in shaping political demands, they are also a major educative or — some would say — propaganda source for the government. The critical and controversial CBS television documentary *The Selling of the Pentagon,* for example, described the public relations activities of the Department of Defense. The film purported to demonstrate the Pentagon's use of scare tactics and sensationalism to arouse citizens to the threat of communism. (The Department of Defense criticized the film for failing to tell the "whole story.")

While some agency public relations work may be little more than self-serving promotion, other educational efforts are quite necessary to the formation of public policy. It seems appropriate that the Department of Transportation remind elected officials and the public of the need for balanced transportation systems and that the Department of Justice remind officials of the need to scrutinize business practices that might adversely affect us. It also may be fitting that generals and admirals remind citizens and public officials of defense needs and develop support for such activities and their agencies. Public agencies require political support if they are to obtain adequate resources from limited public treasuries. The difficulty is that self-serving and misleading presentations may hinder rather than advance the knowledge of citizens and politicians. While the educative function of bureaucracy is an important and necessary one, it can waste public money when carried to excess, and it can distort national priorities. At a more fundamental level, government agencies often help create the very public opinion that is supposed to be a democratic constraint upon their activities.

THE SCOPE OF
PUBLIC BUREAUCRACY

In 1801 only slightly more than 2000 individuals worked for the federal government. Today, it employs roughly 2.8 million people. Whereas at the end of the eighteenth century the total federal expenditures for all civilian and military programs amounted to 7 million dollars, the fiscal year 1975 outlay was 324.6 billion dollars. This figure is expected to and should continue to expand into the 1980s.[8]

These facts point to the obvious conclusion that government has expanded considerably from the early days of the country. Today, the scope and size of public bureaucracy are vast, and most of this growth has come quite recently. For example, in 1950 6.4 million people worked for the government; since that time the country has witnessed an increase in public employment of over 100 percent. Although it is common to cite the expansion of the bureaucracy as evidence of a "march of power" to Washington, such is not really the case, for state and local public bureaucracies are in the aggregate not only larger but also have been expanding at a far more rapid pace. For example, between 1950 and 1972, employment by state governments rose by more than 163 percent, while local governments increased their employment rosters from 3.2 million to 7.9 million during this period, an increase of almost 150 percent. At the same time, employment in federal agencies rose by only 33 percent.[9] Table 1.1 illustrates this growth trend of local and state bureaucracies. From it we can see that the percentage of federal government employees compared to state and local government employees has dropped considerably. Budgetary pressures may curb the rate of growth in the future but a permanent reduction in the number of government workers is unlikely.

The growth in public employment is paralleled by the rise in government expenditures. The total budgets of all levels of government now represent roughly one-third of the gross national product (the total of all goods and services produced in the country in one year) and it has been predicted that they could reach 50 percent of the gross national product within fifteen years if present spending patterns continue.[10]

Indeed, the scope of public bureaucracy is reflected in many ways. Not only can it be understood by the extent of budgetary outlays and by

TABLE 1.1   Government Employment and Population, 1946–76

Fiscal year	Government employment				Population	
	Federal executive branch[1] (thousands)	State and local governments (thousands)	All governmental units (thousands)	Federal as percent of all governmental units	Total United States (thousands)	Federal employment per 1,000 population
1946	2,666	3,305	5,971	44.6	141,936	18.8
1947	2,082	3,568	5,650	36.8	144,698	14.4
1948	2,044	3,776	5,820	35.1	147,208	13.9
1949	2,075	3,906	5,981	34.7	149,767	13.9
1950	1,934	4,078	6,012	32.2	152,271	12.7
1951	2,456	4,031	6,487	37.9	154,878	15.9
1952	2,574	4,134	6,708	38.4	157,553	16.3
1953	2,532	4,282	6,814	37.2	160,184	15.8
1954	2,382	4,552	6,934	34.4	163,026	14.6
1955	2,371	4,728	7,099	33.4	165,931	14.3
1956	2,372	5,064	7,436	31.9	168,903	14.0
1957	2,391	5,380	7,771	30.8	171,984	13.9
1958	2,355	5,630	7,985	29.5	174,882	13.5
1959	2,355	5,806	8,161	28.9	177,830	13.2
1960[2]	2,371	6,073	8,444	28.1	180,671	13.1
1961[2]	2,407	6,295	8,702	27.7	183,691	13.1
1962	2,485	6,533	9,018	27.6	186,538	13.3
1963[3]	2,490	6,834	9,324	26.7	189,242	13.2
1964[3]	2,469	7,236	9,705	25.4	191,889	12.9
1965	2,496	7,683	10,179	24.5	194,303	12.8
1966	2,664	8,259	10,923	24.4	196,560	13.6
1967	2,877	8,730	11,607	24.8	198,712	14.5
1968	2,951	9,141	12,092	24.4	200,706	14.7
1969[4]	2,980	9,496	12,476	23.9	202,677	14.7
1970[2]	2,884	9,869	12,753	22.6	204,875	14.1
1971[2]	2,823	10,257	13,080	21.6	207,045	13.6
1972	2,770	10,640	13,410	20.7	208,842	13.3
1973	2,722	11,065	13,787	19.7	210,396	12.9
1974	2,794	11,501	14,295	19.5	211,909	13.2
1975 (est.)	2,802	(5)	- - - - - -	19.1	213,651	13.1
1976 (est.)	2,802	(5)	- - - - - -	18.6	215,379	13.0

[1] Covers total end-of-year employment in full-time permanent, temporary, part-time, and intermittent positions except for summer workers under the President's Youth Opportunity Campaign; and beginning in 1970, excludes various disadvantaged worker-trainee programs.

[2] Includes temporary employees for the decennial census.

[3] Excludes 7,411 project employees in 1963 and 406 project employees in 1964 for the public works acceleration program.

[4] On Jan. 1, 1969, 42,000 civilian technicians of the Army and Air Force National Guard converted by law from State to Federal employment status. They are included in the Federal employment figures in this table after and including 1969.

[5] An official projection of State and local government employment is not available. The percentages shown for these years are consistent with a range of reasonable estimates based on recent trends in population and State and local government activity.

Source: *Special Analyses: Budget of the United States Government, Fiscal Year 1976* (Washington, D.C.: U.S. Government Printing Office, 1975), p. 136.

the numbers of individuals who work for government, it can also be understood by recognizing the heterogeneity of the governmental agencies that dot the organizational landscape. The increasing functions of government have led to the establishment of a large number of separate organizational structures, as shown for the federal government in table 1.2. Many of these separate departments and agencies can exert direct or indirect influence on the life of every person who lives in the United States. To cite but one example, the levels of employment and inflation may be directly affected by the monetary policies of the Federal Reserve Board or by decisions made by the departments of Agriculture, Commerce, and State. Of course, other policies and agencies also have an impact on the economy. State and local agencies can also affect the economic health of their jurisdictional areas, and in some cases even the nation, as in the case of New York City's financial crisis.

The scope of public bureaucracy can also be understood if we recognize not only the immense differences *between* public organizations but also the myriad of interests and suborganizations reflected *within* each public organization. Viewed in this light, a public organization becomes a complex environment representing a tremendous diversity of values, skills, and behavior. Nowhere is this internal heterogeneity more clearly illustrated than within the federal Department of Health, Education, and Welfare, which has no less than one hundred quasi-autonomous organizational units, as noted in table 1.3.

Thus, public bureaucracy is large, at all levels of government; it is expensive; and it is complex. Beyond this, its scope and complexity are reflected by the countless *professions* and *skills* of public employees, which represent a broad and often competing array of interests and talents. Found throughout the formal structure of public bureaucracy is an impressive array of lawyers, biochemists, land-use experts, educators, engineers, transcribers, and many others, whose interactions cause both creative growth and professional conflict (see chapter 2 for a more detailed discussion of this point). A series of necessary technical processes also abound, including budget analysis, job-description analysis, personnel evaluation, cost-benefit measurement, decision-making dynamics, guidelines formulation, testing, and program measurement. Conceivably, every skill that contemporary university students are developing could find a place within the public bureaucratic enterprise.

Why is this so? Could we not have a return to simpler, less cumbersome mechanisms for the implementation and management of public policies? Undoubtedly, current economic difficulties will contribute to some staff cutback or reduced rates of growth in many agencies, at least in the short run. But the growth of public administration has roots that make radical decreases improbable. In fact, unemployment and other problems produce demands for *more* public-service jobs and programs. The complexity and size of public bureaucracy are a manifestation of the

TABLE 1.2   List of Major Federal Agencies and Number of Personnel

Paid Civilian Employment in the Federal Government, by Agency: 1960 to 1973

Agency	1960	1965	1969	1970	1971	1972	1973[1]
All agencies[2]	2,398,704	2,527,915[3]	3,076,414	2,921,909	2,862,894	2,811,779	2,777,586
Legislative branch	22,886	25,947	29,577	30,715	32,280	33,688	32,782
Judicial branch	4,992	5,904	6,708	6,887	7,730	8,243	8,585
Executive branch	2,370,826	2,496,064	3,040,129	2,884,307	2,822,884	2,769,848	2,736,219
Percent Dept. of Defense	44.2	41.4	44.1	41.4	39.9	39.1	39.2
Percent Postal Service	23.7	23.9	24.3	25.2	25.4	25.2	24.3
Executive Office of the President:							
White House Office	446	333	344	311	600	596	583
Office of Management and Budget	434	524	582	633	727	703	692
Council of Economic Advisers	32	46	53	59	59	70	61
Executive Mansion and Grounds	70	71	72	73	74	72	72
National Security Council	65	38	46	75	83	81	77
Office of Economic Opportunity	(x)	1,259	3,311	2,797	2,845	2,271	2,035
Office of Emergency Preparedness	1,833	372	455	465	397	383	515
Office of Science and Technology	(x)	70	74	89	68	70	68
All other	39	136	230	240	393	1,336	1,531
Executive departments:							
Agriculture	98,694	113,017	125,034	116,012	117,699	114,975	107,990
Commerce	49,300[4]	33,668	36,470	57,674[4]	34,314	33,977	35,540
Defense	1,047,120	1,033,775	1,341,587	1,193,784	1,127,237	1,082,657	1,072,522
Office of the Secretary	1,865	2,297	2,576	2,375	2,153	2,018	1,974
Department of the Army	390,046	366,726	500,877	443,369	421,047	400,502	395,102
Department of the Navy	347,760	333,271	433,870	376,340	350,198	341,543	336,605
Department of the Air Force	307,449	291,500	332,865	306,323	293,141	279,893	272,390
Other Defense activities	—	39,981	71,399	65,377	60,698	58,697	66,451

TABLE 1.2 continued

Paid Civilian Employment in the Federal Government, by Agency: 1960 to 1973

Agency	1960	1965	1969	1970	1971	1972	1973[1]
Health, Education, and Welfare	61,641	87,316	112,514	108,044	110,504	112,974	117,425
Housing and Urban Development[5]	11,105	13,777	14,949	15,190	16,953	16,445	18,639
Interior	56,111	70,711	74,649	73,361	70,393	71,173	67,484
Justice	30,942	33,222	36,415	39,257	44,299	47,334	47,741
Labor	7,096	9,527	10,803	10,991	12,123	13,430	13,523
State	37,983	39,552	42,195	39,753	38,694	36,199	34,588
Agency for International Development	14,443[6]	15,098	16,290	14,974	13,991	12,061	11,154
Transportation	(x)	(x)	64,099	65,985	70,346	69,217	67,933
Treasury	76,179	88,761	88,579	92,521	96,833	104,613	111,057
Independent agencies:							
Action[7]	(x)	(x)	1,443	1,317	1,134	1,762	1,964
American Battle Monuments Commission	461	439	408	404	401	398	389
Arms Control and Disarmament Agency	(x)	175	170	177	179	186	164
Atomic Energy Commission	6,907	7,329	7,467	7,347	7,206	7,131	7,337
Board of Governors, Federal Reserve System	598	667	863	1,016	1,185	1,215	1,198
Canal Zone Government	2,625	3,028	3,293	3,318	3,281	3,263	3,460
Civil Aeronautics Board	755	846	652	682	656	679	661
Civil Service Commission	3,579	3,789	5,561	5,508	5,738	5,711	6,142
Commission on Civil Rights	82	109	177	153	216	200	195
Environmental Protection Agency	(x)	(x)	(x)	(x)	7,133	8,854	9,197
Equal Employment Opportunity Commission	(x)	19	620	850	856	1,315	1,426
Export-Import Bank, U.S.	237	308	328	358	379	380	391
Farm Credit Administration	245	235	234	235	241	232	211
Federal Aviation Administration[8]	38,132	45,257	(x)	(x)	(x)	(x)	(x)
Federal Communications Comm	1,403	1,541	1,501	1,537	1,577	1,662	1,703
Federal Deposit Insurance Corp	1,249	1,544	2,215	2,478	2,655	2,679	2,625

(continued)

TABLE 1.2 continued

Paid Civilian Employment in the Federal Government, by Agency: 1960 to 1973

Agency	1960	1965	1969	1970	1971	1972	1973[1]
Federal Home Loan Bank Board[9]	1,000	1,300	1,292	1,273	1,309	1,356	1,268
Federal Maritime Commission[10]	(x)	251	238	233	277	269	273
Federal Mediation and Conciliation Service	347	422	445	450	436	439	429
Federal Power Commission	859	1,163	1,164	1,132	1,165	1,171	1,128
Federal Trade Commission	782	1,157	1,210	1,330	1,355	1,382	1,440
General Services Administration	28,211	36,524	39,715	37,945	39,772	37,510	37,792
Information Agency	10,915	11,628	10,833	10,262	9,933	9,442	9,372
Interstate Commerce Commission	2,381	2,427	1,827	1,755	1,661	1,676	1,765
Nat'l Aero. and Space Admin.[11]	10,232	34,049	33,929	32,548	30,506	28,382	27,765
Nat'l Capital Housing Authority	331	423	(x)	(x)	(x)	(x)	(x)
Nat'l Credit Union Admin	(x)	(x)	(x)	419	489	525	499
National Foundation on the Arts and Humanities	(x)	(x)	137	103	175	280	447
National Labor Relations Board	1,750	2,252	2,338	2,144	2,237	2,407	2,376
National Mediation Board	129	135	143	126	100	109	112
National Science Foundation	734	1,116	1,252	1,211	1,168	1,223	1,129
Panama Canal Company	11,436	11,936	12,734	12,571	12,056	11,865	11,558
Railroad Retirement Board	2,234	1,767	1,750	1,734	1,780	1,749	1,689
Renegotiation Board	284	184	203	236	240	225	215
St. Lawrence Seaway Development Corporation[12]	159	164	(x)	(x)	(x)	(x)	(x)
Securities and Exchange Comm	980	1,420	1,396	1,454	1,429	1,603	1,550
Selective Service System	6,230	7,587	9,273	8,395	7,416	7,377	6,976
Small Business Administration	2,244	3,751	4,296	4,269	4,616	4,438	5,132
Smithsonian Institution	1,555	2,334	2,676	2,641	2,715	2,986	2,912
Soldiers' Home	1,041	1,134	1,136	1,126	1,143	1,125	1,095
Tariff Commission	271	298	267	242	269	293	278

TABLE 1.2 continued

Paid Civilian Employment in the Federal Government, by Agency: 1960 to 1973

Agency	1960	1965	1969	1970	1971	1972	1973[1]
Tax Court of the United States	153	154	157	(13)	(13)	(13)	(13)
Tennessee Valley Authority	14,993	16,797	19,722	22,244	25,829	25,415	23,644
U.S. Postal Service[14]	562,868	595,512	739,002	726,472	716,752	696,840	665,224
Veterans Administration	172,338	167,059	175,074	168,719	179,535	184,369	192,021
All other	1,038[15]	555[15]	527	579	1,043	1,149	991

X Not applicable.
[1] As of Jan. 31.
[2] 1970 and 1971 exclude Youth Program employees and Public Service Career employees.
[3] Includes 33,480 appointments under the Youth Opportunity Campaign.
[4] 1960 includes 15,574 temporary piece-rate workers on 1960 census; 1970 includes 24,278 enumerators on the 1970 census.
[5] Includes Housing and Home Finance Agency transferred in 1965.
[6] International Cooperation Administration, predecessor of AID.
[7] Formerly Peace Corps; became an independent agency in 1971.
[8] Established in 1958. Transferred to Dept. of Transportation, April 1967.
[9] Became an independent agency in 1955.
[10] Became an independent agency in 1961.
[11] National Advisory Committee for Aeronautics became National Aeronautics and Space Administration in 1958.
[12] Transferred to Dept. of Transportation, April 1967.
[13] Beginning 1970, included in Legislative Branch.
[14] Post Office, an executive department through 1970, reorganized and became U.S. Postal Service, an independent agency, as of July 1, 1971.
[15] Includes Virgin Islands Corporation; agency terminated June 30, 1966.

Source: U.S. Civil Service Commission, *Annual Report* and *Monthly Release of Federal Civilian Manpower Statistics*.
Source: *Statistical Abstract of the United States* (Washington, D.C.: U.S. Government Printing Office, 1973), pp. 404–405.

times, created not by a single factor but by a series of elements. At bottom, they result from the interdependencies and demands produced by technological advance and specialization. There are, however, specific forces in American society that help explain the enormous growth of public bureaucracy.

TABLE 1.3   The Citizen's Easy
Reference Guide to HEW

I.   Office of the Secretary (Secretary, Under Secretary, 8 Assistant Secretaries, General Counsel, 9 Agency Heads, 10 Regional Directors)
         Office for Civil Rights
         Office of Human Development
         Office of Consumer Affairs

II.   *Education Division*
       A.   *Office of Education:* includes Bureau of Elementary and Secondary Education, Bureau of Occupational and Adult Education, Bureau of Equal Educational Opportunity, Bureau of Education for the Handicapped, Bureau of Higher Education, Institute of International Studies, National Center for Educational Statistics, National Center for Educational Technology, National Center for the Improvement of Educational Systems, Office of Indian Education.
       B.   National Institute of Education: includes a National Council on Education, Office of the Director, and a series of ad hoc task forces.

III.   *Public Health Service.*
       Includes Food and Drug Administration (which itself includes: Bureau of Biologies, Bureau of Drugs, Bureau of Foods, Bureau of Radiological Health, Bureau of Veterinary Medicine, National Center for Toxicological Research, Executive Director's Office of Regional Operations); National Institute of Health (which includes: National Cancer Institute, National Heart and Lung Institute, National Institute of Mental Health, National Library of Medicine, National Institute of Arthritis, Metabolism, and Digestive Diseases, National Institute of Allergy and Infectious Diseases, National Institute of Child Health and Human Development, National Institute of Dental Research, National Institute of Environmental Health Sciences, National Institute of General Medical Services, National Institute of Neurological Diseases and Stroke, National Eye Institute, Clinical Center, Fogarty International Center, Division of Computer Research and Technology, Division of Research Resources); Health Resources Administration (which includes: Bureau of Health Resources Development, National Center for Health Services Research, National Center for Health Statistics); Health Services Administration (which includes Bureau of Community Health Services, Bureau of Quality Health Assurance, Indian Health Service, Bureau of Medical Services); Center for Disease Control (which includes: National Institute for Occupational Safety and Health, Bureau of Epidemiology, Bureau of Health Education, Bureau of Laboratories, Bureau of Smallpox Eradication, Bureau of State Services, Bureau of Training, and Bureau of Tropical Diseases); and Alcohol, Drug Abuse and Mental Health Administration (which includes: National Institute on Alcohol Abuse and Alcoholism, National Institute on Drug Abuse, National Institute of Mental Health).

(continued)

IV. *Social and Rehabilitative Service.*
   Includes: Assistant Payments Administration, Community Services Administration, Medical Services Administration, Rehabilitation Services Administration, regional social and rehabilitation services offices.

V. *Social Security Administration.*
   Includes: Bureau of Retirement and Survivor's Insurance, Bureau of Disability Insurance, Bureau of Health Insurance, Bureau of Supplementary Security Income for the Aged, Blind, and Disabled, Bureau of Data Processing, Bureau of District Office Operations, Bureau of Hearings and Appeals, and ten regional commissioners.

Source: Adapted from U.S. Government Organization Manual (Washington, D.C.: U.S. Government Printing Office, 1975).
Authors' Note: Some agencies like HEW are constantly undergoing revisions. The reader should be cautioned that this chart reflects the typical complexities of large-scale organizations but need not be a totally descriptive statement of the current structure of HEW. Nor does this list include the inordinately complex web of divisions, branches, and other organizational entities that are located within the various offices and bureaus.

Public Bureaucracy as a Response to Political Issues

Public organizations are usually created in response to a problem perceived or articulated by a salient interest group within the political environment. And people in modern society, well - educated and often holding important jobs, are frequently in a position to levy considerable pressure on government, especially in politically democratic nations. Key economic groups, such as corporate executives, truck drivers, and teachers, can back up their wishes with publicity campaigns, political contributions, or more drastic measures such as strikes. The salient group may also be urban residents who make a claim on government for more effective housing programs or it may be a group of scientists who argue for an expanded governmental role in the fight against cancer. Public bureaucracy, therefore, becomes a means of achieving goals within the political system. Arguments that bureaucracy has become too large often fail to perceive the tide of continuous demands made by the public itself.

The spiral of perceived needs and demands has led to a continuing expansion of the public bureaucracy. During the years of the Great Society of President Lyndon Johnson, for example, many new public programs were created in response to the riots and activism of the 1960s.[11] The increasingly apparent flaws in the criminal justice system led to the establishment of the Law Enforcement Assistance Administration, which has since distributed millions of dollars to state and local governments to upgrade their police and law enforcement programs.

In 1970, the problems of the environment, such as air and water pollution, led to the creation of the powerful Environmental Protection Agency. Financial difficulties and the threatened demise of a system of shared powers because of the growth of federal power gave rise to the theme of "new federalism." There emerged a spate of new state and local government programs, as evidenced by the establishment of revenue sharing, wherein the federal government turns over a portion of the money it collects to state and local governments. The depressed economic state of the mid-1970s resulted in special comprehensive employment legislation, which subsidized the salaries of local government employees.[12] There existed not only need in the above examples but also demands by groups and individuals that those needs be met. While there may be a threshold at which new bureaucratic growth cannot occur without serious damage to society, the inherent dynamics of the American political system as a "demand-response" system probably means that long-term growth will continue, although it is probable that persistent economic problems will slow it down.

Growth of Public Bureaucracy as Affected by an Increase in Knowledge

Increasing technological developments as well as an increase in studies of social problems provide new and alternative policy choices. Because of the pace of development of scientific theory and technology (computers, satellites, teaching methods, etc.), previous solutions to problems become outdated more rapidly than ever before. In modern society, the present quickly becomes the past, and the "novel" solution to public needs more speedily becomes the anachronism, sometimes leaving the victims of its experiments in its wake (for example, transportation schemes that wreak havoc on communities).[13]

Public bureaucracy is continuously challenged by the need to adapt in order not to become obsolescent (but perhaps continue to survive). In this adaptation process, expansion or differentiation of function often results, leading not to the demise of the bureaucracy but to a larger and more complex bureaucracy. Because of the "knowledge revolution" associated with this increase in technological capacity we may become inspired to attempt even more and to create even newer bureaucratic frameworks to develop and refine our new inspirations. Thus, while an increasing technology may provide us with new tools to do more, an ever increasing knowledge base may inspire us to challenge or want even more.[14] Properly used, new technological developments and administrative strategies can assist government to accomplish responsibly its tasks. But with a narrow perspective, new techniques can become ends in themselves and thereby subvert more important goals. They can also subvert personal freedoms and democratic political controls. Computerized records on individual citizens, for example, may threaten personal privacy by enabling the government to amass large "dossiers." These could be used against members of political opposition groups or parties as well as against other citizens.

Public Bureaucracy as a Response
to Certain Deficiencies
of the Private Enterprise System

While the survival of both private- and public-sector bureaucracy depends on their individual ability to respond to "market" needs (economic versus political markets), the continued growth of public-sector bureaucracy is affected by the dimensions of private-enterprise activity in several ways.

First, public bureaucracy is often called upon to respond to needs that private-sector bureaucracy cannot or will not provide. The motive for private-sector involvement is generally profit, while the public-sector motive is that the action be compatible with the public interest. Thus, in the private sector, goods and services are rendered on a profit-making basis, a form of economic calculation generally irrelevant in public-enterprise decision making. For example, we do not expect or wish that the degree of fire protection be determined by means of a monetary-profit standard. Through our taxes, then, we subsidize the provision of goods and services that might not be provided through private-sector profit motivations. Neither, as the anguished history of mass transit in the United States has demonstrated, do we necessarily expect that mass transit be supported solely on a calculation of economic profitability. While profits would be theoretically possible by raising fares to meet the costs, such a move might be counterproductive because it would discourage potential users. Thus, it may be in the "public interest" for government to subsidize deficits of publicly owned mass transit companies in order to keep them active.[15] Effective means of transportation for workers are necessary to a healthy economy.

Second, public bureaucracy often expands because of the *excesses* of private-enterprise activities. Public organizations are often established for the express purpose of checking and controlling the behavior of private bureaucracy. The most dramatic example can be seen in the rise of the regulatory agencies. Beginning with the establishment of the Interstate Commerce Commission (ICC) in 1887 to control, among other things, the fare structure of the railroads, a series of quasi-independent public organizations has been created largely to regulate the abuses of private enterprise. The Federal Communications Commission (FCC) regulates the use of airwaves for broadcasting purposes; the Civil Aeronautics Board (CAB) monitors the rates and assigns flight routes of the competing airlines; and the Environmental Protection Agency attempts to protect the environment. In addition to many other examples at the federal level, state governments also have their share of public bureaucracies designed to control the activities of private companies. Insurance boards and public utility commissions are two common examples. Of course, as we shall see, many of these public regulatory bureaucracies often fail to police effectively the sectors they were established to regulate.

We can also see that public bureaucracy has grown because private-sector bureaucracy has refused to address critical problems on its own. The rise of the Environmental Protection Agency, for example, can be attributed to both public and governmental dissatisfaction with the weak efforts undertaken by private industry to curtail industrial pollution.[16] The growth of the Department of Housing and Urban Development is evidence not only of a reawakened public commitment to the problems of the cities, but also demonstrates a counterbalancing to private-sector activity, such as exploitative private construction of buildings that may damage the viability of a business or housing area.[17] Additionally, businesses themselves have often requested assistance and support requiring the expansion and creation of public bureaucracies. Airlines, for example, have benefited greatly from federal support for the construction of airports as well as the provision of safety services such as air traffic control.

The increasing scope and size of public bureaucracy has the capacity of presenting us with a nightmarish future of increased administrative ineffectiveness or a future of increased opportunities, benefits, and service to the public. Most likely, it will present a host of serious problems in addition to a number of benefits. While expanding public-sector bureaucracy certainly curtails individual autonomy in many areas, its continued growth may help provide new opportunities to solve old problems and to provide new freedoms. For example, those who argue for an improvement in national health planning and services hope that with the increased government involvement more equitable and effective health services will be provided. The new opportunities reflected in increased bureaucratization (growth of the bureaucracy), however, come at a cost. To illustrate, professionalism within public bureaucracy, while increasing the talent pool, also encourages alliances with independent professional associations. Among other things, this challenges the traditional hierarchical control within organizations. Increased bureaucratization also challenges the ability of legitimate formal political centers, such as the executive and legislative arms of government, to check organizational activity and leads to decreased citizen control and awareness.[18]

Unfortunately, then, public bureaucracy, established to broaden public benefits and opportunities, can develop into rigid organizations removed from the control of elected public officials. In a democratic political system that fate is unacceptable.[19] Ensuring control over a responsive and capable bureaucracy working toward well-defined ends must be a continuous matter of concern for the public and its elected representatives alike. The opportunities reflected by the development of new public goals can easily be undermined if the skills and sensitivities necessary for effective administration of policy are lacking. While we recognize the fact that many complex goals cannot be achieved without a bureaucratic, hierarchical structure, we should continue to challenge and perfect this form of organization and, where possible, consider other types of public organizations, such as temporary problem solving units with limited structural impediments.

THE CRITICISMS OF PUBLIC BUREAUCRACY

Having discussed the growth of public bureaucracy and its immense size and diverse scope, it is essential to consider the "price." An awareness of administrative accomplishments and survival capacity does not require that we serve as apologists for bureaucratic bungling, administrative recklessness, or public-sector inaction. While we must recognize that public bureaucracy has served as the major vehicle for providing public services, we cannot ignore the various challenges that bureaucracy must meet and problems it must solve if it is to serve as an effective and responsive public instrument. In many ways, public bureaucracy is an orphan of the American political system. Unlike the three constitutionally defined branches of government, it lacks a clear constitutional basis for its existence. Each agency responds differently to varying environmental constraints. Some move aggressively, some quite passively. While some try to gain power by soliciting interest-group support for their activities or "co-opting" potential adversaries, others react principally to internal professional or technical pressures and demands. Bureaucratic behavior is therefore quite diverse and the choice of one strategy of action may preclude the selection of another.[20] In the process of responding to its relevant environment as it perceives it at that time, an agency may fail to satisfy other values or interests. Inevitably, we can expect criticism of public agencies, since their actions and decisions cannot please everyone and must disappoint some.

Not only is public bureaucracy criticized because of its policy-making role, by means of which some are disadvantaged, but it is also challenged by proponents of other forces or values. Some, for example, argue that the routinized, specialized, and overly structured patterns of public organization ignore the needs of individual citizens and complicate redress for injustices committed by bureaucracies. Others argue that bureaucracies have a biased interpretation of the public interest and respond primarily to specialized and narrow interests. It is commonly argued that agencies often get caught in a web of expediency — doing whatever satisfies their clientele (the groups with whom they work), shunning any broad or comprehensive interpretation of the "public interest." Regulatory agencies such as the Interstate Commerce Commission have been frequently charged with kowtowing to the demands of their clients.

There is much uneasiness today about these alliance patterns. Instead of bureaucracy being concerned with survival per se, many argue that it must develop a *moral* consciousness over what it is doing and why. Should and can organizations develop a sense of moral purpose apart from political expediency? Dvorin and Simmons, in a brief but timely work entitled *From Amoral to Humane Bureaucracy,* note that:

> *Constitutional democracy can best be served by a public service which is unabashedly aware of its great power and determined to commit its total sources to the ceaseless struggle for the maintenance of the dignity of man. . . .*
>
> *The public bureaucracy must accept major responsibility for the re-ordering of the more limited, selfish values which are represented by a global technology dividing into ever-increasing specialization, in favor of more fundamental values which contribute to human dignity.*[21]

The search for human dignity is a perennial problem, especially in a nation such as ours, which is philosophically based on ideals of human worth and freedom. But how do we achieve this in modern society? Do we do it by imposing federal regulations? Is the path to be achieved by structuring a "moral review" division within all public agencies, responsible for monitoring the social effects of agency actions?

Consider the telling commentary on bureaucracy reflected by the tribulations of Ernest Fitzgerald, the Department of Defense employee who publicized the scandalously high cost overruns in defense contracts. Fitzgerald was summarily dismissed from his job because of "insubordination" and it took lengthy Civil Service Commission hearings to get him reinstated. Such actions demonstrate the probable difficulties for persons who attempt to stress broad public goals that embarrass their superiors or run counter to agency policy. By the same token, well-meaning employees may be wrong, narrow, or biased, and by taking such action delay or prevent the accomplishment of desirable policy.

Perhaps morality should be imposed by the political realm. But if the political system is as fragmented as is the American separation-of-powers and checks-and-balances system, then how can it be imposed politically? Possibly blaming amorality on public bureaucracies is the wrong approach. After all, the bureaucracy may reflect society's values and its culture. Instead of castigating the bureaucracy for "amorality" perhaps we should examine the moral basis of the broader political system, of which the bureaucracy is but a part.

We will never purge bureaucracy of all its failings, but, as the foregoing discussion illustrates, the charges leveled against public bureaucracy reflect considerable and continuing anxiety over the role performed by bureaucracy within the political system. One scholar of public affairs put it very accurately when he noted that the role of public bureaucracy has become such a source of contention within the political system that liberals, conservatives, and moderates — although politically diverse — could be unified in spirit under an "antibureaucracy" banner. As James Q. Wilson noted:

> *The federal bureaucracy, whose growth and problems were once only the concern of the Right, has now become a major concern of the Left, the Center, and almost all points in between. Conservatives once feared that a powerful bureaucracy would work a social revolution. The Left now fears that this same bureaucracy is working a conservative reaction. And the Center fears that the bureaucracy isn't working at all.*[22]

Can public bureaucracy function in a responsible and effective manner while taking into account the moral imperative for human dignity? To assist us in comprehending this question and also in responding to it, we shall view bureaucracy within a structured framework of three categories: "machine bureaucracy," "humane bureaucracy," and "political bureaucracy."[23] Each represents a useful approach to understanding bureaucracy while at the same time defining the various problems confronting it.

Machine Bureaucracy

Bureaucracy was seen in traditional management theory as the most effective mechanism to accomplish complex goals. At least in its ideal form, bureaucracy can be viewed as analogous to a well-tuned machine. A machine is, after all, composed of identifiable and functionally necessary parts that operate interdependently to achieve efficiently some common purpose. Thus, bureaucracies are, in part, comparable to machines that use raw supplies or materials and transform them into some desired end product. Bureaucracies are designed to transform public-sector inputs (ideas, money, personnel, etc.) into desired public products. The basic dimensions of this "bureaucracy as machine" model were first stated by the architect of "ideal-type" bureaucracy, Max Weber, a nineteenth-century German sociologist. He observed that "bureaucracy is like a modern judge, who is a vending machine into which the pleadings are inserted together with the fee and which then disgorges the judgement together with its reasons mechanically derived from the code."[24]

TABLE 1.4   The Problems of Public Bureaucracy: Three Contending Approaches

	Machine Bureaucracy	Humane Bureaucracy	Political Bureaucracy
	Increase organizational efficiency and mechanical effectiveness	Increase development of needs and values of public employees	Increase accountability to plurality of political interests and to appropriate political institutions
Examples of commonly perceived problems of bureaucracy	—competition between organizational units —ineffective management strategies —lack of efficiency —lack of evaluative measures to determine effectiveness of programs or efficiency of personnel —lack of technical skills	—managerial/worker conflict —loss of personal identity —loss of civic identity —few opportunities to participate in decision making —inadequate material and motivational incentives	—overcentralization of administration —lack of accountability —inadequacy of formal political control —lack of adequate citizen redress for bureaucratic abuses
Examples of suggested solutions	—reorganize —provide structural mechanism for inter- and intraagency cooperation —measure agency productivity or employee efficiency —manage by objectives —improve technical skills of employees	—increase training efforts —develop new managerial styles —induce temporary organizations —provide for rotation schemes —increase material and psychological rewards —provide for an employee bill of rights —enrich jobs	—improve legislative oversight —establish little city halls —encourage citizen participation —establish ombudsmen —decentralize
Benefits	—the application of skills and expertise in a non-political environment to achieve stated goals effectively and efficiently	—the cooperative efforts of psychologically healthy personalities toward public goals	—accountability to a diversity of citizen needs and to formal political centers

This bureaucracy-as-machine concept, however, raises two diametrically opposed challenges. First, bureaucracy can be brought to task because it is *too much of a machine,* discouraging the attainment of individual needs within the organization. This view of bureaucracy as an inhuman monster is reviewed below and further discussed in chapter 4. The second criticism (quite paradoxically) is that bureaucracy is *not adequately machinelike.* From this perspective the need is to restyle the machine, redesign its structure, synchronize its parts, and better evaluate its output and performance. It is common to find public bureaucracy assailed because it is "inefficient," structurally handicapped, and because chains of command and leadership are ignored, and technical skills and know-how are absent.

This "breakdown of the machine," while exemplified in many ways, is often characterized by the maze of paperwork that defines much of the everyday world of public organizations. While some paperwork is always necessary for efficient information flow and accurate record-keeping, modern bureaucracy's preoccupation with forms (1 million different forms, filled out at an annual rate of 19.5 billion) has become a synonym for inefficiency, inaction, and even absurdity. One congressional investigation committee discovered that the paperwork costs of public bureaucracy — including the man-hours consumed by government employees processing forms — total about 18 billion dollars a year, matched by another 18 billion dollars per year in man-hours consumed by individuals and private businesspeople, who must comply with the reportage requirements of the government.[25] These costs represent nearly 15 percent of the federal budget. Senator Thomas McIntyre, attempting to emphasize the impact of such staggering figures, indicated that the 36 billion dollars spent annually on paperwork could pay for well over 2 million low-cost housing units.[26]

Indeed, the paperwork problem is only the tip of the iceberg, symptomatic of more serious problems of the bureaucratic machine. Caught in its own maze of agreements, memoranda, program guidelines, and other "red tape," bureaucracy's ability to act quickly and to comprehend where it has been and to determine where it should go is often lost. We will see later that even new management techniques designed to improve performance can themselves become ends, requiring workers to spend hours compiling required reports.

Other charges that bureaucracy is inefficient are equally commanding. A continuing array of reports by the Joint Economic Committee of Congress demonstrates that the far-flung activities of public bureaucracy produce major omissions and inefficiencies. Whether the attack is on the Forest Service for improperly managing the nation's forests or upon HEW for ineffectively monitoring health programs, the challenge is equally serious: can we revitalize the bureaucratic machine so that it moves with effectiveness, speed, and efficiency in accomplishing public goals?

Critics of machine breakdown do not argue that bureaucracy should be replaced. On the contrary, they argue that it should be perfected. Competition among agencies should be resolved through better use of interagency coordinating committees; goals should be better identified through the application of more sophisticated managerial skills and practices; obsolescent bureaucratic structures should be abolished in favor of new structures; and efficiency and effectiveness should be enhanced by performance measurement and productivity incentives.

The need to make bureaucracy more efficient and rational is not solely the product of recent thought. After the Civil War, for example, efforts to improve bureaucratic functioning included the establishment of a merit system so that expertise, and not politics, could determine administrative careers. Since then, a continuing list of presidential commissions and boards has investigated the efficiency and structure of bureaucratic activities, and there has been continued support for the development of new technical tools and skills to be applied in the administration of public services.

The Taft Commission on Economy and Efficiency (1910), the President's Committee on Administrative Management headed by Louis Brownlow (1936), the two Hoover Commissions (1947 and 1953), the "Landis Report," commissioned by President John F. Kennedy to investigate the plight of the regulatory agencies (1960), and the Ash Council (1971), established by President Nixon to suggest government reorganization needs, were all devices created to recommend means of untangling the confusing practices and structures of administrative agencies.[27] The fact that our history is replete with such commissions is evidence not only of a continuing concern with improving the management of public programs but also of the perennial difficulty in achieving the goals of such investigatory bodies.

But the problem of improving performance remains and is more complicated than ever given the increased size and complexity of the public sector. Moreover, increased efficiency can have a definite price, namely, the possible exclusion of other values or effective responses to other important challenges. An organization's ability to better its machine capacities will be affected not only by performance-improvement opportunities and techniques but also by countervailing pressures to satisfy other needs. Among these are the requirements of humane bureaucracy.

Humane Bureaucracy

While some contend that the path to responsive administration lies in better equipping organizational machines to solve problems efficiently and effectively, others argue that bureaucracy is an anachronism in a world of quickly accelerating professionalism, technological change, and democratic values. Efficiency advocates seek to perfect bureaucracy, but those concerned with the impact of bureaucracies on individual needs would redesign the machine to achieve a more liberated and humane organizational arrangement.

Individuals who seek the development of more humanistic bureaucracy strive for a more liberated worker, freed from the hierarchical and impersonal role positions that bureaucracies have traditionally imposed. "Man is born free and yet we see him everywhere in chains,"[28] noted Rousseau in speaking of the demise of political liberties and freedom. His cry has been adopted by those who believe that organizations are but another imprisoning element, suffocating creativity, the utilization of multiple skills, and the enhancement of meaningful work relationships among human beings. Weber, that theorist of the efficiency model of bureaucracy, once noted of the bureaucrat: "The individual bureaucrat cannot squirm out of the apparatus in which he is harnessed. . . . In the great majority of cases, he is only a single cog in an ever-moving mechanism which prescribes to him an essentially fixed route of march."[29]

Challengers of the traditional concept of bureaucracy hope to see a metamorphosis in which new forms of flexible structures will be better equipped to solve the complicated problems of the future and will give greater dignity and meaning to the individuals within their ranks. In *Future Shock,* Alvin Toffler refers to the organization of the future as "ad-hocracy . . . the fast-moving information-rich, kinetic organization . . . filled with transient cells and extremely mobile individuals."[30] In this apparatus, individuals — representing a mosaic of skills and capabilities — will be transferred from one project to another, never maintaining permanence in any one location. New-style managers will monitor the efforts of ad hoc groups assembled to tackle one problem then disbanded and shunted off to other problem-solving enterprises. Hierarchical posturing will become less. and less significant, with much greater emphasis on an individual's capacity to participate meaningfully in the problem or task before the group unit. Frederick Thayer notes: "When the organizational revolution has run its course, when societies have been transformed as they must be if we are to survive, the world of organizations will be one of innumerable small face-to-face groups characterized by openness, trust, and intensive interpersonal relations."[31]

Perhaps the chief architect of this emerging organizational thought has been Warren G. Bennis, a social psychologist and consultant to major industries. Bennis has argued that the pace of technological change, the increasing sophistication of the worker, and the diversity of professional skills currently required in problem solving exceed the capacities of traditional forms of organizations. Thus, he argues that organizations of the future will be "temporary organizations" or "adaptive structures" — changing form and appearance as new problems must be met:

> The social structure of organizations of the future will have some unique characteristics. The key word will be "temporary." These will be adaptive, rapidly changing temporary systems. These will be task forces organized around problems to be solved by groups of relative strangers with diverse professional skills. The group will be arranged on an organic rather than mechanical model; it will evolve in response to a problem rather than to programmed role expectations. The executive thus becomes the coordinator or "linking pin" between various task forces. He must be a man who can speak the polyglot jargon of research, with skills to relay information and to mediate between groups. People will be evaluated not according to rank but according to skill and professional training. Organizational charts will consist of project groups rather than stratified functional groups.[32]

Critics of traditional bureaucracy who emphasize humanistic values advocate the need for individual growth and fulfillment through such strategies as upward mobility, job enrichment, and the like. These goals seek to adapt organizations to the needs of individuals. The quest of the humanists is to broaden the skills, capacities, and values of organizational members to enhance creative growth. These techniques, they argue, help guarantee that public policy is developed and implemented by psychologically and professionally mature adults rather than by skeletal entities in a rigid bureaucratic world. Implicit in this concern is their belief that organizations will be more responsive to external, especially political, values and needs if they demonstrate a concern for internal values and needs. (This theme will be discussed in chapter 4.) The issue of responsiveness to political values is both complex and of central concern to the role of public bureaucracy in a democratic society.

Political Bureaucracy

Up to this point, the challenges that we have discussed deal primarily with *internal* dimensions of bureaucracy at either the technical or human level. These challenges, however, may encourage the view that bureaucracies are "closed systems," responsive only to their own needs. But public bureaucracy is first and foremost political bureaucracy. Yet it is often criticized for being insensitive and nonresponsive to a diverse set of political values and interests, for responding to *some* political values and not others.

A common charge, for example, is that public organizations fail to speak for a broad base of interests within the political system.[33] Yet the structuring of public organizations according to function or interest (agriculture, transportation, defense, etc.) makes difficult a broad perspective by their employees. Another criticism concerns the propensity of public bureaucracy to articulate and foster the interests of large, well-established clientele groups, while less organized interests, including the public as a whole, are not adequately considered.

Additionally, it is often argued that Washington bureaucracy, or even agencies of state government, are too geographically removed from local communities to be politically responsive to their needs. Agency-established guidelines determined by a centralized office often seem to have little in common with the needs of the local communities. This problem has given rise to the call by some for bureaucracy to decentralize itself so that policies better tailored for local use can evolve. Little city halls, designed to provide easier access and quicker response through neighborhood offices in cities, are an expression of this ideal. The rise of the concept called "new federalism" also reflects the philosophical notion that better, more democratic administration will occur if state and local governments regain a greater voice vis-à-vis the federal level. The call for decentralization, however, raises complex issues that will be discussed in Chapter 5.

Others attempting to come to terms with the need to make bureaucracy accountable for its actions to political values press for the need for citizen participation in policy formulation. They argue that public bureaucracy will be better able to serve its heterogeneous clientele if individual citizens are allowed fuller access to the administrative process. Indeed, a real challenge to public bureaucracy lies in developing its capacity to encourage such participation. Many individuals understandably are not optimistic. Robert Alford, for example, has noted:

> *The principles of bureaucracy and participation are to some extent incompatible. There is continual pressure toward bureaucratization of more and more city services — the expansion of agencies with specially trained personnel entrusted with the performance of specific decisions and functions. Yet there is continual emphasis on the broadest possible public and group participation in decision-making processes, through voting, public meetings, informal influence on pressure groups, petitions, and all other conceivable means of applying influence on public leaders. These are incompatible principles. Bureaucratization implies the insulation of decision-makers from outside influences, by definition not as competent as experts are to judge the relevant range of facts, nor to balance the objectives desired. Participation implies the right and the duty of the public to intervene in the determination of decisions.* [34]

Still others argue that public bureaucracy must make itself more accessible by "opening its doors" to greater public inspection. The evolution of the Freedom of Information Act (or "sunshine laws" as they are popularly called in some cases) allows citizen access to government records. The perennial call for the creation of ombudsmen, people who investigate citizen complaints against particular bureaucracies, indicates that one problem of bureaucracy is its excessive self-protectiveness and the resulting "bureaucratic mystique."

Finally, others maintain that bureaucracy must be made more accountable to formal political centers such as the legislatures, elected executives, and courts. The degree of political control that should be established has never been resolved. Some scholars favor limiting political intrusion to the problem-solving and administrative realm, while others want extensive direction and control of the bureaucracy by the political leaders.[35] Arguing for the "mastership of the public" over the independent tendencies of bureaucracy, Herman Finer asked:

> *Are the servants of the public to decide their own course, or is their course of action to be decided by a body outside themselves? My answer is that the servants of the public are not to decide their own counsel; they are to be responsible to the elected representatives of the public and they are to determine the course of action of the public servants to the most minute degree that is technically feasible.*[36]

Although such positions have some validity, the notion of politically accountable bureaucracy presents several difficulties. For example, legislative review, including oversight by a legislature's specialized committees, has not proven to give effective, continuous checks on agency actions. In fact, legislative "controls" have sometimes made bureaucracies even less responsive to broad public interests because legislatures or their committees have become captive to particular clientele interests.[37] Agricultural committees, for example, are typically comprised of representatives from farming districts. Thus, there may be little incentive to apply pressure on agricultural agencies to emphasize broad public interests over organized agricultural interests. Moreover, legislative systems are not monolithic centers of policy review or debate. They are heterogeneous bodies with multiple interests reflected by their specialized committees and subcommittees. Legislators typically hold only a narrow range of intense interest and expertise among the many policy areas of modern public administration.[38]

Efforts at political control of bureaucracy by the executive branches of state and federal government similarly have been disappointing. Executive reorganization of public administration, for instance, generally has fallen into a quagmire of interest-group politics and agency reluctance.[39] With such limited or narrow political review, clientele groups or internal bureaucratic pressures such as demands by experts can exert a far greater influence than that envisioned by advocates of political responsibility.

In sum, the concept of political bureaucracy concerns itself with an essential requirement of democratic society — the need to view external demands and controls as a legitimate constraint as well as impetus for administrative actions. The ultimate purpose of government, after all, is to serve the needs of society. Though unanimous agreement on the precise goals and values to be achieved by public bureaucracy will never be possible, there is still nearly universal agreement that it should be servant and not master. The problems associated with political bureaucracy focus on some of the most fundamental aspects of the nature of American democracy.

VALUES IN PUBLIC BUREAUCRACY

As we have seen, public bureaucracy is not and cannot be a neutral participant in American society. It represents an integral part of a governmental system that not only profoundly affects the quality of life but also helps determine who will be the prime recipients of the basic resources of society, such as money, employment opportunity, education, medical care, and so on.

The values emphasized by government administrators and agencies are crucial because they play a principal role in determining the direction of public policy and the treatment of citizens and government workers. Indeed, the very structure of bureaucracy as well as the tools it employs and the procedures it follows have their roots in values. The term "value" here refers to basic standards and principles that guide action. We believe that contemporary values of American public bureaucracy, incorporating many diverse aspects, can be subsumed under the three broad categories of machine, humane, and political. Though the implications of these values will be treated more fully in later chapters, it can be briefly noted here that their philosophical underpinnings include the ideas that government should effectively serve the people and should restrict their freedom as little as possible, that all individual human beings are significant in their own right, and that government should be controlled by the people and their elected representatives.

Machine-bureaucracy values.   An organization oriented primarily to "machine" values emphasizes the utilization of technical skills and procedures in formulating and implementing public policy. Emphasis is placed upon organizational procedures to assure that technical, not individual or political, values affect decisions. Expertise, measurement of alternative policies, objective rule making, and task accomplishment are central. These values include a concern for detail, timeliness, and efficiency. Usually, but not necessarily, emphasis is maintained on the hierarchical flow of authority and knowledge within the organization. Output evaluation and the maximization of all energies are emphasized.

Humane-bureaucracy values.   An organization oriented primarily to "humane" values prizes individual worth and human development above technical needs or values. It is primarily oriented to its internal needs but the underlying premise is that as these needs are met, it can more effectively cope with its external clientele. Proponents of the humane approach argue that individual citizens dealing with the agency will be treated more humanely and with greater sensitivity and that greater social justice will be achieved by satisfying internal humanistic values, such as increasing minority representation among employees.

Among the major attributes of humane-bureaucracy values is a concern for the health and vitality of the organization as a social unit. Emphasis is placed on career-development programs, individual freedoms, job enlargement and enrichment, as well as on developing new organizational forms or strategies that might enhance the creative development and utilization of the employees.

Political-bureaucracy values.   Among the major values of political bureaucracy is that public employees be aware of the legitimacy of political demands; that they understand that an organization must be held accountable for its actions to the public and its elected and appointed leaders; and that within a democracy citizens and public officials as provided through law can make claims against the bureaucracy and anticipate a timely response. Citizens can also be protected from capricious or harsh treatment through procedural guarantees. Access and the sharing of power and influence in policy matters are recognized as necessary features of public policy making within a democracy.

Political-bureaucracy values are broader than mere responsiveness to pressures that determine an agency's survival. They are also concerned with equalizing opportunities for citizens and recognizing the legitimacy of alternative and competing political values. Moreover, they compel a recognition of the importance of formal political control and supervision of agency activities, and they counter such behaviors as corruption, improper political influence, and hostility by public employees.

Political-bureaucracy values, then, refer to a broad scope of elements forcing the organization to come to grips democratically with its external environment.

VALUES INTEGRATION

We make no claim as to which value framework is always most or least desirable. In fact, each can reinforce or sometimes conflict with the others. A multiple approach, however, can help provide for an internal check-and-balance value system within the bureaucracy itself. A bureaucracy that is oversensitive to political values and interests can wreak as much havoc as a bureaucracy dominated by a sterile, impersonalistic machine approach. Indeed, some of our governmental problems today, e.g. the financial plight of many major urban centers such as New York, are due partly to excessive political responsiveness to demands by groups that cut across all strata of society. Governments do

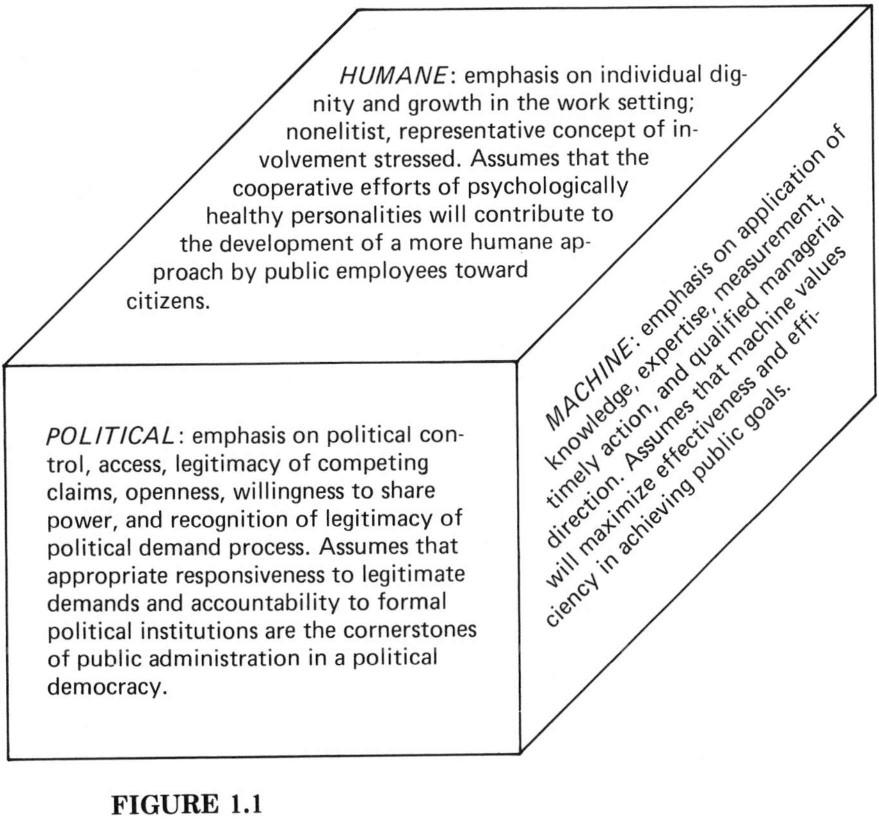

HUMANE: emphasis on individual dignity and growth in the work setting; nonelitist, representative concept of involvement stressed. Assumes that the cooperative efforts of psychologically healthy personalities will contribute to the development of a more humane approach by public employees toward citizens.

MACHINE: emphasis on application of knowledge, expertise, measurement, timely action, and qualified managerial direction. Assumes that machine values will maximize effectiveness and efficiency in achieving public goals.

POLITICAL: emphasis on political control, access, legitimacy of competing claims, openness, willingness to share power, and recognition of legitimacy of political demand process. Assumes that appropriate responsiveness to legitimate demands and accountability to formal political institutions are the cornerstones of public administration in a political democracy.

FIGURE 1.1

not have unlimited financial resources. Conversely, overemphasis on machine values may cause important dimensions of humane values to be lost leading to unnecessarily harsh treatment of public employees as well as citizens. By the same token, an over emphasis on the rights and needs of employees can weaken the democratic controls of the electorate. Thus, these three value systems — machine, humane, and political — should be seen as important, yet each can create serious problems if over-emphasized.

The three-part scheme depicted by figure 1.1 represents our view that organizational value choices are not a matter of "either-or" but a collective force of three important dimensions. We wish to stress the promise and potential of creating a capacity within bureaucracy to max-imize its awareness and sensitivity to all three values rather than seizing one at the expense of the others. Of course, it will sometimes be necessary to emphasize one or two perspectives. But the capacity of public agencies to adapt to each and capability to accomplish each is essential. Greater capacities and a broader orientation to machine, humane, and political values could alleviate some of the more persistent problems of public bureaucracy.

In a complex social system, organizations must be able to develop complex orientations and be encouraged to break beyond the safe con-fines of a dominant influence or perspective. Yet, the ability to maximize responsiveness to machine, humane, and political values is seriously con-strained by important *internal* and *external* forces. It is to these dimen-sions of public bureaucracy that we now turn our attention.

NOTES

1. Max Weber, "Bureaucracy," H. H. Gerth and C. Wright Mills, eds., *From Max Weber: Essays in Sociology* (New York: Galaxy Books, 1946), pp. 196 - 244.
2. The complex nature of policy making is discussed in Austin Ranney, ed., *Political Science and Public Policy* (Chicago: Markham, 1968).
3. This interpretation of politics draws, of course, upon Harold D. Lasswell, *Politics: Who Gets What, When, How* (New York: McGraw-Hill, 1936).
4. An important early statement on the interdependence of politics and administration was made by Paul H. Appleby in *Policy and Administration* (University, Ala.: University of Alabama Press, 1949).
5. The aggressiveness of bureaucracy in preserving its domain is discussed by Peter B. Natchez and Irving Bupp, "Policy and Priority in the Budgetary Process," *American Political Science Review* 68 (September 1973).

6. See, for example, Edward C. Banfield, "Making a New Federal Program: Model Cities, 1964 - 1968," Allan P. Sindler, ed., *Policy and Politics in America: Six Case Studies* (Boston: Little, Brown, 1973), pp. 124 - 159.

7. Norton Long, "Bureaucracy and Constitutionalism," *American Political Science Review* 46 (September, 1952): 808 - 818.

8. United States Office of Management and Budget, *The United States Budget in Brief: Fiscal Year 1977*, p. 56.

9. Based on "Government Employment and Payrolls: 1950 to 1972," *Statistical Abstract of the United States* (Washington, D.C.: U.S. Government Printing Office, 1973), p. 433.

10. See "Budget Message of the President," February 3, 1975. Office of Management and Budget, *The United States Budget in Brief: Fiscal Year 1977*.

11. Many of these programs reflect the problems analyzed by the Kerner Commission. See, National Advisory Commission on Civil Disorders, *Report of the Commission* (Washington, D.C.: U.S. Government Printing Office, 1968). The limits of some of these programs are explored by James L. Sundquist and David W. Davis, *Making Federalism Work* (Washington, D.C.: The Brookings Institution, 1969).

12. This is more formally referred to as the "CETA Program," an acronym for the legislation that created it: the Comprehensive Employment Training Act of 1974.

13. Many of the critical issues related to the pace of technological change are discussed in Albert H. Teich, ed., *Technology and Man's Future* (New York: St. Martin's Press, 1973).

14. The management and control over the direction of new knowledge is an important issue of modern society and organizations. It is discussed in Edward I. Friedland, "Turbulence and Technology: Public Administration and the Role of Information Processing Technology," pp. 134 - 150, and Orion White, Jr., "Organization and Administration for New Technological and Social Imperatives," pp. 151 - 168, both in Dwight Waldo, ed., *Public Administration in a Time of Turbulence* (Scranton: Chandler, 1971).

15. This liberalized interpretation of mass transportation is reflected in more recent legislation that provides greater financial support to mass transportation, e.g. the Federal Aid Highway Act of 1973.

16. The legal role of the Environmental Protection Agency in curbing environmental abuse is covered by Frederick R. Anderson, with Robert H. Daniels, *NEPA in the Courts: A Legal Analysis of the National Environmental Policy Act* (Washington, D.C.: Resources for the Future, 1973).

17. On the establishment of HUD, see Jay S. Goodman, *The Dynamics of Urban Government and Politics* (New York: Macmillan, 1975), pp. 52 - 53, 84.

18. See Barbara Hickley, *Stability and Change in Congress* (New York: Harper & Row, 1970), pp. 186ff.

19. We define democratic political systems, very briefly, as those characterized by free, open elections, with at least some realistic chance of alternation of political elites on the basis of those elections. One of the key consequences of such systems should be increased citizen impact through elected representatives, and, sometimes, by direct participation.

20. The literature on bureaucratic behavior is extensive. But several representative sources include Herbert A. Simon, *Administrative Behavior*, 2nd ed. (New York: Macmillan, 1961); Victor Thompson, *Modern Organization* (New York: Knopf, 1961); James G. March and Herbert A. Simon, *Organizations* (New York: Wiley & Sons, 1958); and Anthony Downs, *Inside Bureaucracy* (Boston: Little, Brown, 1966).

21. Eugene P. Dvorin and Robert H. Simmons, *From Amoral to Humane Bureaucracy* (San Francisco: Canfield Press, 1972), pp. 11, 17.

22. James Q. Wilson, "The Bureaucracy Problem," *The Public Interest* (Winter 1967).

23. In his interesting book, *Political Bureaucracy* (Glenview, Ill.: Scott, Foresman, 1973), chap. 1, Lewis C. Mainzer argues that these three problem areas constitute central challenges to contemporary bureaucracy. We agree with the threefold classification but believe that today's problems demand a greater emphasis on machine and humane values, without abandoning political values.

24. Cited by Warren Bennis, "Changing Organizations," *Journal of Applied Behavioral Science* 2 (1966): 250.

25. See U.S. Congress, Senate, Select Committee on Small Business. Subcommittee on Governmental Regulation, *Hearings: The Federal Paperwork Burden,* Part 1, 92nd Cong., 2nd sess., 1972, p. 1.

26. Ibid., p. 522. For other discussions of this perennial problem see also, U.S. Congress, House of Representatives, Committee on Public Works, Subcommittee on Investigations and Oversight, *Hearings: Red Tape Inquiry into Delays and Excessive Paperwork in Administration of Public Works Programs,* 92nd Cong., 1st sess., 1971.

27. See, for example, James M. Landis, "Report on Regulatory Agencies to the President Elect" (Washington, D.C.: Office of the President, December 1960), and U.S. Congress, Senate, Committee on Government Operations, *Hearings: Executive Reorganization Proposals,* 92nd Cong., 1st sess., 1971.

28. Jean Jacques Rousseau, *The Social Contract,* John Somerville and Ronald E. Santoni, eds., *Social and Political Philosophy* (New York: Doubleday Anchor, 1963), p. 205.

29. Gerth and Mills, *From Max Weber,* p. 228.

30. Alvin Toffler, *Future Shock* (New York: Bantam Books, 1971), p. 144.

31. Frederick C. Thayer, *An End to Hierarchy! An End to Competition* (New York: New Viewpoints, 1973), p. 50.

32. Warren G. Bennis, *Organization Development: Its Nature, Origins, and Prospects* (Reading, Mass.: Addison Wesley, 1969), p. 34. But see also his "A Funny Thing Happened on the Way to the Future," *American Psychologist* 25 (1970): 595 - 608.

33. See, for example, Louis M. Kohlmeier, Jr., *The Regulators: Watchdog Agencies and the Public Interest* (New York: Harper & Row, 1969); Jewel Bellush and Stephen M. David, eds., *Race and Politics in New York City: Five Studies in Policy-Making* (New York: Praeger, 1971); and Richard L. Berkman and W. Kip Viscusi, *Damning the West: Ralph Nader's Study Group Report on the Bureau of Reclamation* (New York: Grossman Publishers, 1973).

34. Robert R. Alford, *Bureaucracy and Participation: Political Cultures in Four Wisconsin Cities* (Chicago: Rand McNally, 1969), p. 25.

35. The classic debate on this problem has been between Professors Friedrich and Finer. See Carl J. Friedrich, "Public Policy and the Nature of Administrative Responsibility," *Public Policy* (Harvard, 1940) and "Dilemma of Administrative Responsibility," Carl J. Friedrich, ed., *Nomos III: Responsibility* (New York: Liberal Arts Press, 1960), pp. 189 - 202; Herman Finer, "Administrative Responsibility in Democratic Government," *Public Administration Review* 1 (Summer 1941): 336.

36. Finer, "Administrative Responsibility," p. 336.

37. See John Manley, *The Politics of Finance* (Boston: Little, Brown, 1970) for an interpretation of the influence of economic interests in legislative policy making.

38. For a brief but useful discussion see Stephen K. Bailey, *Congress in the Seventies,* 2nd ed. (New York: St. Martin's Press, 1970), chap. 5.

39. See Frederick Mosher, ed., *Governmental Reorganizations* (Indianapolis: Bobbs Merrill, 1967).

The Environment of
Public Bureaucracy

The preceding chapter discussed the role of public bureaucracy in the American political system. It gave particular emphasis to the vast scope of bureaucracy and its importance in the development and implementation of government policy decisions. We suggested that public bureaucracy could be studied by means of a three-part framework that centers upon machine, humane, and political values. These values, we suggested, were all legitimate and necessary in democratic public administration. Before further examining each of the three, however, we should first consider briefly the external and internal environment within which public organizations operate, because this environment affects profoundly the applications of machine, humane, and political values.

As figure 2.1 shows, the setting in which public administration operates is defined by multiple elements and constraints. These elements and constraints also define the degree to which the administrative system can adopt and adapt to evolving values and political interests. The impact of the environment of public bureaucracy on administrative action provides the focus of this chapter.

This environment includes a constitutional framework that delimits possible avenues of change. Within the constitutional constraints — separation of powers, federalism, etc. — there exist many possible alternatives of administrative activity. But there seems little likelihood of such revolutionary changes as the establishment of a parliamentary system on the British model or the destruction of federalism by abolishing the present fifty states. Hence, this book will consider strategies for dealing with bureaucracy within the present constitutional framework.

Similarly, certain cultural and political forces set a somewhat flexible boundary around possible administrative changes. It is unlikely, for

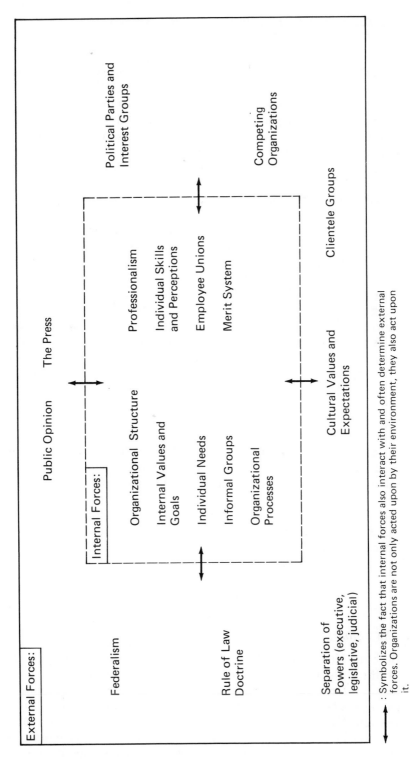

FIGURE 2.1

example, that the American public would support a movement to nationalize all major industry and set up a socialized economy, even though the public has accepted the gradual role of increasing government intervention in the economy. We shall assume, moreover, that the tradition of "rule of law" will continue to provide substantial opportunity without criminal penalty for individuals, groups, and parties to influence or attempt to oppose government activity. Barring some cataclysmic crisis such as nuclear war or complete economic breakdown, it seems probable that the democratic character of the American political system will survive despite modifications.

Human and group characteristics also delimit possible methods for improving public administration. We shall assume, for example, that public employees will continue to exhibit a concern for their own welfare and not totally forsake self-interest for the needs of the "public." We shall also consider informal group mechanisms, professional values, and other internal forces as constraints. For the foreseeable future we do not view as feasible the creation of a utopian society in which people or leaders behave unselfishly and industriously to obtain the "common good" without concern for personal gain. Plato, Karl Marx, and B. F. Skinner, among others, have suggested that such societies might be achieved, and there seems to be no final proof regarding their potential.[1] But we shall be more modest in suggesting mechanisms for altering human values and behavior. America is not likely soon to become a society of selfless humanitarians.

In sum, there are limits, but fairly wide limits, for improving the public administrative system in America. Furthermore, the environmental features discussed in this chapter will be viewed from both a positive and negative perspective. The constraints of constitutionalism, political and cultural forces, as well as internal characteristics of organizations, can contribute to the successful achievement of public policy as well as impede it.

THE EXTERNAL ENVIRONMENT

The Constitutional Framework

Both the United States Constitution and the state constitutions provide for three distinct branches of government: the executive (the president and governors), the legislative, and the judicial. Similarly, many urban governments have legally separate power centers defined by their charters. Separation of political institutions is intended to prevent abuse of power by politicians as well as by the majority of the electorate, whom the constitutional framers viewed. with considerable distrust.[2] The powers of and, hence, potential for abuse by politicians are limited by dividing political responsibilities among competing branches of government. The resultant system of checks and balances, including a number of other protective provisions, such as the division of the federal and state legislatures (with the exception of Nebraska) into two houses, sets up political systems that at first glance are divided neatly into separate institutions with separate responsibilities in law making, law execution, and law adjudication. As often noted, however, "separation" of powers is ordinarily a system of shared powers in which each branch performs functions of the others. And actual practice has greatly expanded the overlapping of these functions. For example, the president can, as allowed by the Constitution, veto acts of Congress and deliver legislative messages, thereby participating in the making of laws. The president, moreover, is actually the principal legislator when he submits legislative programs and otherwise provides legislative leadership. The Supreme Court in the preceding century began to declare acts of Congress and the president unconstitutional, through the doctrine of judicial review.

The separation of institutions and sharing of powers has great significance for the administration of public policy. The executive branch, in which most government departments and agencies are located, technically maintains responsibility for administering the law. Elected chief executives (presidents, governors, mayors) formally head the public bureaucracy. But actual control is dispersed. For example, presidents lack autonomy in authorizing funds for subordinate agencies because of Congress's role in the budgetary process. President Nixon's efforts to curtail programs by impounding funds approved by Congress were successfully challenged in federal court. Indeed, the prime purpose of the Congressional Budget and Impoundment Control Act of 1974 was to increase legislative balance in agency spending and budget control over executive dominance in the budget process. Among other things, this act provided for a congressional budget office. Governors and mayors in varying degrees also face constraints.[3] But, experienced administrators realize that they depend on multiple avenues of support and control. The presidential appointee of a national agency must attempt to attract support not only from key career administrative subordinates and elected superiors but also from congressional committees and other political power centers if he or she is to receive adequate funding, staffing, or authority. The power to administer is not an automatic requisite of high administrative or political office but must be gained through bargaining, persuasion, and other more subtle means.[4]

From a positive standpoint, sharing of powers by different branches of government provides multiple points of access to the political system. The failure of one branch of government to respond favorably to a particular group or sector of society may be offset by the willingness of another structure, e.g., a congressional committee, to be more supportive. Also, agency heads can sometimes build up a measure of independence from chief executives, allowing themselves greater freedom to follow the dictates of their professional consciences and thereby respond to interests or issues neglected by the formal political centers.

Some take comfort in the delaying effect of a fragmented power structure. To achieve major policy innovations such as the establishment of nationalized gun control or medical care requires the acquiescence of multiple power centers. Therefore, such changes can be blocked at a variety of points.[5] Conservatives are seemingly the prime beneficiaries of this inertia, yet fragmented systems of power benefit all resisters of change, which at times might be liberals attempting to block more conservative policy positions.

Yet, separation and sharing of powers exact certain costs. Speedy action may be delayed on problems requiring a fast response. Majority sentiment may be stalemated by a tiny minority, as in the case of a few powerful committee chairmen in Congress resisting nationally supported legislation. Planning becomes uncertain when political executives cannot assure their agency heads of legislative approval of funding. Politicians running for office, especially for executive positions such as the presidency, cannot honestly promise implementation of their election platforms. Too many obstacles may arise in other branches. In fact, certain components of the bureaucracy, such as independent regulatory agencies, are by law excluded from direct executive control and constitute an additional source of fragmentation and autonomy.

The Legal Tradition

The concept of "rule of law" is basic to the democratic form of government. This central tenet stipulates that laws and not individuals safeguard constitutional freedoms. No person is above the law, and all are limited by it — especially government officials.

Though imperfectly achieved in practice, this legal tradition does have profound implications. It limits significantly the actions of government workers and constrains capricious and discriminatory behavior. Government officials ordinarily cannot spend monies unappropriated or unauthorized by legislators. They have difficulty withholding benefits mandated by law. Even if, for example, an administrator in the Veterans Administration held strongly racist attitudes, he would have difficulty consistently withholding benefits from minority veterans.

Administrative-procedure laws and other regulations help define the legitimate and permissible boundaries of bureaucratic action. The Administrative Procedure Act of 1946, for example, defined the rights of parties in litigation before a government agency — the right to counsel, the right to a fair hearing, the right to redress, and the right to understand clearly the charges or allegations being presented. The Freedom of Information Act of 1967 provides citizens with a legal basis for obtaining information or data from governmental agencies. These and similar laws are becoming increasingly important as government agencies acquire growing amounts of information on citizens and as computer technology facilitates the accumulation and dissemination of such information.

But the rule of law has to rest on firmer ground than statute alone. It must be a part of the value structure of the millions of bureaucrats who compose our public service. If it is accepted only as a formal guideline, it will lack the power that only deep-rooted conviction and identification can produce. Millions of Americans have been discriminated against because of their race despite the thirteenth, fourteenth, and fifteenth amendments to the Constitution. Local, state, and even some federal administrators have resisted the 1954 Supreme Court decision requiring schools to integrate "with all deliberate speed." Despite a host of federal and state laws and agencies aimed at ending discrimination on the basis of sex, age, race, religion, or national origin, such discrimination continues to occur within all levels of government as well as within the private sector.[6] Even where discrimination is not involved, countless citizens have been ill-treated by overzealous or sometimes indifferent public officials oblivious to the letter and spirit of the law. The most egregious and well known recent instance of public servants operating above the rule of law was Watergate, in which the president himself violated national statutes as well as his constitutional oath in an effort to protect his political power base.[7]

Another limitation of the rule of law involves effectiveness and efficiency. Adherence to rigorous procedures often produces major delays in dealing with crucial policy issues. Enabling various interests to present their case in various forums of government and to challenge government decisions in the courts can slow action during emergencies, such as a major recession or energy crisis. Individuals may have needed benefits withheld because of time-consuming procedural delays. Additionally, the rule-of-law principle often forces a focus on narrow legal issues rather than on broad aspects of public policy. The needs of society and of individuals may go unmet because of narrow interpretations of the law by attorneys and other employees in the public service.

Although the rule-of-law doctrine affects the behavior of all administrative agencies, its impact is most strongly reflected in the regulatory agencies of government, which are granted a quasi-judicial function. Set up to monitor and control the activities of specific sectors of the economy, often with legislated political independence from executives, these agencies frequently have become subservient to the groups they are supposed to regulate. The Interstate Commerce Commission, the Securities and Exchange Commission, the Federal Trade Commission, and the Food and Drug Administration all have quasi-judicial functions. Their purpose is to enforce regulatory legislation and to make legal decisions involving such matters as licensing requests, consumer complaints, and disputes related to fair competitive practices. The neutrality of these agencies has apparently increased due to the appointment of "administrative judges," examiners who are civil servants with independent status within government agencies, to hear cases. These individuals are usually highly qualified lawyers with considerable experience. Although the regulating process and hearing procedures are severely limited by law and by the strategies of litigation,[8] and decisions by these agencies can be appealed through the federal court structure, the courts have resisted accepting regulatory cases for review, in part because of their lack of technical expertise.[9] Thus, the regulatory agencies have been granted considerable license in the determination of administrative law. This has resulted in an extensive backlog of cases, delays in adjudication, and mounting legal expenses as cases move slowly through the labyrinth of the required legal procedures.[10]

The delay, however, which takes its toll on timely action, seems necessarily unavoidable in a legal system that affords countless opportunities for litigants to challenge the power of administrative agencies. One must recall, after all, that the encumbrance of bureaucratic agencies with legal constraints results in part from the public's distrust of unrestrained bureaucratic action, so while legal procedures emanating from the rule of law often provide important protection against bureaucratic abuse, they often simultaneously cripple the efforts of an agency attempting to prevent an abuse of law by an offending party or company.[11]

Thus, rule-of-law principles, while attempting to ensure that constitutional principles and guarantees are followed, often preclude speed of governmental action and policy setting. But, in addition to this, it has also become obvious that many regulatory agencies fail to use the full legal powers that they may have in forcing private industries to correct deceptive or illegal practices. Witness, for example, the lengthy interaction between the Federal Trade Commission and the makers of Geritol, who maintained that their product cured "tired blood." Making use of a series of legal maneuvers, the Geritol manufacturers were able to continue this allegedly deceptive advertising about their product. The American Bar Association lambasted the failure of the Federal Trade Commission (FTC) to force Geritol to modify its advertising. The FTC, fearful of being labeled "antibusiness," did little more than elicit gentlemen's agreements from the company that it would refrain from advertising in the future.[12]

The rule of law, then, constitutes an important force in limiting the action of public officials and providing procedural safeguards. But, as history has indicated, the principle sometimes can be violated in practice as well as in spirit. Even where followed, moreover, it may impede effective and timely action. Nevertheless, in helping provide public access and protecting individual rights it represents a crucial underpinning of public bureaucracy in any political democracy.

Federalism

A third major force affecting the operation of bureaucracy is federalism. The peculiar history of the United States, especially the establishment of separate American colonies and the reaction to British rule, helped engender a belief that centralized power was the antithesis of democratic government. After independence from Britain was achieved, the Articles of Confederation produced a loose alliance of states without a strong unifying national government. The Constitution corrected some of the weaknesses of the Articles of Confederation by providing a stronger central government while maintaining a decentralized structure.

Federalism means, of course, that two or more governments have jurisdiction over the same geographic area. In Boston, for example, law-enforcement officers from the FBI (national), Massachusetts state police, and Boston city police may arrest citizens for various crimes. Though some functions, such as those concerning foreign policy, reside exclusively in the national government and some are constitutionally reserved to the states, most administrative functions in fact overlap. Federal, state, and city governments, for example, have a significant role in welfare policies. Such overlapping of functions and jurisdictions necessitates cooperation but inevitably produces conflict. And it has profound consequences for administrative responsiveness.[13]

On the positive side, federalism helps provide for the preservation of local and regional values, at least for the electoral majority in local areas. Additionally, the potential for citizen access is normally increased because governments are closer and state and local legislators represent fewer constituents than their national counterparts. Administrators of state and local governments may be more attuned to local problems and may have more sources of information on which to base decisions. Furthermore, the size of administrative agencies and number of hierarchical layers within them are often smaller than their national counterparts. In smaller political units, citizens may feel an increased sense of participation and even trust of government officials, who can seem less remote.

On the negative side, the multiple layers of government resulting from federalism produce duplication and cause problems of coordination, delay, and difficulty in pinpointing responsibility. Many public programs cannot be neatly layered and subdivided into areas of autonomy, thus, the structural "neatness" of federalism belies the confusing strands that contribute to public programs.[14] Moreover, voters have a greatly increased burden in attempting to understand and control the elected officials of multiple governments.

Further, national decision makers attempting to formulate and administer policy concerning national problems such as energy management have to contend with state and local officials who sometimes resist or ineffectively administer policy. And local officials may view federal officials in a similar bad light, judging them arrogant, blind to reality, and insensitive to local uniqueness. Lack of common standards and laws adds to the confusion and fosters countless judicial appeals. From the viewpoint of local officials, flexibility is lost and time wasted in meeting national guidelines for the expenditure of grant monies from the federal government. National law, on the other hand, may be ignored or impeded by local and state officials unsympathetic to federal guidelines on equal employment opportunities as well as other aspects of civil rights.

Federalism may be an inevitable feature of such a large and diverse nation as the United States. Although it has undergone considerable transformation over the years, it still remains a component of the bureaucratic system. While the general policy-setting trend has been in the direction of the national government, we have seen that state and local governments have expanded rapidly. Hence, the problems and opportunities of a federal structure of government will continue.

Political Attitudes

The politically relevant beliefs and attitudes of people help determine their reaction to public bureaucracy. Of particular importance are orientations toward the nation, system of government, and, of course, public bureaucracy itself. Also important are social values that may determine the likelihood of people obeying laws and cooperating with government officials. Probably the most basic one is belief in the legitimacy of government.

The significance of political culture is apparent when we consider that the most effective means of enforcing government policy is voluntary citizen compliance. No modern government could force the bulk of its population to obey rules and regulations against its wishes. Even the so-called totalitarian governments such as that of the Soviet Union must be rooted in public support for their long-term survival; tyranny and terrorism cannot be sustained indefinitely against large numbers of people in highly interdependent, contemporary societies.

Potentially disruptive political sentiments among deprived ethnic minorities or hostile majorities illustrate the point that fragmented societies such as the U.S. have a high stake in stimulating greater support. Yet, certain aspects of the political culture of the United States well serve the administrative system. The great majority of people in this country identify themselves as Americans, support the system of government, and demand integrity in their public officials. To be sure, their notions of democracy may be rather vague and they may exhibit somewhat authoritarian and intolerant attitudes with respect to such matters as race and radical organizations.[15] But on the whole the American public remains loyal to the country and to the idea of constitutional democracy, though they may be quite critical of politicians or of the performance of a particular institution, such as Congress. Even with the increasing distrust of government generated by the Vietnam war, Watergate, and unfulfilled promises of racial and sexual equality, a strong reserve of support for the country and its form of government remains. It is not solely fear that motivates compliance with tax, traffic, and other regulations but also a sense of civic duty. In contrast to many countries, Americans tend to be honest in their dealings with government. They also tend to expect comparatively fair treatment from public officials.[16] Most people would not try to cast double ballots or steal large items of government property even if they had no fear of getting caught. Their compliance greatly facilitates the administration of policy and usually surmounts a generalized, weak contempt for "bureaucrats," a term that in popular usage connotes rigid and perhaps ineffectual people.

Regrettably, the public's tendency to obey and to ignore can produce some rather serious consequences. Most obviously, the ideal of political democracy is popular control, not public apathy. In the 1972 presidential election, for example, only about 55 percent of the voting-age population cast ballots, and elections for senators and congresspeople, as well as local elections, often elicit less than a 50 percent turnout of eligible voters. Recent studies show clearly that public political participation is minimal and skewed heavily in favor of the more highly educated, affluent, and organized sectors of American society.[17]

The danger, of course, is that apathy may facilitate corruption or other forms of abuse. Yet, despite recurring reports of scandals concerning intermittent corruption in the legislative, executive, and judicial branches of government in the United States, its exact extent is difficult to document.[18] The degree of corruption in America should not be overstated. However, the fact that even a few judges, legislators, governors, and American presidents have been involved in such matters is cause for concern and illustrates the need for vigilance. Administrative corruption also occurs, as in the case of certain police forces in large cities.[19] As one would expect, administrative corruption seems to be more frequent at local levels and in the enforcement and permit/licensing functions of government. Yet, on the whole, most public employees, who represent a fair cross-section of American citizens, seem to be quite honest in their conduct.

In addition to public support (or apathy) and to comparatively high levels of honesty in the public sector, two other cultural norms are major elements of the external environment of bureaucracy. One of these is efficiency, which commands that bureaucracy act with speed, minimum cost, and with the application of expertise. This, as we have noted, is the basis of "machine" bureaucracy. The other is political responsiveness, which is reflected by norms such as representativeness, accountability, and openness. The motivating belief behind this value is that government agencies should be the servants of the people.

The values of efficiency and political responsiveness often conflict in practice. A financially sound municipal budget may require that citizen demands for a swimming pool or new high school be postponed. Similarly, timely development of an effective annual budget may be impeded by procedures that provide maximum access to the decision-making process by groups within the community. Yet both efficiency and political responsiveness acquire legitimacy from the political culture.

Political Parties and Interest Groups

Political parties and interest groups also affect the actions of bureaucracy. A primary function of political parties in many countries has been to assemble and articulate interests and to translate them into public policy through the authoritative decision-making centers of government. Where party discipline exists, parties can exercise a major role in the formulation of policy. Party discipline typically produces united voting along party lines in legislative bodies. In parliamentary systems, such as that of the United Kingdom, party effectiveness is further enhanced because the legislative and executive functions are combined in Parliament rather than separate.

But in the United States, the two major political parties do not as effectively represent separate and distinct interests.[20] To win decisively, parties must serve as umbrella organizations, hoping to attract as wide a basis of support as possible; this limits their ability to speak for one particular group or set of interests. Also, the separation between executive and legislative branches and the fragmentation of power within many legislatures mean that governors, mayors, and presidents cannot ensure passage of their legislative programs and that the policy making is less cohesive.

Yet parties have significance at the national level and wherever party competition exists. Though they may assemble and articulate interests imperfectly, it can be said that as a general tendency the

Democratic party represents less affluent and more liberal sectors of society as well as minorities. Republicans tend to be somewhat wealthier, more conservative, and oriented toward business interests.[21] Of course, there is much overlap, as in the case of conservative southern congresspeople. American parties may also help unite executive and legislative branches, especially when both are of the same party. Moreover, within legislatures they can help elicit support or opposition to part^ular policy proposals.

While neither disciplined nor reflective of specific sectors of American society, parties do help shape public policy. But the fact that they are not authoritative determinators of public policy per se provides increased freedom and flexibility for organizations as they attempt to shape it. Thus, political parties may effectively contribute to the power of bureaucracies by being comparatively weak voices in the articulation of public policy.

Interest groups are private organizations seeking to influence public policy. They may represent economic as well as philanthropic groups. The National Association of Manufacturers and the AFL-CIO are prime examples of economic interest groups. The American Humane Society illustrates a noneconomic interest group that seeks to achieve social goals. In recent years Common Cause, the Center for Responsive Institutions, and other organizations have emerged as interest groups attempting to represent the public as a whole against the power of narrow economic organizations. Of great consequence have been civil rights groups, such as the Southern Christian Leadership Conference and the NAACP.

The attempts of interest groups to influence public policy focus on public bureaucracies as well as upon elected legislators and executives. Such efforts are quite rational because of the major role public bureaucracy plays in the formulation and implementation of public policy. Furthermore, contact between public administrators and representatives of private interests is often inevitable and in many ways desirable. Government agencies need information from and often the cooperation of private organizations to carry out their tasks. Officials in the Federal Energy Administration, for example, clearly require data from oil companies in order to plan intelligently. This data should, however, be balanced by information provided by consumer and environmental groups.

As the beneficiaries or victims of government policy it is understandable that interest groups would want to influence government decisions. Their desire to play a role is also democratic in the sense that private-interest organizations provide for a kind of representation that may be lacking through elected politicians. Small or specialized interests might be swallowed up in the electoral process, which provides representation on a geographic basis. It seems perfectly appropriate, for instance, that national student organizations argue before the Civil Aeronautics Board for the retention of youth air fares.

In short, access to public bureaucracy by interest groups can provide a crucial form of democratic representation because interest groups reflect different "publics." Individuals, after all, tend to work through groups, so group representation can support the principle of democratic government to the extent that it allows a variety of competing interests to present their cases to public bureaucracy. Multiple sources of information and pressure can provide a diversity of influences on policy matters, though multiple inputs do not guarantee equal influence upon those making policy decisions.

From a negative standpoint, widespread group intervention can present a confusing array of opinions to public administrators. Wallace Sayre and Herbert Kaufman, authors of a major study of urban government, attribute the lethargy, sluggishness, and status quo orientation of big-city bureaucracy to the confusion generated by competing group demands.[22] Not only inaction but also self-serving policies may emerge from pluralistic group activity if public organizations feel free to emphasize goals that advance the power and security of certain groups over others. Perhaps a more serious problem involves an agency being "captured" by a single interest group, as in the case of regulatory agencies becoming subservient to interests they are supposed to regulate.

This amalgamation of private interest and public agency may arise from a number of causes. Public officials and private organizations may hold similar professional values. Also, high-level public administrators, such as members of regulatory commissions, may be recruited from the regulated industry itself. Of great consequence in a political democracy is the fact that government organizations ordinarily require public support if they are to thrive. An antagonistic powerful interest group can bring enormous pressure to bear through the legislative system. Agencies viewed as "difficult" may fail to have budget requests granted and public administrators may find themselves demoted or transferred if they too consistently resist influential private groups.[23]

Interest-group activity can have a profound impact on legislative policy making through direct lobbying as well as through the electoral process.[24] Lobbying refers to efforts by individuals or groups to influence the decisions or actions of government officials. It may take many forms, such as providing information and organizing letter-writing campaigns. Through campaign contributions interest groups can have a great effect on the outcome of elections. Both lobbying and electoral support can be legitimate expressions of democratic processes. To the extent that the activities of interest groups remain ethical and broadly representative of the political system as a whole, democratic public administration may be served. But financial and organizational advantages may result in the more powerful sectors of society dominating activity in public organizations.

Competing Organizations

Last, we should briefly note that an important part of an organization's environment may be other public organizations in competition with it. Competition is fostered by overlapping and often conflicting organizational goals and limited system resources (such as money and personnel). Competition between organizations — and often between subdivisions within the *same* organization — compromises the potentially autonomous powers of agencies and provides an important check on bureaucratic abuse of power. This competition, however, is often minimized by the organizations themselves agreeing upon their jurisdictional and functional limits and tacitly respecting each other's terrain.[25]

THE INTERNAL ENVIRONMENT

Public organizations also display certain internal characteristics that profoundly affect their performance. These internal environmental features can sabotage the official goals of organizations or, properly channeled, aid in the achievement of them.

Professionalism

One of the consequences of an increasingly complex and technologically sophisticated society is the growing number of professions. Such occupations as statistician, electronics engineer, and medical technician are now important professions in the national economy. Moreover, jobs that previously required little training now demand professional education. Police officers have been typically considered working-class public servants. Now, university training in criminal justice has begun to professionalize this field. Some communities, such as Berkeley, California, require that applicants for police jobs have university degrees, and it is not unusual to find patrolmen or sergeants holding master's degrees.

It is not only the growing technical requirements of occupations that stimulate greater professionalism. Occupational groups themselves support greater training in order to improve their capacity to work effectively and to elevate their status and power vis-à-vis other occupations. Exclusive educational and examination requirements, which are typically controlled by private professional organizations, provide financial and status rewards to members. If private professional associations can restrict membership, or if training requirements are so arduous as to limit qualified personnel, the demand for services can produce high salaries and elite status. Universities, which have an interest in maintaining enrollments, contribute to professionalization by offering new programs for old fields.

A variety of government professional positions, such as personnel officer, are primarily concerned with administrative support duties. But the government employs virtually every class of professional to be found in the private sector. Economists, physicians, attorneys, scientists, and a host of others occupy key government posts. Their education and continuing links with their professions through journals, conferences, and membership in professional organizations help determine their actions as employees of government. In fact, their entrance into government may be determined by educational requirements and licensing exams controlled directly and indirectly by a private professional association external to government.[26]

Professionalism contributes to the machine capacity of government agencies and provides skills and talents essential to fulfilling public goals. Engineers in state highway departments and medical personnel in city hospitals illustrate the point that life and death decisions often depend upon the professional judgment of government specialists. In addition to skills, professionalism produces other values of benefit to public administration. A professional mentality involves a commitment to do one's job well. Moreover, professionals typically view their jobs as careers, not just as a nine-to-five occupation to bring in money for the necessities and pleasures of life. Professionalism may also enhance the desire to be of service and usually engenders honesty. Though still human, professionals seem far less likely than others to accept bribes or to compromise standards for the sake of political expediency.

This integrity, however, may produce undesirable side effects. In a democracy, public policy is usually the result of compromise. Yet by its characteristic adherence to strict standards, professionalism produces hostility to compromise and sometimes hostility to broad public programs. In other words, professionalism may impede control of public administrators by elected representatives. Also, professionalism may foster a rather scornful or patronizing view of ordinary people who do not have the special insight and knowledge of the professional group. Hence, citizens dealing with professionals in government may sense a certain aloofness, an emphasis upon procedure, and a lack of concern for everyday human problems.[27]

While professionalism may foster a narrow, mechanistic view, certain countertrends serve to ameliorate these undesirable consequences. First, social problems such as poverty, energy shortages, and environmental pollution are so complex that interdisciplinary cooperation is required of the various professionals dealing with them.[28] Second, while professionalization tends to pull the process of decision making down the administrative hierarchy to the level of the expert and the specialist, other technological developments, such as new budgeting techniques, tend to push decisions back up to higher levels. However much one may recoil against the authoritarian structure of bureaucratic organizations, administrators near the top may be forced to take a broader view of their agencies' operations. In part this results from the fact that top-level bureaucrats are more accountable to elected politicians. Also, their work is less specialized and reflects a broader external environment.

Professionalism, therefore, produces multiple consequences. Its positive or negative impact can depend on the circumstances of the particular case. One of the most telling commentaries on professional solidarity occurred in 1953 when the director of the National Bureau of Standards, Dr. Allen V. Astin, was asked to resign by the secretary of commerce because of his refusal to certify the usefulness of a particular battery additive developed by an inventor. The Republican administration then in office had a probusiness orientation, and the inventor had successfully mobilized political support for his case. On the basis of Bureau of Standards testing, however, the product appeared useless.[29]

Dr. Astin was "a distinguished scientist well-known for his contributions to the development of the proximity fuse since World War II."[30] His firing was interpreted by the scientific community as an attack upon scientific objectivity and the professional integrity of scientists. The fact that Astin was a government employee was second to the fact that he was a professional scientist. As author Samuel Lawrence notes: "Members of the Federation of American Scientists and the Washington Chapter of the Association of Atomic Scientists (largely physicists) mounted a frontal assault. They issued angry press releases, called meetings, badgered the administration, and sought to call public attention to the government's alleged assault on science."[31] In the end, Astin was reinstated.

Employee Unions

During the 1950s and 1960s there was a massive rise in membership and an increase in the power of public-sector unions. Although public employee unions have a heritage that goes back to the late 1880s, they had never before demonstrated such strength, a change that can be attributed in part to the large increase in the number of public-sector employees. Also of great influence on the unions' recent dramatic rise to prominence was the wave of demands for democratization that swept the world following World War II.

These and similar events provided mutual reinforcement and gave impetus to public-sector unionism. For example, strikes by public employees in one city helped generate similar action in other cities. Also, competition between unions generated some of the increase in areas such as education. Further, government employees became increasingly dissatisfied with the salary gap between public and private employees and unionization gave them the power to demand parity. Professionalism also stimulated some union demands, with government professionals seeking a greater voice in policy decisions affecting the quality of their service. Nurses and teachers, for example, sought improved services to students and patients as well as salary increases and better working conditions. Finally, the economic recession and government budgetary problems of the mid-1970s produced a situation in which workers concerned with losing their jobs were motivated to join unions for protection.

A survey undertaken in 1969 by the Federal Bureau of Labor Statistics in cooperation with the International City Management Association revealed that two out of every three local government employees belonged to an employee association of some kind.[32] In fact, between 1960 and 1970, union membership increased by 100 percent for local and state government employees. The American Federation of Teachers increased its membership by well over 200 percent (56,000 to 205,000) and the State, County, and Municipal Workers' Union increased from 210,000 in 1960 to 445,000 in 1970.[33]

At the state level the increasing impact of unionization of public employees has led to a flurry of legislative attempts to provide a statutory framework for collective-bargaining issues, since specified procedures accepted by unions and management help prevent costly deadlocks. Between 1958 and 1969 twenty states enacted legislation delineating permissible collective-bargaining activities for state and local government employees.

The increasing impact in unionism at the state and local government levels is matched at the federal level, where slightly over 50 percent of all federal employees belong to a union or employee association of some type.[34] Between 1960 and 1970 membership in such unions as the American Federation of Government Employees and the American Postal Workers Union increased 94 percent (from 535,000 to 1,036,000).

Union demands for public investment in employee training programs, retirement programs, and annual salaries mean that unions now share the "power of the purse" with legislative bodies. They also help shape policy decisions. One study indicates that the increase of 88 percent in salary compensation to public employees between 1960 and 1970 may be largely attributable to public employee unions.[35] In some instances, collective-bargaining agreements have led to a reduction in program delivery. An extreme example of this occurred in 1968 when the

Youngstown, Ohio, school doors were closed because the community was unable to pay for negotiated salary agreements.

Another consequence of unionization has been to limit management discretion and innovation. The police commissioner of Detroit in 1970 instituted a requirement that future promotions on the force be dependent upon completion of at least one year of college. The Detroit police union killed this idea by threatening to block future union negotiations with the city. Even though strikes by government employees are generally outlawed, work-stoppage tactics have nevertheless had a measurable impact. For example, in 1965 there were 42 strikes involving about 12,000 government employees (146,000 workdays lost); in 1970 there were 412 strikes involving over 330,000 government employees resulting in over 2 million lost workdays.[36]

On the positive side, employee unions engender a number of benefits. They help limit arbitrary managerial action and assist in the protection of individuals. Since approximately one in six Americans is employed by government, the magnitude of these protections seems clear. Unions can also stabilize employee-management relations by stimulating the development of viable collective-bargaining procedures. Some governmental units now accept binding arbitration, in which both sides agree to accept the decision of a neutral arbitrator, in the event that bargaining and mediation do not result in agreement between unions and management. Of great importance is the point that unions may reflect professional goals and therefore demand the upgrading of public services.

Unionization has, therefore, brought several important benefits along with its liabilities. There seems little doubt that unions will continue to be an important force in public administration in coming years.[37]

The Merit System

A chief defining characteristic of American public service is the merit system, a method of recruitment and promotion designed to ensure employee selection on the basis of ability, not political influence. The assassination of President Garfield in 1881 by a disgruntled job seeker stimulated a reform effort that resulted in the Pendleton Act of 1883. Carefully defining procedures for hiring in the public service, the Pendleton Act began to make significant inroads on the spoils system, under which people had been selected on the basis of political influence and often fired when new politicians were elected.

The merit system provides for a competitive examination procedure to determine one's eligibility for government service and for a system of promotion and compensation based on merit, not partisan loyalty. It implies a standardized and routinized procedure not only for entry into but also for movement through the levels of governmental bureaucracy.

Of course, the system operates imperfectly because of such factors as preference points for veterans and difficulties in measuring true ability through examinations. The implied basis of the merit system — "the right person for the right job" — has created a complex system of job descriptions and job specifications so that the individual can ascertain the requirements of his job in order to be safeguarded from intemperate management. Security in service — protection from the fluctuations of party control of the government — is an added important attribute. The merit system, in short, is intended to be the basis of neutrality, continuity, and stability for workers in public service.

Although not all positions in the federal government are competitive civil service jobs, the approximately 85 percent of the work force now covered by civil service is a significant increase from its more modest beginnings in 1883, when only 10 percent of the federal positions were covered.[38] Various strategies sometimes enable civil service rules to be manipulated, yet this may facilitate not only patronage appointments but also flexibility for administrators seeking the most qualified person for the job. The goal of the merit system to insulate employees from politics appears to have been largely achieved at the federal level as well as in many states. Significant strides have also been made at the local level, often because of federal regulations requiring civil service procedures prior to the distribution of federal funds to local jurisdictions.

The values the civil service system has helped maximize have not come without cost. The categorization of tasks according to pay classification and job description formats have to some degree so standardized and regimented responsibilities that they have often dampened the development of flexibility in job design and problem solving and frustrated the administrator seeking more novel approaches. The standardization of promotion, benefits, and the like often induces a laxness in the bureaucracy in which commendable achievement is not automatically rewarded, nor inferior workers weeded out. Equally unfortunate is the fact that the "neutrality" provided by the merit system often adds to bureaucratic recalcitrance in acting decisively or with sensitivity to individual employee or citizen needs. In the zeal to separate politics from administration, the merit system may have also insulated administration from the legitimate political value and human needs that lie beyond the walls of the organization.

Organizational Structure

Organizational structure influences administrative decisions and contributes to the values and behavior of public employees. We have seen, for example, that public organizations are predominantly bureaucratic, that is, constructed on a hierarchical, chain-of-command principle wherein rules supposedly determine personal conduct. The hierarchical principle does, of course, concentrate great power at the top, with administrative leaders commanding and coordinating the activities of thousands of subordinates.

Yet hierarchy produces other consequences. Employees may be reluctant to forward negative information to their superior for the understandable reason that it may reflect badly on them. When an employee's promotion or retention depends upon making a good impression, it is not surprising that many people will attempt to cover up or minimize their mistakes. Unfortunately, the tendency to withhold negative information means that superiors often have inadequate information upon which to make decisions.

This problem is especially serious because top-level administrators often lack technical expertise in particular policy areas and have become increasingly dependent upon expert professionals.[39] In other words, although administrators are charged with making good decisions, they may lack information necessary to that task. The uncertainties of the consequences of decisions add to the conservatism of high-level officials. In policy areas such as housing, poverty, and the environment, so many variables determine outcomes and so much is beyond the control of administrative leaders that they may make only minor policy adjustments rather than risk the uncertain outcome of radical change.[40] Carried to excess, this decision-making strategy can seriously impede the innovative and responsive capacities of organizations.

Hierarchical organization, however, does help establish accountability, since specific individuals can more easily be held responsible for administrative actions. The formal hierarchical positions of people also help to determine their attitudes. Public administrators are likely to take on the values of their position. Career officers in the military, for example, ordinarily acquire a strong sense of duty, and they feel a personal responsibility to help defend their country.[41]

Other structural characteristics of public organizations may also help determine bureaucratic responsiveness. The division of bureaucracies into specialized agencies, offices, and units is standard. It allows organizational agencies and subunits to develop expertise on particular problem areas or to handle particular functions. This concentration can help produce efficiency and competence. Units may be established on the basis of serving particular clientele or geographic area. They also may be established to perform a particular purpose (e.g. health services) or process (e.g. auditing).

Specialization, however, may produce administrative problems. Specialized units can acquire a narrow perspective in which broader organizational goals are ignored. Financial departments, for example, may become so obsessed with procedures and record-keeping that they weaken the organization's capacity to accomplish its primary goal. Another common problem with organizational subunits is competition or conflict. The classic line-staff conflict may involve a unit concerned principally with support (staff) in opposition to a unit charged with providing the organization's chief service (line). Administrative personnel (staff) and professors (line) in universities, for instance, may each fail to appreciate the problems and contributions of the other. Even though line-staff functions may overlap, each unit may perceive itself as performing the one vital task of the organization. Competition among units, even those with similar roles, manifests itself in requests for budget increases, new personnel, and broadened decision-making authority.

Public agencies sometimes experience difficulty because of the geographic separation of their offices. Most employees of the federal government work in outlying regions, not in Washington, D.C. Similar patterns of separation occur in state agencies. The separation of field from state central office may engender communications difficulties and complicate the task of coordinating and directing activities. On the one hand, administrators in the field may feel that they better understand local conditions and that they can be more responsive to local needs. Central-office administrators, on the other hand, may become frustrated with field representatives failing to follow policy guidelines established in Washington or in state capitals.[42]

Human Considerations

Organizations are staffed by people who bring many different attitudes, values, and personal characteristics with them. Some of these characteristics may be culturally defined, such as a tendency to exhibit a high degree of interpersonal trust, which facilitates cooperation. Other cultural values may have mixed consequences. Competitiveness may sometimes stimulate productivity but it may also generate hostility and divert individual attention to personal goals.[43]

In addition to broad cultural values, public employees bring personality characteristics into their places of employment.[44] Public managers must contend with insecurities, hostilities, and various forms of neuroses in some of their subordinates, coworkers, and superiors. Much of the time spent on personnel matters by administrators may be consumed by people who, superficially at least, are "problems." It is true, of course, that nonconformists, zealots, and others who require special attention may be a creative, innovative force. Their "maladjustment" may reflect merely an understandable resistance to the regimentation characteristic of much bureaucratic activity.

Employees inevitably hold various perceptions of their own self-interest, a fact that is understandable but that complicates the development of effective and responsive administration. A frequent source of conflict of interest may involve the ambitions of individual administrators versus the tasks and goals of government organizations. These conflicts do not ordinarily involve outright dishonesty but instead result from organizational incentives such as promotion opportunities. Responding to public needs, for example, may require that an administrator openly argue against his or her superior's orders. Now, a degree of obedience is not only helpful for the coordination and control of public policy but is a quality needed by employees who wish to have successful careers. Nevertheless, submissiveness may seriously weaken the service orientation of public organizations. The needs of a citizen may become secondary to the security needs of employees. Less excusable are pressures on an employee's time. Dealing with special cases or making exceptions ordinarily takes extra effort. A natural response is to make decisions that will demand the least amount of work.

The degree to which individuals respond to task requirements, develop a positive attitude toward the service clientele, and identify with organizational objectives can be viewed as dependent upon the "psychological contract" they make with their organization. For some individuals a demanding and challenging organizational setting is a requisite for participating and producing. For others, this setting may be an anathema to their expectations and interests. Thus, to be effective, organizations must be able to mete out different inducements — both tangible and intangible — to individuals to secure their contributions.[45]

Unfortunately, however, many organizations attempt to provide only tangible and material inducements, and many of these serve to reward only a fixed level of minimum performance expectations, creating an atmosphere of conservatism.[46] Thus, the capacities of bureaucracy are in large measure determined by the maze of expectations and work-related values within the organization. The degree to which capacities are maximized is affected by an organization's ability to recruit and sustain the activities of individuals who show concern for the needs of the people served by the organization.

Another important element affecting administrative behavior is the existence of informal groups. Organizational charts may specify the hierarchical chain of command as well as communications networks and formal rules. But human friendships, peer group support, or alliance networks may in practice radically alter these formal structural principles. Administrative work is partly a political art, requiring the ability to elicit support and cooperation to accomplish tasks. It is therefore natural for public employees to form friendship groups. These informal structures, whose composition or nature no organizational chart can predict, may establish their own rules of behavior and standards of performance.

On the one hand, informal groups and supportive ties may be quite beneficial. An organizational subunit can develop a strong esprit de corps that includes a high commitment to service; informal hierarchical networks can bypass ineffective people; and friendship ties can augment an administrator's formal powers. On the other hand, informal structures can subvert organizational goals. It is not uncommon that conformity to group norms takes priority over the accomplishment of public goals, thereby encouraging mediocrity. Friendship cliques, moreover, can alienate workers excluded from the clique, while cabals, which are secret, informal groups, may have some form of administrative sabotage or personal revenge as their primary goal. In short, informal organization is probably an inevitable part of administrative life, and it can be a powerful tool for achieving machine, humane, and political values, but it can also be a powerful impediment. In any event, it must be an important consideration for the operation of any bureaucratic structure.

Organizational Processes

Finally, the behavior of bureaucracies is largely defined by the nature of the organizational processes that continuously transpire within them. Although we cannot review all of the processes, communication, decision making, staffing, and budgeting are indicative of the range of these dynamics. While each of the processes of administration can contribute to bureaucratic capacities, they may also detract from them.

For example, no organization can survive without the communication of ideas and data. Although communication lies at the heart of administration, there is no one most effective way to communicate, nor is there any guarantee that an attempted communication is actually understood. Efforts by organizations to improve the flow of communication often lead to excessive rigidity in communication channels as well as communication overload. This problem is common where data collection exceeds the organization's ability to filter or synthesize it.[47]

Roberta Wohlstetter's account of the attack on Pearl Harbor provides a telling commentary on the potential seriousness of communication gaps. She argues that prior to the attack, American officials suffered not so much from a lack of information as from an overabundance of often irrelevant information. Also, communication between strategic elements of the intelligence arms of government was often abysmally slow and was often filtered through large numbers of people. Many communications, moreover, contained conjectures that often were accepted by recipients as fact.

In the absence of effective interagency communication and without consistent communication between Washington and the theater commands, individuals operated in an idiosyncratic manner, accepting as significant their *portion* of the messages flowing throughout the haphazard communications network. Stressing the importance of the communications process to the ability of the United States to predict an attack by Japan, Wohlstetter emphasizes the problem of lack of effective communication between central headquarters and field stations:

> *The Office of Naval Operations sent more information and evaluations to Honolulu than did the Army and almost invariably worded its messages in a way that the Army would have considered somewhat alarmist. The Army messages were infrequent and very cautiously worded. However, both services used a type of phrasing that left a great deal to the discretion of the local commander, both as to his interpretation of the intent of the message and the possible actions that he might put into effect as a result. The same message was sometimes intended as an alert order for one service, but not for the other. . . .*
>
> *Communication between Washington and the theater in 1941 was at such a rudimentary level that local interpretations were not subject to check. There was no standard procedure for acknowledgment or follow-up. Most top officials in Washington had only the haziest idea of what information was sent as a matter of course to the theaters, and since intentions were excellent, everybody assumed, much as we do today, that all essential or critical items of information were being sent out quickly. Admiral Turner, for example, was unaware that Kimmel did not have his own MAGIC decoding unit at Pearl Harbor. He also believed, like Admiral Stark and other Navy leaders, that the top-secret information received by both services in Honolulu was identical, that Short and Kimmel exchanged immediately whatever information they received, that there was a good press coverage in Honolulu, and that all the key officers read the daily papers with good judgment. As we have seen, none of these beliefs was justified.[48]*

Unfortunately, there are no universal, infallible rules for establishing effective communications. The number of actors involved in a communications network introduces human frailties at every turn. The tendency to decipher matter in terms relevant to one's own experiences and predilections means that the original intention of a communication may become distorted.

A second example of the impact of administrative processes concerns decision making. Decisions occur at every level of organizations: decisions related to what to do, how to do it, and when to do it. They may be decisions of obvious import to the organization or decisions seemingly irrelevant, which only later demonstrate their importance.

In ideal terms, goals are officially stated and administrators make decisions that will achieve them. Viewed in this manner, organizational decision making appears to be a quite simple process. But such a view distorts the basic characteristics of goals and the basic elements of organizational communications patterns outlined earlier. For example, organizations often hold multiple, conflicting, and unspecified goals, and administrators may lack vital information on problems because of faulty communications. Also, a simplistic view of the decisional process fosters a static view of organizational decision making.

In an interesting essay some years ago on decision making in organizations William Dill developed a simplified model of the decision-making process that affords us a means of briefly illustrating its complexities.[49] Noting that decision making can be viewed in terms of phases, he developed a five-part schema:

(1)   Agenda building: defining goals and tasks for the organization and assigning priorities for their completion.

(2)   Search: looking for alternative courses of action and for information that can be used to evaluate them.

(3)   Commitment: testing proposed "solutions" to choose one for adoption by the organization.

(4)   Implementation: elaborating and clarifying decisions so that they can be put into effect; motivating members of the organization to help translate decisions into action.

(5)   Evaluation: testing the results of previous choices and actions to suggest new tasks for the organizational agenda or to facilitate organizational learning.

Unfortunately, the Dill schema structures the process too rigidly. In reality, the process is not entirely rational.[50] "Goal definition," for example, is an imperfect task subject to the vagaries of temperament, skill, and organizational environment. "Search" procedures, although aided today by extensive technological contributions, are often equally subjective and diffuse given the complexity of the problems being considered. "Testing" mechanisms are sometimes little more than artificial abstractions, and controlled tests may develop conclusions that do not apply in real-world settings. "Implementation" is typically quite complicated and reflects the whole gamut of administrative problems compressed into one concept, and "evaluation" may be prejudiced by the biases of the observer.

In sum, certain necessary processes of administration pose formidable problems for public administrators. Nevertheless, we shall see in the remaining chapters that certain techniques can facilitate the communications process and improve administrative decision making.

THE SETTING OF PUBLIC ADMINISTRATION

We have seen that public organizations confront a number of external and internal forces in their daily activities. These forces define the setting in which they must operate. At times these forces help enlarge the role of bureaucracy (as in the case of the relative weakness of political parties), and at other times they limit the activities of bureaucracy. Thus, organizations are immersed in a framework that imposes both constraints and liberties upon them.

Awareness of the consequences of these countervailing forces upon bureaucracy is critical to understanding the unique nature of bureaucratic capacity and democratic control. While check-and-balance systems seemingly help ensure that no power center will abuse its power for long, excessive checks impede organizational decisiveness. At other times, competition among political branches may give the bureaucracy excessive freedom as it watches from a protected middle position the separate political branches joined in battle. While interest groups serve as an important mechanism for representing citizen needs, organizations can often be captured by the aggressive activities of a few interests, limiting broader public representativeness.

In addition, there is an interrelated implication to the complexity of pressures and processes that define the administrative environment. With a competitive external environment and a dynamic, multifaceted internal environment, adherence to uniform organizational goals is usually impossible. The complexities of the administrative environment, the competing environmental pressures, and the imperfections that mark the internal workings of organizations often lead to the displacement or alteration of some organizational goals. The issue of goal displacement is quite complex, and we shall not review all possible considerations. It may be noted, however, that while sometimes such goals are self-serving, they may also sometimes well serve the public, particularly where politically or administratively established rules work to subvert the wider responsiveness of an organization.

Administrators ordinarily pursue a number of goals simultaneously, emphasizing different ones at different times. Some of these goals may be incompatible, and environmental pressures may cause administrators to sacrifice earlier goals and replace them with newer ones. A principal goal of almost all organizations is survival — and often growth by increasing size, budget, and functions. It is occasionally assumed that self-serving goals of this kind subvert the public-service purposes of administrative agencies. Yet it is perfectly natural for professionals and administrators who value their work to see the survival and strengthening of their organizations as a vital part of the public welfare. It is not surprising nor inherently wrong that officials of the National Aeronautics and Space Administration, the U.S. Army, or the administrators of a state college view their functions as vital to the welfare of society. Responsiveness to the public interest may decrease, however, when such dedication supplants an organization's primary function, subverts political control, degrades the treatment of citizens, or results in the inhumane treatment of employees.

Public organizations are not solely creatures of their environment. While they must to some extent adapt to external and internal conditions, they can have great ability to shape the forces around them.[51] We have noted, for example, such techniques of generating external support as building alliances with private groups and pursuing public relations campaigns. The three-dimensional value framework discussed in the preceding chapter is of vital importance in minimizing the negative consequences of organizational efforts to adapt to or manipulate the environment. Thus, while adaptation to environment is an important and necessary component of all organizational systems if they are to survive, the *direction* and *kind* of adaptation determines the values that the organization will reflect and the effectiveness of its actions. Let us, therefore, look at the three dimensions in greater detail.

NOTES

1. Plato's *The Republic* discusses means for developing unselfish "philosopher-kings"; Marxists, of course envisage an egalitarian society. From a more contemporary setting, B. F. Skinner has argued against the values of individualism. See his *Beyond Freedom and Dignity* (New York: Knopf, 1971).
2. See Catherine Drinker Bowen, *Miracle at Philadelphia* (Boston: Little, Brown, 1966), and David G. Smith, *The Convention and the Constitution: The Political Ideas of the Founding Fathers* (New York: St. Martin's Press, 1965). The classic criticism of the interests that motivated the Constitutional Convention is Charles A. Beard, *An Economic Interpretation of the Constitution of the United States* (New York: Macmillan, 1913, 1935).
3. A comparison between national and state chief executives is made by Joseph E. Kallenbach, *The American Chief Executive: The*

Presidency and the Governorship (New York: Harper & Row, 1966). The comparative power of American governors is reviewed by Joseph A. Schlesinger, "The Politics of the Executive," Herbert Jacob and Kenneth N. Vines, eds., *Politics in the American States: A Comparative Analysis* (Boston: Little, Brown, 1971), pp. 210 - 237. For those interested in the diffusion of power and influence in local government, see Wallace S. Sayre and Herbert Kaufman, *Governing New York City: Politics in the Metropolis* (New York: W. W. Norton, 1960, 1965). A classic statement on urban pluralism is Robert A. Dahl, *Who Governs? Democracy and Power in an American City* (New Haven: Yale University Press, 1961).

4. See Richard E. Neustadt, *Presidential Power: The Politics of Leadership* (New York: Wiley & Sons, 1960).

5. A lively discussion of the politics of health policy making is found in Eric Redman, *The Dance of Legislation* (New York: Simon & Schuster, 1973).

6. The persistence of discrimination even in the face of legal action is reviewed by Thomas R. Dye, *The Politics of Equality* (Indianapolis: Bobbs Merrill, 1971).

7. An assessment of this problem can be found in a useful series of original essays on Watergate by Donald W. Harwood, ed., *Crisis in Confidence: The Impact of Watergate* (Boston: Little, Brown, 1974).

8. See American Bar Association, *Report of the ABA Commission to Study the Federal Trade Commission* (Chicago: American Bar Association, 1960); Louis M. Kohlmeier, Jr., *The Regulators: Watchdog Agencies and the Public Interest* (New York: Harper & Row, 1969); James M. Landis, "Report on Regulatory Agencies to the President-Elect" (Washington, D.C.: Office of the President, December 1960). Congressional documents are also a rich source of data on the problems of regulatory administration. See, for example: U.S. Senate, Committee on Commerce, Subcommittee on Surface Transportation, *Hearings: Interstate Commerce Commission Oversight*, 91st Cong., 2nd sess., 1970, and Library of Congress, Legislative Reference Service, *Separation of Powers and the Independent Agencies: Cases and Selected Readings*, Document No. 91 - 49, 91st Cong., 1st sess., 1969.

9. See Martin Shapiro, *The Supreme Court and Administrative Agencies* (New York: Free Press, 1968).

10. See especially American Bar Association, *Report of the ABA,* and Landis, "Report on Regulatory Agencies."

11. Joseph C. Palamountain, Jr., *The Dolcin Case and the Federal Trade Commission,* Inter-University Case Program No. 79 (Indianapolis: Bobbs Merrill, 1963).

12. American Bar Association, *Report of the ABA.*

13. The promise and constraints of federalism are reviewed by Daniel Elazar, *American Federalism: A View from the States* (New York: McGraw Hill, 1966), and Richard Leach, *American Federalism* (New York: W. W. Norton, 1970). An important statement on

"new federalism" is made by Michael D. Reagan, *The New Federalism* (New York: Oxford University Press, 1971).

14. Two important statements on the lack of functional neatness in the administration of programs in federalism are made by Morton Grodzins, *The American System: A New View of Government in the United States* (Chicago: Rand McNally, 1966), and Terry Sanford, *Storm Over the States* (New York: McGraw Hill, 1966).

15. See Donald J. Devine, *The Political Culture of the United States: The Influence of Member Values on Regime Maintenance* (Boston: Little, Brown, 1973), and Ira Sharkansky, *The United States: A Study of a Developing Country* (New York: David McKay, 1975).

16. See U.S. Senate, Committee on Government Operation, Subcommittee on Intergovernmental Relations, *Confidence and Concern: Citizens View American Government: A Survey of Public Attitudes* (committee print), 93rd Cong., 1st sess., December 3, 1973; Daniel Katz et al., *Bureaucratic Encounters: A Pilot Study in the Evaluation of Government Services* (Ann Arbor, Mich.: Institute for Social Research, University of Michigan Press, 1975); and Gabriel Almond and Sidney Verba, *The Civic Culture: Political Attitudes and Democracy in Five Nations* (Boston: Little, Brown, 1963).

17. A classic analysis of participation in American politics is provided by Lester Milbrath, *Political Participation* (Chicago: Rand McNally, 1965). A cross-cultural interpretation can be found in Almond and Verba, *The Civic Culture.*

18. For theoretical discussions, see Arnold J. Heidenheimer, ed., *Political Corruption: Readings in Comparative Analysis* (New York: Rinehart & Winston, 1970).

19. For practical examples, as well as techniques, of corruption and patronage consult Martin and Susan Tolchin, *To the Victor: Political Patronage from the Club House to the White House* (New York: Random House, 1971).

20. The coalition, umbrella aspect of political parties forms part of the analysis of Judson L. James, *American Political Parties: Potential and Performance* (New York: Pegasus Press, 1969).

21. Herbert McClosky, Paul J. Hoffman, and Rosemary O'Hara, "Issue Conflict and Consensus among Party Leaders and Followers," *American Political Science Review* 54 (June 1960): 405 - 427.

22. Sayre and Kaufman, *Governing New York City.*

23. The interaction between administrators and interest groups forms an important part of the case studies on smoking and housing. See, for example, A. Lee Fritschler, *Smoking and Politics: Policymaking and the Federal Bureaucracy* (Englewood Cliffs, N.J.: Prentice Hall, 1969, 1975), and Harold Wolman, *Politics of Federal Housing* (New York: Dodd, Mead, 1971).

24. Lobbying by interest groups is discussed in Lester Milbrath, *The Washington Lobbyists* (Chicago: Rand McNally, 1963), and Lewis A. Froman, Jr., "Some Effects of Interest Group Strengthening

State Politics," *American Political Science Review* 60 (December 1966): 952 - 962.

25. The concept of organizational territoriality is discussed in Anthony Downs, *Inside Bureaucracy* (Boston: Little, Brown, 1966), especially pp. 211 - 222. Boundaries of organizations are discussed by Victor A. Thompson, *Organizations as Systems* (Morristown, N.J.: General Learning Press, 1973). Competing organizations are discussed by S. Terreberry, "The Evolution of Organizational Environments," *Administrative Science Quarterly* 12 (March 1968): 590 - 613.

26. Frederick C. Mosher, *Democracy and the Public Service* (London: Oxford University Press, 1968).

27. Discussions of the impact of professionalism on organizations are found in Mosher, ibid., and Robert Wood, "When Government Works," *The Public Interest* 18 (Winter 1970): 39 - 51. See also Jewell Bellush and Stephen M. David, eds., *Race and Politics in New York City: Five Studies in Policy-Making* (New York: Praeger, 1971), and Alan A. Altshuler, *The City Planning Process: A Political Analysis* (New York: Cornell University Press, 1965), esp. pp. 392 - 405.

28. Mosher, *Democracy*.

29. Samuel A. Lawrence, *The Battery Additive Controversy* (Syracuse, N.Y.: Inter-University Case Program, 1962).

30. Ibid., p. 13.

31. Ibid., p. 24.

32. U.S. Department of Labor, *Municipal Public Employee Associations Bulletin,* No. 1702 (Washington, D.C.: U.S. Government Printing Office, 1971), p. 1.

33. U.S. Department of Labor, Bureau of Labor Statistics, "Labor Union and Employee Association Membership: 1970" (Press release, September 13, 1971).

34. See Inter-Agency Committee on Federal Labor Relations, *Labor-Management Relations in the Federal Service: Report and Recommendations, Executive Order 11491* (Washington, D.C.: U.S. Government Printing Office, 1969), p. 31.

35. See *New York Times* (August 2, 1972), p. 15.

36. Cited in "Statement of the National Association of Manufacturers," in U.S. Congress, House, Committee on Education and Labor, Special Subcommittee on Labor, *Hearings: Labor-Management Relations in the Public Sector,* 92nd Cong., 2nd sess., 1972, p. 580.

37. For two useful views on the evolving role of unions see Felix Nigro, "Collective Bargaining: The Implications for Public Administration," *Public Administration Review* 32 (March-April 1972): 120 - 126, and Gus Tyler, "Why They Organize," *Public Administration Review* 32 (March-April 1972): 97 - 101.

38. A breakdown of the composition of the federal civil service can be found in U.S. Civil Service Commission, Bureau of Manpower In-

formation Systems, *Occupations of Federal White Collar Workers* (Washington, D.C.: U.S. Government Printing Office, 1969).

39. On the problem of knowledge management see James D. Carroll, "Noetic Authority," *Public Administration Review* 29 (September-October 1969): 492 - 500.

40. See David Braybrooke and Charles E. Lindblom, *A Strategy of Decision* (New York: Free Press, 1963).

41. Role orientation, however, may be complex. See Emmette S. Redford, *Democracy in the Administrative State* (New York: Oxford University Press, 1969), pp. 46 - 49.

42. The problem of area and administration is reviewed by Professor James W. Feslevin, "The Basic Theoretical Question: How to Relate Area and Function," *Public Administration Review*, Special Issue on the Administration of the New Federalism, (September 1973): 4 - 14.

43. On the potential positive significance of achievement norms to societies see David C. McClelland, *Motivational Trends in Society* (Morristown, N.J.: General Learning Press, 1971).

44. A good treatment of the organization worker is provided by Edgar H. Schein, *Organizational Psychology* (Englewood Cliffs, N.J.: Prentice Hall, 1965).

45. The theory of psychological contracting within organizations can be found in James G. March and Herbert A. Simon, *Organizations* (New York: John Wiley & Sons, 1958). See also Chester I. Barnard, *Functions of the Executive* (Cambridge, Mass.: Harvard University Press, 1938).

46. The concept of individual conservatism is treated by Downs, *Inside Bureaucracy.*

47. On the problem of communication overload see Downs, *Inside Bureaucracy,* and Gordon Tullock, *The Politics of Bureaucracy* (Washington, D.C.: Public Affairs Press, 1965).

48. Roberta Wohlstetter, *Pearl Harbor: Warning and Decision* (Stanford: Stanford University Press, 1962).

49. William R. Dill, "Administrative Decision-Making," Sidney Mailick and Edward Van Ness, eds., *Concepts and Issues in Administrative Behavior* (Englewood Cliffs, N.J.: Prentice Hall, 1962), pp. 29 - 48.

50. On the limits of rationality in the decision-making process see March and Simon, *Organizations,* and Daniel Katz and Robert L. Kahn, *The Social Psychology of Organizations* (New York: Wiley & Sons, 1966), esp. chap. 10.

51. For a stimulating discussion from this viewpoint see Charles Perrow, *Complex Organizations: A Critical Essay* (Glenview, Ill.: Scott, Foresman, 1972).

Machine Bureaucracy

We noted earlier that one of the major tasks confronting modern public bureaucracies is their need to develop more effective organizational capacities to respond to public needs: the ability to plan, decide, and implement is vital. The "machine" techniques seek to achieve this through a focus on organizational structure and through strategies designed to improve the rationality of decision making. From the "machine" perspective sound management is seen primarily as the result of proper structural design, effective procedures, technical skills, tools of analysis, and effective supervision of employees. Political controls and human considerations are from the "machine" perspective often seen as impediments or, at best, necessary evils.

THE THEORETICAL LEGACY

In traditional management theory, bureaucracy is viewed as the most rational means of achieving a given purpose. Bureaucracies consist of a hierarchical structure, formalized rules for guidance, and qualified personnel who perform in accordance with their defined roles. The virtues of bureaucracy, then, are seen in its ordered, hierarchical form, its reliance on regulations, and its expertise. Emotionalism, personalism, cliques, etc., should dissipate in the wake of purposeful bureaucracy operating with machine - like precision and efficiency. Although we now have a more comprehensive understanding of organizations and their environment, which precludes wholesale adoption of such a rigid interpretation, the legacy of these beliefs is still with us, affecting much of contemporary organizational life and expectations.[1]

The machine metaphor usually elicits images of the "scientific management" period early in this century during which there was a focus — at times an obsession — on rigid *principles* of management that, when applied, would purportedly make organizations more effective and efficient. But not only does the image remain a viable contemporary force, the belief that organizations should be effective, rational delivery systems represents an ageless expectation. The persistent force of this approach to bureaucracy can be best understood by reviewing briefly its theoretical basis.

Classical Weberian Thought

The concept of bureaucratic "rationality" is generally attributed to the German sociologist Max Weber (1864 - 1920).[2] In what is now viewed as the classic theory of impersonal, efficient, rational bureaucracy, Weber outlined the conditions that generated and perpetuated the development of bureaucratized society. Although he felt that the impersonalism and the creation of a "caste" of technocrats that were inevitable with the generation of bureaucracy represented contradictions to the principles of democracy, he believed that the bureaucratization of society was inevitable and once established would be difficult to destroy or supplant.[3]

Bureaucracy, he believed, was inevitable and indispensable. Basically it was seen as a rational, unemotional instrument for the attainment of desired ends. It was compartmentalized according to necessary tasks and functions. Rules, laws, and regulations governed individual contributions. The existence of a hierarchy created superior-subordinate relationships and helped guarantee dependable lines of communication and authority. A broad base of skilled individuals with a career commitment applied their knowledge within their respective organizational confines. Over this broad domain, a management applying objective standards meted out tasks and responsibilities. Thus, bureaucracy was viewed as rational because it was a means of curbing individual impulse and emotion, because its form and structure were related to goal attainment, and because of its technological superiority over other forms of organization.

What of the plight of the individual bureaucrat? In the Weberian interpretation, he is "forged to the community of all the functionaries who are integrated into the mechanism."[4] Not only is the individual bureaucrat unable to interject his personal biases into the activities of the organization, but the citizens "served" by this rational instrument cannot be allowed to interfere with the practice of administration by expertise, for "chaos" would result. "Bureaucracy," Weber noted, "rests upon expert training, a functional specialization of work, and an attitude set for habitual and virtuoso-like mastery of single yet methodically integrated functions."[5] Involving the citizen in the activities of this intricate and delicate balance of skills and expertise could only diminish the rationality of the instrument.

We have learned through experience that hierarchy is not infallible, that individuals do not necessarily enslave themselves to their organization, that expertise does not preclude biased judgment, and that the meshing of organizational functions may be more art than science. Nevertheless, the goals of rational bureaucracy remain viable. The reasoned application of expertise, the integration of specialized functions, and the control of specified activities remain important prerequisites for effective and responsive bureaucracy.

Scientific Management

The belief in the need to sustain (or create) more effective organizations took a more practical and operational turn in the early part of the twentieth century in the United States. In reaction to the negative effects caused by the intrusion of blatant politics into the activities of government, many scholars and political leaders concerned themselves with the creation of a "science" of management that could enhance organizational effectiveness. The antipolitics stance evidenced by the scientific management movement in the United States was reflected in the reform writings of Woodrow Wilson, in which he urged that the conduct of public management be made "more businesslike."[6] Principles were generated with flurry and enthusiasm. Better government, it was presumed, could be achieved by uncovering and then applying "rules" of management and organization.

Frederick Winslow Taylor, by profession a mechanical engineer but widely used as a consultant by many industries seeking improved product and worker output, and his followers developed "laws" of management and organization to ensure more efficient use of personnel.[7] Unconvinced of the ability of organizational man to work undirected toward the achievement of complex goals, the efforts of these theorists were directed toward concepts of human engineering. Typical were time-motion studies which analyzed worker time requirements for task completion.

Taylor, perhaps unwittingly, cast the bureaucrat in the light of the Pavlovian dog, incapable of independent thought, responsive only to materialistic reward:

> *Perhaps the most prominent single element in modern scientific management is the task idea. The work of every single workman is fully planned out by the management at least one day in advance, and each man receives in most cases complete written instructions, describing in detail the task he is to ac-*

> *complish, as well as the means to be used in doing the work. And the work planned in advance in this way constitutes a task which is to be solved. . . . This task specifies not only what is to be done but how it is to be done and the exact time allowed for doing it. And whenever the workman succeeds in doing his task right, and within the time limit specified, he receives an addition of from 30 per cent to 100 per cent to his ordinary wages. These tasks are carefully planned, so that both good and careful work are called for in their performance, but in no case is the workman called upon to work at a pace which would be injurious to his health. The task is always so regulated that the man who is well-suited to his job will thrive while working at this rate during a long term of years and grow happier and more prosperous, instead of being overworked.[8]*

Organizations were viewed as productive machines, with management orchestrating all efforts toward increased output. The fact that humans might balk at rules and managerial dominance was countered by Taylor's belief that monetary rewards were the prime stimulus of work. Taylorism was thus compatible with the model fashioned by Weber, for its goals were comparable: efficiency, control, and the smooth attainment of organizational purposes.

Successors to Taylor were also committed to bureaucratic rationality. Luther Gulick and Lyndall Urwick, both management consultants and frequent advisers on management matters to President Franklin Roosevelt, took a "step-by-step" approach to the principles of authority and control:

(1)   First step: Define the job to be done.

(2)   Second step: Provide a director to see that the objective is realized.

(3)   Third step: Determine the nature and number of individualized and specialized work units into which the job will have to be divided.

(4)   Fourth step: Establish and perfect the structure of authority between the director and the ultimate work division.[9]

Although the task of administration appears simple when perceived in this manner, each of these four steps has severe inherent limitations. Take, for example, the injunction to "define the job to be done." At various levels throughout the organization, the potential for clear job definition may vary. In the real world, the actions of other organizational subunits may be beyond one's control and thus job definition may vary from precise tasks to general statements of policy. The fourth step, "establish and perfect the structure of authority between the director and the ultimate work division," also contains a problem. Most modern managers would like to see this step implemented, but authority in organizations is not always hierarchical. Responsibility, control, and influence may be dependent upon relations between organizational sub-units competing for dominance in particular policy areas. Informal organizations often wield significant amounts of power. Professional perspectives may also weaken control from the top. Scientists and other experts may have certain values and standards not easily overridden by directors from above.[10]

The quest for rational management principles was also undertaken by the French industrialist and management theorist Henri Fayol, who proposed certain administrative criteria typical of management theory in 1916:

(1)   See that the plan of operations is carefully prepared and strictly carried out.

(2)   See that the human and material organization are suitable for the objects, resources, and needs of the undertaking.

(3)   Establish a management which is competent and has singleness of purpose.

(4)   Co-ordinate operations and efforts.

(5)   Make decisions which are clear, distinct, and precise.

(6)   Make careful selection of staff — each department with a competent and energetic head: each employee where he can be of most service.

(7)   Define duties clearly.

(8)   Encourage the desire for initiative and responsibility.

(9)   Reward men fairly and judiciously for their efforts.

(10)   Impose penalties for mistakes and blunders.

(11)   See that discipline is maintained.

(12)   See that individual interests do not interfere with the general interest.

(13)   Pay special attention to unity of command.

(14)   Ensure material and human order.

(15)   Subject everything to control.

(16)   Avoid red tape.[11]

These postulates seem rooted in common sense but in reality are of little operational assistance. To ask that "duties be defined clearly" has little meaning because no administrator can control the perception skills of all of his or her subordinates. Duties can be easily misunderstood or avoided. And to command the avoidance of "red tape," while still emphasizing adherence to the other management requirements, seems contradictory.

While providing a useful beginning to the study of organizations, these approaches neglected crucial considerations. Responsive bureaucracy was viewed as an extension of sound management principles. But what kind of responsiveness was this? It was primarily a responsiveness to principles of hierarchy, chain of command, and span of control (the number of subordinates a manager could effectively supervise). Of course, the importance of such concerns should not be minimized, for they are necessary to the smooth running of the organizational "machine." But these bureaucratic principles ignored the problem of responsiveness to employees, to the general public, to specialized clientele, and to government leaders. Management and bureaucracy were seen to stand apart from the political hurly-burly. They were purified, cleansed of all of the confusion of the larger environment. Good bureaucracy was scientific bureaucracy, inherently beneficial, without reference to the rest of the world.

CONTEMPORARY PERSPECTIVES

The impact of Weber and the developers of scientific management theory still persists. Although the theory has been modified and elaborated, its broad outlines are still visible. The beliefs in the value of *efficiency*, in the need to *de-politicize* administrative decisions, in the significance of formal *structure*, and in the ability to *prescribe solutions* to ailments have not changed.

There is, however, a difference between management science today and its predecessors. An increased understanding of the complexities of organizations, an awareness of their sociological and psychological properties, and an appreciation of the difficulty of implementing change differs from what now, in hindsight, seem to have been overly simplistic interpretations. There is likewise a greater awareness of some of the negative consequences of hierarchy and chain of command. Along with this evolution in our thinking about organizations, new and complex techniques and tools have been developed as aids to management. The concept of bureaucratic "rationality" today is more dependent upon calculations and conclusions drawn from complex analytical frameworks, rather than emerging from any single doctrine or "principle" of management.

The broader focus of contemporary management science is reflected in the kinds of skills now valued by organizations. Greater use of economic analysis, more large-scale organizational planning and re-structuring, more comprehensive evaluation and measurement, and the expanded utilization of computer-facilitated technologies demonstrate that the *tools* of machine bureaucracy are the major difference between contemporary and traditional management science. The goals of rationality, efficiency, and effectiveness, however, remain the same.

Today, the machine bureaucracy perspective focuses on the purpose and capacity of organizations. They are viewed as instruments to achieve particular goals, with certain operational devices utilized to ensure the attainment of these goals. If not achieved, then a new strategy must be devised: the failure is not in the goal but in the way its implementation was attempted. Behind machine bureaucracy theory and practice lies an optimistic note: problems are solvable, either through structural modification or new skill implementation. Machine bureaucracy adherents are the perennial optimists, believing that if "politics" and "emotion" can be kept out of the situation, then wisdom and technical expertise will prevail.

While we have argued that public administration and politics are inseparable (see chapter 1), and that in fact administrative decisions reflect political consequences, machine bureaucracy is premised upon the need to sustain nonpolitical, rational goal achievement: organizations must be able to make decisions based upon knowledge and expertise and should develop a capacity to review program effectiveness without bias. Yet, these concerns do not preclude an awareness that machine-derived solutions will have political consequences. Unfortunately, many adherents of political bureaucracy fail to understand that machine bureaucracy capacities might be useful in enhancing political values and goals, and hence deny the usefulness of machine strategies for evaluation or analysis. By the same token, obsessed supporters of machine bureaucracy fail to appreciate the significance of political bureaucracy values or humane bureaucracy goals. The "true believers"[12] are found in all three camps of public administration.

The manifestations of machine bureaucracy are visible in four organizational areas: *structure, procedure, evaluation,* and *management.* By emphasizing these four components, machine bureaucracy adherents believe that nonfunctioning, ineffective organizational frameworks can be revitalized. This "rational" policy-making system is illustrated in figure 3.1. On the surface it is neat, comprehensive, logical, laden with skills and expertise, and rational. Everything seems "to be in its right place," with adequate supervision and monitoring. It is assumed that there are people in this process, but they appear only to fulfill expectations that others have about them.

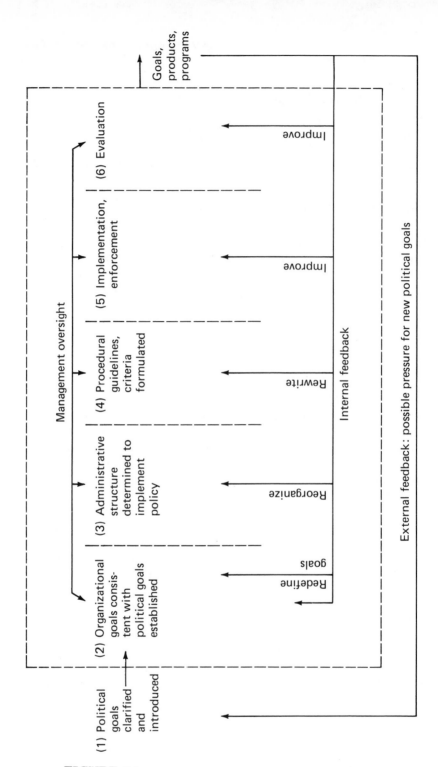

FIGURE 3.1

Structure

A major dimension of machine bureaucracy is its emphasis on an organization's *structural* capacity. We all recognize that a critical problem of modern public organizations is overly complex or outdated structures. The perennial suggestion for "reorganization" is a reflection of this belief. Implicit in much of the concern for structure of public bureaucracy is the presumption that there is a *best* way to organize the activities of the organization.

Although there is undeniably a political motivation behind many reorganization moves, restructuring often goes beyond mere political motives. It is based on the hope of achieving increased organizational effectiveness through heightened structural capacities. For example, the effort to modernize the Post Office Department into a self-sufficient postal corporation with more autonomy and less fiscal dependency on Congress, although certainly not producing the quick benefits anticipated, was based on the belief that better service at a lower cost could be achieved by restructuring its framework.[13] Restructuring is generally interpreted to imply the rarely attempted large-scale reorganization, but many public agencies continuously reshape their framework using internal-reorganization guidelines. Indeed, constant small-scale reorganization and reshuffling of units seem to be strategies employed by many public agencies.

A salient example of the kind of restructuring often suggested can be seen in the comprehensive 1970 report of the Blue Ribbon Defense Panel, composed of fifteen prominent citizens and headed by Gilbert W. Fitzhugh, then chairman of the board of the Metropolitan Life Insurance Company.[14] The Department of Defense employs tens of thousands and contains myriad organizational components. Because it is composed of many different types of professionals, structural change poses threats to numerous occupational groups. In response to these and other sources of resistance to cost-saving strategies, the panel made suggestions for improving the department's organizational structure. The recommendations reflect a deep-rooted belief in the notions of hierarchical control and rationality:

(1) The *organization* of the department must be responsive to the direction, control, and authority of the president and the secretary of defense in all areas of departmental operations.

(2) The *lines of authority* and responsibility within the department must be made clear and unmistakable so that delegation of authority and responsibility will not result in loss of individual accountability.

(3)   The *chain of operational command* must be unencumbered, and flexible enough to operate reliably and responsibly in both peace and war.

(4)   The organization of the department must permit and *facilitate objective assessments* and innovative, but nonduplicative, long-range planning for structuring and equipping of forces.

(5)   The organization of the department must be streamlined to reduce substantially the manpower assigned to staff activities.

(6)   The *"span of control"* of the secretary must be reduced.[15]

If it were not for the date of the report, one might believe that these recommendations were written at the height of the scientific management movement!

As we noted in chapter 1, American history is replete with presidential commissions and boards established for the purpose of redefining organizational missions and perfecting their structural basis.[16] The comprehensive proposals made by the Nixon administration to reorganize the federal bureaucracy reflect the persistence of the belief that organizational restructuring will not only enhance political control of the bureaucracies but will also make them more sensitive to the goals for which they were originally established. The reorganization proposals submitted to Congress by President Nixon in 1971 were the result of a six-member presidential commission headed by Roy Ash, formally known as the President's Advisory Council on Executive Reorganization. Stressing the importance of structure to governmental performance, the council recommended the reorganization of seven major federal agencies and several independent agencies into four new agencies. The seven affected departments (Agriculture; Commerce; Health, Education, and Welfare; Housing and Urban Development; Interior; Labor; and Transportation) were to be dissected and regrouped into departments serving four basic needs: Economic Affairs, Natural Resources, Community Development, and Human Resources.

The administration argued that reorganization would bring government closer to the people by decentralizing certain federal programs, that new management strategies would be allowed to flower in a more professional environment, that greater authority would be granted to cabinet secretaries to mold and enforce departmental policies, and that efficiency would become the guiding doctrine of the public service. Stressing the need to take politics (interest groups) out of the public bureaucracy, supporters of the reorganization scheme argued that a lessened role for interest groups was desirable if government was to be made responsive to the public as a whole.[17]

These themes of efficiency, rigorous accountability, and goal attainment were emphasized, but the scientific management "mystique" created by the supporters of the president's reorganization proposals, who presented them as the only solution for making the government bureaucracy responsive to political (presidential) control, was not shared by Congress, and it voted them down. Although Congress argued that the creation of four superbureaucracies would not guarantee any more effective management than had been witnessed in the past, the real reason for the defeat of the reorganization proposals can be traced to what Congress saw as their far-reaching effects — enhancing the president's control of the bureaucracy, thereby undermining the maze of congressional-agency and agency-clientele relationships that had been nurtured over the years and that acted to check presidential direction of the bureaucracy.

At the state level, structural modifications in organizations are also often viewed as a prerequisite to effective and responsive government. Some gubernatorial candidates have waged campaigns on a slogan of introducing efficiency and structural soundness into state government through reorganization. Since 1965, no fewer than sixteen states have undergone major restructuring of their bureaucratic apparatus. In some states, such as Florida and Michigan, restructuring has been achieved primarily by weeding out useless or antiquated agencies. In other states, such as Massachusetts and Maryland, a comprehensive restructuring of the bureaucracy has occurred through the initiation of a cabinet form of administration, theoretically directly responsible to the governor, whereby previously independent and scattered agencies are consolidated into major organizational units (headed by secretaries, who form the cabinet), such as "human services," "environment," or "transportation."[18]

Thus, changing the arrangement of organizational building blocks is a constant activity in public administration. While the effects of restructured bureaucracies are sometimes invisible or disheartening, machine bureaucracy adherents still view restructuring as a critical step in the establishment of efficient organizations.

Procedure

As we have already noted (chapter 2), a defining characteristic of public bureaucracy is its reliance on procedures and guidelines in directing individual and organizational behavior. Although the worth of sound procedures is generally accepted, what exactly constitutes "sound procedure" and how an agency can establish it are a matter of debate and speculation. Public bureaucracy would be paralyzed in the absence of good procedures, yet it is often incapacitated because of poor procedures.

Benefits and programs provided to state and local governments by the national government are determined according to guidelines that are fashioned at a central federal agency. Any flaws in these guidelines result in failures in the program. For example, the landmark programs of the Great Society of Lyndon Johnson — model cities, the Office of Economic Opportunity, and others — were conceptualized and fostered through the creative process of "politics" involving multiple participants, but were dependent upon guidelines and other regulations to attain their goals. When it was discovered that state and local governments were apparently misallocating health funds administered by the national Department of Health, Education, and Welfare, the response by HEW was to establish *monitoring procedures* to correct their deviant practices.[19] When state, local, and private organizations failed to implement rigorously the requirements of the National Environmental Policy Act, which called for the submission of Environmental Impact Statements, the Environmental Protection Agency issued more definitive operational procedures.[20]

Consider, also, the American Bar Association (ABA) report on the Federal Trade Commission (FTC). One of the faults cited by the ABA was inadequate agency *guidelines* by which employees could decide whether or not a case or complaint before the agency was worthy of further investigation.[21] In the absence of guidelines employees made subjective judgments, and patterns of inequitable investigation and enforcement by the FTC resulted. However, many problems are occasioned not by the absence of procedures or guidelines but by the existence and application of unsound ones. For example, the General Accounting Office recently criticized the Food and Drug Administration for failing to establish adequate guidelines related to surveillance of drug manufacturing practices, thereby allowing on the market certain deficient products.[22]

At the heart, then, of many discussions of agency effectiveness are the standards and guidelines that become the basis for prescribing agency involvement. Whenever there is a criticism of a particular agency, bureau, or division, the common reaction is to research quickly the existing guidelines or procedures for flaws in need of correction, since procedures establish the mechanisms and standards through which goals are achieved. We must not believe that by removing them we will be any closer to achieving responsive bureaucracies, but must instead concentrate on ways of formulating sound ones.

Consider, for example, the ways in which the lack of guidelines can expose us to organizational abuse. The fact-finding committee established by HEW in 1972 to investigate experimentation in the early 1930s on untreated venereal disease victims sponsored by the U.S. Public Health Service, since absorbed by HEW, and certain southern state and local health departments, criticized the lack of procedures preventing such experimentation.[23] Although the report made by the committee pointed out that the experiment, which used only black males, was "ethically unjustified" in 1932, it did note that this judgment was "acutely sharpened" by hindsight. Further, when this experimentation process was first publicized in Tuskegee, Alabama (the site of one of the experiments), even top HEW officials admitted they did not know of its existence. The inception of these experiments, and their continuation (in terms of follow-up research), unknown to many into the early 1970s, demonstrates the difficulty of monitoring all the activities of the government, be they programs or grants. The solutions recommended by the task force were largely procedural in nature, emphasizing the need for stronger guidelines concerning government-sponsored research on human beings. The report concluded that stronger *rules* and *regulations* were needed to curb unnecessary and unethical government experimentation.

Proceduralism, thus, is a double-edged sword. By their presence procedures often confuse and frustrate administrative efforts; in their absence, action is haphazard and subject to improprieties. One of the dilemmas of modern bureaucracy is that procedures may simultaneously safeguard and befuddle citizens. Worse, the increasing scope of government operations means that procedures designed to protect individuals may serve to undermine individual freedom as well as public control by restricting the range of autonomous action or personal preference. This is a fact that many adherents of machine bureaucracy fail to recognize.

Evaluation and Program Analysis

Although the structural and procedural aspects of organizations have long been matters of concern, recent years have witnessed increased interest in the technical evaluation of organizational output. Although measuring the "efficiency" of organizational efforts has long been a tenet of machine bureaucracy, current efforts are more oriented to *evaluating* the "effectiveness" and the "productivity" of organizational enterprises — judging the quality as well as the quantity of their activities.

This heightened awareness of the need for evaluation of quality can be attributed to several sources. First, increased frustration on the part of both citizens and public officials, stemming from an inability of many organizations to achieve their goals, has created a mood conducive to reviewing agency efforts and activities. Second, increasing economic constraints on organizations are forcing them to evaluate for themselves their expenditures of financial and human resources. Third, a new awareness that we have been spending billions of dollars on public programs and have failed to undertake any comprehensive and continuous evaluation of these expenditures is creating a new evaluation impulse. As table 3.1 demonstrates, of the nearly 3.9 billion dollars spent in 1969 for selected federal programs, less than one-half of 1 percent was spent for contracted evaluation efforts and only 76 in-house staff members were utilized for evaluation.

TABLE 3.1 1969 Funding and In-House Staff for Evaluation of Selected Programs[a]

Department	(1) Estimated 1969 Obligations (Millions)	(2) Estimated 1969 Federal Evaluation Contracts and Grants (Millions)[b]	(3) Percentage for Evaluation[b] [(2)/(1)]	(4) Estimated In-House Professional Evaluation Staff
Total (selected programs)	3,877	17.0	0.4	76
Department of Labor (selected programs)	1,010	4.1	0.4	28
Manpower Development and Training Programs[c]	240	0.3	0.1 ⎫	28
Programs funded under the Economic Opportunity Act[d]	665	2.8[l]	0.4 ⎬	
Work Incentive Program[e]	105	1.0	1.0 ⎭	
Department of Health, Education, and Welfare (selected programs)	1,610	4.0	0.3	26
Maternal and Child Health Programs[f]	210	1.4	0.7	13
Vocational Education[g]	250	0.1[m]	0.03	1+
Title I, Elementary and Secondary Education Act	1,120	0.6	0.05	9
Follow Through[h]	30	1.9	6.3	3
Office of Economic Opportunity (selected programs)	1,003	6.5	0.7	14
Community Action Program (local initiative programs only)[i]	331	2.2[n]	0.7	7
Head Start[j]	330	2.4	0.7	2
Job Corps[k]	295	1.9[o]	0.6	4
Legal Services Program	47	0[p]	0	1
Department of Housing and Urban Development (selected programs)	254	2.4	0.9	8
Model Cities	254	2.4	0.9	8

[a]Because of delays in fiscal year 1970 appropriations and because of the lack of agency evaluation plans, 1970 funding estimates and evaluation funding estimates are still not available for most programs.

[b]Including contracts for development of evaluation systems but *excluding* costs for in-house staff, administrative costs for monitoring activities, and some costs for data collection.

Because of the use of multiple funding sources for evaluation and becaue of the lack of overall agency evaluation plans, these figures must be considered "best estimates" only.

cInstitutional programs (delegated to HEW) and on-the-job training programs.

dNeighborhood Youth Corps, Operation Mainstream, New Careers, Concentrated Employment Program, Special Impact Program; includes JOBS program but excludes Job Corps.

eDelegated from HEW.

fGrant-in-aids programs for maternal and child health services and crippled children's services, project grants for maternity and infant care, family planning, and comprehensive health care for children, and appropriations for research and training.

gVocational Education Act of 1963 and George Barden Act only.

hFunded from the Head Start program appropriation.

iDoes not include national emphasis programs, such as Head Start and the Legal Services Program.

jNow transferred to HEW.

kNow transferred to Department of Labor.

lIncludes $750,000 OEO share of the Comparative Manpower Program Evaluation Study on the Job Corps, MDTA (Institutional), NYC (Out-of-School), JOBS, and New Careers programs.

mApproximately $350,000 was obligated during fiscal year 1968 for Vocational Education evaluation.

nIncludes costs for program impact and program strategy evaluations of CAP, including local initiative programs but excluding national emphasis programs such as Head Start and the Legal Services Program.

oExcludes OEO share of cost of the Comparative Manpower Program Evaluation Study. (See footnote l above.)

pLegal Services Program expended approximately $300,000 for monitoring contracts.

Source: Joseph S. Wholey, John W. Scanlon, Hugh G. Duffy, James S. Fukumoto, Leono M. Vogt, *Federal Evaluation Policy: Analyzing the Effects of Public Programs* (Washington, D.C.: The Urban Institute, 1970, p. 79.

In addition, the development of new technologies and skills has produced new capacities for evaluation. We must emphasize, however, that increased sophistication in analysis can be used by agencies to justify the need for increased expenditures or responsibilities. Data can be presented in a variety of ways, and administrators are usually inclined to show themselves in the best possible light. Thus, the issue of "evaluating the evaluators" may present a real challenge for public administrators within the next few years. Although we recognize the inherent bias that can stem from selecting one skill or technique over another, it is fair to say that aids to calculation (computers, cost-benefit analysis, program evaluation review techniques, and the like) have had an immeasurable impact on organizational evaluation efforts.

Finally, increased evaluation has occurred because organizations within the public bureaucracy that by law or position have influence over the budget or policy decisions of other agencies have either "suggested" or "required" that those agencies employ evaluative strategies. Typical examples of these "critical" agencies would be the Office of Management and Budget and the General Accounting Office at the federal level,[24] or central offices of "administration and finance" commonly found within most states as staff appendages to the office of the governor.

It is not uncommon for these staff agencies to view the activities of the line agencies (agencies that have direct contact with the public) as self-serving, costly, and needing comprehensive self-evaluation. Perhaps they do not "understand" the "unique" problems of the functional area for which the line agencies are responsible, but it is quite natural for the critical staff agencies to believe that evaluation is not only necessary but also possible. One finds that because of their influence, line agencies are encouraged to at least ritualistically undertake program evaluation. This clash between line and staff perspectives and jealousies may have unfortunate consequences. On the one hand, program performance actually may be hampered by external staff evaluators who do not comprehend the problems and needs of line agencies. On the other hand, resistance by line agencies to potentially helpful evaluation can seriously impede evaluative efforts.

The role of critical agencies was reflected in a recent statement by the federal Office of Management and Budget, which stressed evaluation through such major initiatives as:

(1)   The development of a panel of senior officials to develop ideas and approaches to enhance program evaluation.
(2)   The development of an inventory of federal evaluative techniques to serve as a knowledge resource.
(3)   The review of agency evaluation plans and efforts.
(4)   The teaching of the attainment of objectives through the continued use of management by objectives, whereby output and individual performance are evaluated according to the degree that goals identified in a participative process are achieved.[25]

Although there is a clear recognition by public administrators of the need for evaluation, there is less consensus on how one actually "evaluates." The two main methods involve measuring *effectiveness* and *productivity*. Let us look at both concepts and applications briefly.

Effectiveness.   How do we know when organizations are effective? What kind of criteria can they employ in determining the effectiveness of their programs? Is effectiveness a qualitative or a quantitative concept? Paul Mott has suggested that "organizational effectiveness" is based upon (1) the quality and quantity of the product and the efficiency with which it is produced, (2) the ability of the organization to adapt to changes and problems by perceiving and resolving them with timeliness, and (3) the ability of the organization to "cope with temporarily unpredictable overloads of work."[26] Although this multidimensional interpretation of effectiveness may be useful for the organizational analyst, we will view effectiveness more simply.

Specifically, we view effectiveness as the organization's ability to achieve stated goals and purposes. This definition presupposes that an organization can identify goals and can apply evaluative strategies to determine the degree to which programs and activities actually maximize the attainment of those goals. If, for example, we argue that penal institutions should be established to "rehabilitate" individuals, then we can measure the degree to which this rehabilitation process has been achieved. We must first define what we mean by "rehabilitate." Then, standards such as degree of recidivism (the frequency with which released prisoners return to jail) might be applied to measure the degree to which the goal was achieved.

But standards and criteria of measurement are not always so obvious. If an agency has as a goal "enhancing educational opportunities for the handicapped," do we use as criteria the number of individuals served by the program (a quantitative indicator) or the life opportunities that are generated (qualitative)? How in fact could life opportunities be measured, since short-run indicators may not be able to measure a long-range impact. For example, many training programs employed by agencies are very "effective" in inducing short-run positive shifts in motivation and attitude, yet may prove to be ineffective in inducing long-term changes in behavior or values.

Can realistic criteria to evaluate effectiveness be developed? Most individuals associated with government evaluation efforts maintain that for most areas, criteria can be developed. It is also recognized that these criteria have to be evaluated themselves to determine the degree to which they prove useful as measuring instruments. And one study group has noted that not everything can or should be evaluated: "Not everything one may want to investigate in federal programs can be evaluated. There are questions that should not be pursued — study cost may be out of line, results might not be obtainable by the time answers are needed, or feasible methods may not exist for tracing certain kinds of effects."[27]

Thus, the push for evaluation may come with some costs, but these are costs that are common to the machine bureaucracy perspective. They demonstrate why public administrators should avoid becoming enamored of any dominant trend in public management. Evaluation efforts long neglected in public agencies may become so overproceduralized that everything becomes geared to the needs of an evaluation team. Other needs and values may become lost. Further, attempts to measure the effectiveness of certain public programs may actually diminish effectiveness in achieving public goals. For example, if departments are rewarded (by greater budgetary allotments) according to the degree that they "improve their effectiveness," excesses of quantity rather than quality performance may arise. If we were to measure the effectiveness of police departments solely according to the number of individuals arrested, would this not be an indirect incentive for police to shun certain forms of preventive work? If public universities are viewed as "effective" according to the numbers of individuals who graduate, and if funds are provided to those schools according to quantity of graduates, would there not be a built-in inducement to sacrifice quality? If the effectiveness of equal opportunity programs is measured solely in terms of the numbers of individuals hired, regardless of the duties they are assigned, would this not contribute to further tokenism? Certainly, an awareness of these pitfalls may produce a more balanced view of effectiveness measurement.

Thus, machine bureaucracy efforts to measure effectiveness confront the problem of machine bureaucracy itself. Comprehensive efforts to measure agency effectiveness require the articulation of goals and criteria through which goals achievement can be measured. These seemingly straightforward tasks necessitate herculean bureaucratic efforts. Staffing, funding, and structural deficiencies have to be resolved. Agencies have to be motivated to undertake such evaluation and to improve themselves on the basis of the results. Thus, even serious efforts at evaluation may be frustrated by the need to establish specific procedural and organizational ("machine") steps in implementing evaluation programs. At that point we will face the issue of evaluating how effective we are in evaluating effectiveness!

Productivity.   Although it was common during the heyday of scientific management to be concerned about the productivity of organizations, productivity measurement within public organizations has returned to vogue only in the past few years. This renewed concern has been engendered by the same factors that gave rise to the current interest in evaluation noted earlier. In addition, the constant urgings for increased government efficiency from the Joint Economic Committee of Congress,[28] headed by Senator William Proxmire, and the publicizing efforts of the National Commission on Productivity,[29] established by President Nixon in 1970 to work on methods for increasing productivity, have further paved the way for considerable productivity measurement at all levels of government.

Generally, productivity is defined as "a measure of the efficiency with which physical inputs — land, labor, and/or capital — are converted into physical outputs — goods and services."[30] Thus, it is distinguished from the concept of "effectiveness" in that the later refers primarily to the impact of goal attainment, while productivity refers to the efficiency of converting energy into output in reaching the goal. Productivity programs, however, often tend to merge the two concepts. For instance, the National Commission on Productivity in its review of police services noted that "for any police activity, productivity must be considered in relation to effectiveness. The two concepts are closely related and at times may be difficult to differentiate."[31] A productivity study jointly prepared by the Civil Service Commission, the General Accounting Office, and the Office of Management and Budget likewise tied the two concepts together when it noted that productivity measurement data should include work measurement data (output), unit costs (input), and effectiveness measurement.[32]

Like effectiveness measurement, therefore, productivity programs require that agencies be able to develop methods of measuring input and output. At the federal level especially this program requirement represents an immediate challenge for agencies, since the Office of Management and Budget now insists that all federal agencies with at least two hundred employees report annually on their productivity efforts and activities. Therefore, approximately fifty federal agencies are now undertaking productivity reviews reflecting the activities of over 60 percent of the civilian government work force.[33]

The problem of attempting to define measures of productivity is the major obstacle to effective productivity programs.[34] But the inherent problems of measurement have not precluded attempts to develop numerous devices. The Postal Service, for example, has defined productivity as a ratio of man-years "to the weighted output of 12 types of mail and six service categories."[35] Using this kind of selective weighting, the Postal Service reports that it has "made significant improvements in productivity."[36] Other productivity indexes attempt to integrate both quantitative and qualitative output. For example, a procedure being tested in the District of Columbia to measure the productivity of solid waste collection uses as output factors not only tons of waste collected but also an "average street cleanliness rating" as well as "the percent of the survey population expressing satisfaction with collection."[37]

To refute the charge that productivity measurement is little more than Taylorism revisited,[38] with its consequent negative impact on the individual worker, some attempts have been made to integrate individual and organizational needs. For example, the Detroit refuse collection productivity program has tied a pay bonus incentive to increases in measured productivity.[39] Although still based on the material reward pattern of Taylorism, current reward methods allow the workers increased options. In Taylor's system, employees had no choice: they worked better at a marginally higher rate of remuneration or they were dismissed. The Detroit program allows the individual worker to choose whether increased productivity is personally desirable given the offered reward structure. Thus, the problem of a potential conflict between material rewards and output demands seems to be recognized by at least some productivity experts.

Regrettably, the press for increased output may tarnish organizational responses to nonmaterial job rewards. Particularly when the maintenance of a job itself is an important individual need, organizations may press for greater output (in order to meet artificial quotas) without any concern for the social-psychological needs of the individual worker. Thus, the way productivity is "packaged" and "sold" to other units of government will have an important effect on the requirements of "humane" bureaucracy. If it is presented as a means of getting "more out of workers" merely by making adjustments in the work environment, then it may prove in fact to be a reintroduction of Taylorism. Consider, for example, one report of the National Commission on Productivity with the appealing title, *So, Mr. Mayor, You Want to Improve Productivity* . . . , which is addressed to local officials.[40] In its review of productivity problems and possible corrective actions there is no hint at all of the possible desirability of introducing certain motivational techniques that might spur greater employee output, such as participatory decision making, flexible work hours, or team-building activities. The focus is more on form than on human dynamics and interactions. Table 3.2 illustrates this glaring omission of many productivity programs. The danger exists, then, that overemphasis on productivity can diminish the values of humane and political bureaucracy which, in turn, might quickly damage the potential benefit of a productivity focus.

TABLE 3.2   Common Problems of Low Productivity and Indicated Corrective Actions

Problem	Possible Corrective Action	Illustrative Examples
Sufficient work not available or workloads unbalanced	Reallocate manpower	Housing complaint bureau schedules revised and temporary help employed during peak winter season
	Change work schedules	Mechanics rescheduled to second shift when equipment is not in use
	Reduce crew size	Collection crew size reduced from 4 to 3 men
Lack of equipment or materials	Improve inventory control system	Inventory reorder points revised to reduce stock-out occurrences
	Improve distribution system	Asphalt deliveries expedited to eliminate paving crew delays
	Improve equipment maintenance	Preventive maintenance program instituted
	Reevaluate equipment requirements	Obsolete collection trucks replaced

Self-imposed idle time or slow work pace	Train supervisors	Road maintenance foremen trained in work scheduling, dispatching, and quality-control techniques
	Use performance standards	"Flat rate" manual standards adopted to measure auto mechanics' performance
	Schedule more work	Park maintenance crews mobilized and work scheduling system installed
Too much time spent on non-productive activities	Reduce excessive travel time	Permit expiration dates changed to reduce travel time of health inspectors
	Reevaluate job description and task assignments	Building inspectors trained to handle multiple inspections
Excessive manual effort required	Mechanize repetitive tasks	Automatic change and toll collection machines installed and toll collector staffing reduced
Response or processing time too slow	Combine tasks or functions	Voucher processing and account posting combined to speed vendor payments
	Automate process	Computerized birth record storage and retrieval system installed
	Improve dispatching procedures	Fire alarm patterns analyzed and equipment response policies revised
	Revise deployment practices	Police patrol zones redefined to improve response time
	Adopt project management techniques	Project control system installed to reduce construction cycle

Source: *So, Mr. Mayor, You Want to Improve Productivity . . .* (Washington, D.C.: National Commission on Productivity and Work Quality, 1974), pp. 18–19.

Techniques for Analysis: Aids to Rationality

The foregoing contemporary perspectives on machine bureaucracy were all designed, among other things, to limit the intrusion of personal bias in the implementation of organizational objectives. Thus, they are aids to organizational neutrality and rationality, not unlike the "rationality" projected by Weber.

According to advocates of the "machine" approach, organizational objectives can be additionally maximized by emphasis and reliance upon specialized analytical *skills* and *tools.* These skills and tools seek to optimize the attainment of "good" policies by more effectively evaluating alternative public policies and by attempting to measure the consequences of potential organizational actions prior to their initiation. It is argued that through the use of rigorous and specialized methods of data collection, analysis, measurement, and work programming, organizations can limit irrational impulses toward action by bias or intuition. Rationality, therefore, can be broadened by the utilization of these tools.

The kinds of analytical tools and strategies frequently employed represent a range of technologies. Obviously, only those agencies with an adequate financial resource base will be able to afford either the personnel or the equipment to receive the potential benefits of these systems. This limitation, however, may not be as serious as one would suspect when we recognize that all instruments of analysis are tools that may be misapplied or utilized in biased ways. Moreover, they may exclude key variables, thus minimizing their presumed "pure" rationality.

Many of the devices used are based on *representations of reality,* such as computer simulations, or reflect laboratory models of selected problem areas. Quantitative or qualitative analysis of these simulations or models in turn becomes the basis of rational decision making. Consider, for example, this question: Should a mayor encourage the creation of new jobs within the core of his or her city? A "simulation" of the city — attempting to reflect its salient socioeconomic factors, such as ethnic makeup, level of education, types of industry, and income levels — would be programmed into a computer and then the "decision" to open up several thousand new jobs would be fed into this "computer city." Based upon the way the computer is programmed (i.e., what values and criteria it is asked to respond to), its decision may be that new jobs would increase pressures on existing housing, add to urban deterioration, and force a tax increase because more workers would be attracted to the city in search of jobs than the limited number of positions could absorb, thus creating a new pool of idle workers.[41] The "experts" could then debate whether or not a faulty set of instructions to the computer caused this "decision" not to add new jobs, or if in fact it reflects the most rational choice. Models can, therefore, be utilized to help analyze problems and can sometimes simplify options between complex and interdependent phenomena.

Although computer simulation is the most common form of modeling, other forms are also used. For example, the Monte Carlo method is a specialized simulation model that employs statistical probability to resolve unique management problems. This simulation strategy might be utilized to develop a mass transit service pattern in a large city that is sensitive to peak hour - slack hour demands that affect customer waiting time. In such a case the simulation run of the transit system would include probability calculations of the degree of system "queuing" (waiting in line) during different time periods and along different points of the transit network. Based on the probability of various queuing patterns at different locations and different time periods, the optimal route flow could be calculated. "Critical path analysis," "program evaluation review techniques" (commonly referred to as PERT), and "decision trees" are three other devices for developing a decision strategy and for tracking probable outcomes and consequences of alternative choices within the established decision net.[42]

The most famous of all of these techniques is cost-benefit analysis, which attempts to assign both "costs" and "benefits" to policy options and thus encourages action only in those areas in which benefits outweigh costs. For example, the decision to construct a highway within a metropolitan area would have to be based on a measurement of projected benefits to commuters, tourists, and service industries as compared to assigned costs in terms of fiscal, social, environmental, aesthetic, and political values. While cost-benefit analysis has proven to be a useful tool for evaluating alternative programs and policies, there are many areas in which costs and benefits cannot be quantified without some peril to objectivity. For example, one researcher, Anthony Downs, has indicated that cost-benefit analysis of many government programs aimed at improving the quality of life in urban areas fails to consider the hidden psychological costs of government programs on residents, such as would occur in a massive program of urban renewal.[43]

It must be noted that cost-benefit analysis is often used by agencies to justify actions they want to undertake. This does not mean that we should not use this tool, but we should be aware of the biased ways in which it can be utilized. One traditional criticism of the Army Corps of Engineers, for example, is that it has always overemphasized the benefits that might accrue from the construction of dams. By overestimating the probability of major floods, the corps has been able to develop highly exaggerated cost-benefit ratios.[44] Clientele groups that support the goals of the corps are not likely to challenge the inflated estimates; the technique, therefore, becomes an important weapon in the arsenal of agency strategy and clientele building.

Management

The key to integrating all of the activities of any organization lies with management. Under traditional scientific theory, management represented a caste within the organization that had more sophisticated understanding of the complexities of the task and the organization and thus was able to orchestrate the efforts of less knowledgeable employees. If goals were not achieved, blame was seldom placed at the door of poor or overzealous management, but upon worker deficiencies, union intrusion, or political intervention.

There have been some modifications in this traditional view that granted management intellectual superiority by virtue of its position within the organizational hierarchy. Some of the increasing awareness has come from managers themselves, who have recognized that their strategies and techniques have limits. And increasing pressure for managerial change has come from a growing number of employees who now view themselves as professionals in their own right and seek a more mature and open organizational environment. Both of these factors have placed increasing visibility on the managerial function, and current thought emphasizes both its *style* and its *tools* as key elements.

The style of management.   A common method of understanding and interpreting managerial styles has been to affix management approaches along a continuum ranging roughly from "authoritarian" to "democratic," with "authoritarian" representing tight managerial control and supervision and "democratic" reflecting the modification of the managerial sense of superiority in favor of employee participation.[45] Between these two extremes lies a range of style options (see figure 3.2). Rensis Likert has also developed a continuum to represent management styles, but he has structured the units more precisely than Tannenbaum and Schmidt.[46] The Likert continuum (figure 3.3) represents control and domination styles at the left with more open and participative styles toward the right. Likert is quite convinced by his research that, given sufficient time, greater motivation, satisfaction, and success are achieved as an organization moves away from "System 1" management and toward "System 4" management.

Another interesting and unique framework for evaluating management style is the Grid® approach. Using this framework, management is identified according to the degree of concern it demonstrates, first, for "people," and , second, for "production." Numerous managerial styles are depicted by the interaction of these two variables. Robert Blake and Jane Mouton, for example, have formalized five basic managerial styles (figure 3.4) varying from a low managerial concern for production and a low concern for individuals ("1,1" management) to a management environment that is supportive both of individual development and high productivity ("9,9" management).[47]

Each of the five styles produces a different effect. For example, under 9,1 there is a managerial obsession with productivity and little concern for the needs or interests of individual workers. Since the environment places a heavy emphasis upon worker "quota" systems, a high degree of efficiency and control is necessary. Power is solidly entrenched in the management hierarchy. Interference in the managerial domain is not tolerated, and formalistic patterns of communications are followed.

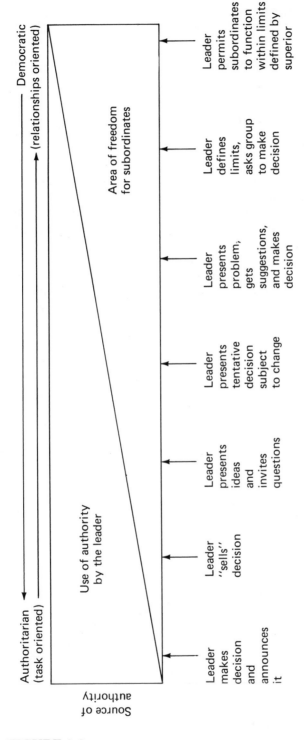

FIGURE 3.2

Source: R. Tannenbaum and W. H. Schmidt, "How to Choose a Leadership Pattern," *Harvard Business Review* (March–April, 1958), p. 96.

System 1	System 2	System 3	System 4
exploitative-authoritarian	benevolent-authoritarian	consultative	participative group

Source: Rensis Likert, *The Human Organization* (New York: McGraw-Hill, 1967), p. 31.

FIGURE 3.3

In contrast, under 1,9 management there is little evidence of concern for organizational output and an extensive concern for human development. Delegation of authority and participatory notions are abundant, and human errors are not penalized. There is concern for full involvement in organizational goal setting and management may be obsessed by such leadership strategies as "management by objectives" and other participation oriented activities. Interestingly, because this managerial style attempts to insure minimum disagreement, creativity, which is often bred out of a full and competitive exchange of ideas, generally does not surface:

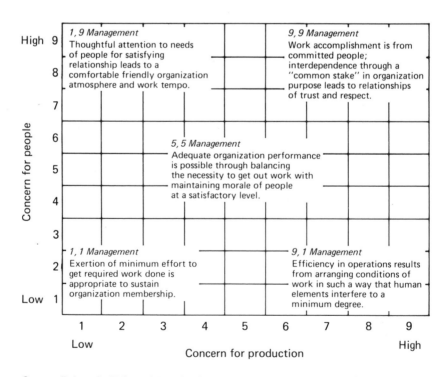

Source: Robert R. Blake and Jane Syrgley Mouton, *The Managerial Grid* (Houston: Gulf Publishing Company, 1964), p. 10. Reproduced with permission.

FIGURE 3.4

> *Creative people . . . are unlikely to accept 9,1 with its authority-obedience assumptions, because it is said to "stifle creativity." When resistance and antagonism are generated, management, in an effort to avoid losing people, swings in the 1,9 direction. The assumption then becomes that the best way to manage is to create good working conditions and to declare hands off with respect to work direction, especially in creative areas. Thus, a country-club atmosphere is produced where the kind of disagreement, intellectual nonconformity and clash of ideas needed for creative and innovative work is absent. Thus, institutions designed to promote creativity become quite comfortable and uncreative places to work.[48]*

As we will discuss in the next chapter, however, it is inaccurate to overstate the causal relationship between management style and organizational output or employee satisfaction. High morale does not necessarily lead to greater output, and one does not motivate a heterogeneous work force with homogeneous strategies of management, even if they are democratic and participative. As we will attempt to indicate, employees are not Pavlovian creatures who respond alike to the same set of stimuli but are complex beings differentially motivated.[49]

Tools of management: MBO, PMS, and MMP.   Style is not the only management strategy for integrating the diverse goals of an organization. Methods such as "management by objective" (MBO), "program management systems" (PMS), and "manpower management programs" (MMP) also attempt to relate organizational activities to organizational objectives and to measure goal attainment. These are systemized efforts to clarify objectives, define the organization's role in relationship to these objectives, and provide a mechanism whereby management can help integrate all activities within the objectives framework.

As has been the case with many management strategies adopted by the government, MBO was first generated in the private sector, where there has traditionally been a more consistent focus on improving organizational output, presumably because of the profit motive basis of private industry. MBO is both a philosophy and a system; it focuses on results and performance and represents a radical departure from the more oppressive characteristics of Weberian and Tayloristic pyramidal bureaucracy. It is supportive of the team approach to problem solving, and thus is a management method that can help induce and expand values salient to humane bureaucracy.

The "management by objectives" method was first used in government by President Nixon, who was concerned that there be established procedures and review mechanisms that would effectively monitor the activities of a far-flung and semiautonomous bureaucracy. Since previous presidential efforts at government-wide reorganization had failed, management by objectives was viewed as an improved strategy for monitoring agency activities. Accordingly, in April 1973, the president sent a memorandum to agency heads directing them to outline their goals and objectives and to develop programs for measuring results. In the directive he noted: "I am confident that this conscious emphasis on setting goals and then achieving results will substantially enhance

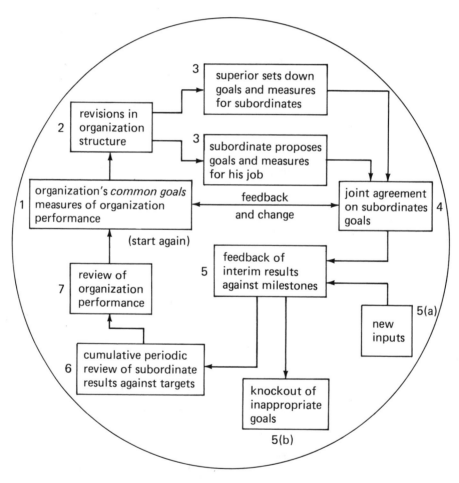

Source: From the book, *Management by Objectives* by George Odiorne. Copyright, ©, 1971 by Pitman Publishing Corporation. Reprinted by permission of Pitman Publishing Corp.

FIGURE 3.5

federal program performance. . . ."[50] Agencies therefore began the intriguing task of goal statement, goal evaluation, and MBO application.

For organizations that have never clearly defined their objectives, MBO may prove to be a useful strategy. The great weakness of MBO is that it may become overritualized and overproceduralized to the degree that creativity and a fresh examination of objectives become impossible. It can also become the victim of self-serving evaluations and goal statement, since unfortunately there is no management strategy that can guarantee honest or objective bureaucratic self-appraisals. For example, introducing MBO in a large scale in what are massive and widely dispersed public bureaucracies has prompted central management units to generate what are popularly referred to as "standard guidance" materials. These guidance materials in many cases define through procedures and formats methods for stating objectives, translating objectives into "work programs," and monitoring methods for reporting both individual and organizational progress toward MBO "milestones." Thus, a system that was generated to break away from bureaucratic standardization and proceduralism has degenerated in places into a monolithic reporting system, in which the only real contribution to the development of objectives is done perfunctorily in a brief annual meeting. Ongoing contribution to objectives statement is thereby foreclosed by a bureaucratic system that has yet to reinforce consistently the notion of employee involvement in management objectives. Many individuals who have pushed MBO within organizations believe in the need for effective management reporting systems, not necessarily employee participation in the decision process; and MBO is thereby perceived as a useful strategy for maintaining administrative control of the system. In addition, for MBO to work effectively an extensive retraining of middle-management would have to occur, because it is at this level that MBO values would have to be reinforced. Upper management has generated the system, but managers at the basic lines of supervision are products of a more pyramidal career experience. Unless this management base can be affected by the spirit and strategies of management by objectives, upper management will continue to send down the hierarchy more and more of its standardized and centralized versions of management by objectives.

Management by objectives does not mean less management, but a new kind of managerial philosophy. Governmental programs that seem insistent on quick evidence of successes for the new, and often trendy, management devices save precious time by eliminating the pretraining and value restructuring that would be the real generators and predictors of program success. Lacking this training for the management base within the bureaucracy, and given the impatience of those who generate and hence demand rapid success of their "invention," continuous streams of guidance will continue to trickle down the bureaucracy. In all of this, the employee who two years ago may have gone to an MBO "training" session and was advised of a new management system that would increase results, diminish paperwork, and lead to greater participation in the organization can only look back upon those assertions with nonproductive cynicism. One official reviewing the inherent danger of MBO pessimistically noted: "The bureaucracy is trying to grab hold of this and generate a huge paper system. MBO is really a management style. But by God the bureaucracy is trying to systemize it."[51]

In addition, although much of the theoretical basis of management by objectives comes from the ideas of organizational democracy and participative management, broad-based participation in MBO efforts is ritualistic only, with upper management retaining its traditional role as the organizational objectives-setter. (Note, for example, in figure 3.5 that although MBO is based on the concept of feedback, it grants to superiors within an organization the major role in determining objectives.) Thus, participation for many subordinates in MBO systems amounts to little more than logging MBO time sheets, which are intentionally designed to record the number of hours the incumbent of a position devotes to a particular objective. Over time, then, there may be serious polarization of perspectives in an organization over the effectiveness of MBO efforts: upper management may inspect the organization and believe that the participants' efforts are tied to an MBO statement of goals and objectives; those further down the hierarchy may view MBO only in terms of their end-of-the-month mad dash to fill out the time sheets, an effort that often involves fabrication of time units that will satisfy management's data needs.

Like MBO, program management system (PMS) is designed to encourage agencies to state objectives, isolate discrete organizational activities, establish operating standards, and generate measures to evaluate programs, with a heavy reliance on cost-benefit analysis. PMS was attempted in the Massachusetts state government in the early 1970s as a means of integrating the activities of the state bureaucracy, thereby introducing rationality into state government. It differed from MBO in that it seemed to require greater precision and rigidity in the classification of program objectives. Yet because of the highly politicized nature of the state government, and because of what was viewed by many as an overzealous implementation strategy on the part of the sponsoring agency, PMS was gradually abandoned.[52]

Manpower management programs (MMP) are one of the closest contemporary links to the traditional tenets of Taylorism.[53] MMP focuses on measuring the time it takes to accomplish particular tasks, and thus is related to traditional time-motion studies. Its key strategy is the development of "standard work times," or the time it should take to accomplish a particular task in a work environment. For example, the

Department of Health, Education, and Welfare will focus on the development of standard work times for activities such as grant processing and monitoring. MMP, therefore, works toward the accumulation of an entire catalogue of standard times for a large range of activities for the purpose of affixing budgetary costs to each. Thus, agencies may become circumscribed in future budget deliberations by current statements of time required to complete tasks. Their full creativity may be marshaled to establish extensive enough standard times for tasks to assure that their budgets will not be jeopardized. So, a device designed to objectify the budget allocation process and restrain costs may in the last analysis have a more costly effect than intended. Indeed, if organizations believe that standard times will become the chief element in budget strategies, tasks that may take ten man-days prior to MMP recording efforts may be listed as needing fifteen man-days so that the need for flexibility and protection is satisfied.

THE LIMITS OF
MACHINE BUREAUCRACY

In reviewing the theoretical and operational characteristics of machine bureaucracy we have emphasized that its chief concern is to maximize organizational "rationality." As we have noted, rationality is not always served by presumably rational instruments because bias, politics, and the inherent limitations of machine tools or strategies distort pure rationality at many points. Nowhere is the frailty of machine bureaucracy more obvious than in the efforts of the federal government in the 1960s to introduce the Program-Planning Budgeting System. Let us look at this episode briefly since it summarizes well so many of the pitfalls to which we have alluded.

On August 25, 1965, President Lyndon Johnson met with his cabinet to announce the initiation of a new administrative program to ensure that agency programs and expenditures met their mandated goals and purposes. This program, first tested by Secretary Robert McNamara in the Department of Defense, was titled the Program-Planning Budgeting System (PPBS) and was intended to be the federal government's major effort at program evaluation and managerial sophistication. In announcing the PPBS effort, President Johnson observed:

> Good government demands excellence.
> It demands the fullest value for each dollar spent. It demands that we take advantage of the most modern management techniques.
> This is what I want to introduce today — a new planning-

programming-budgeting system developed by our top management experts led by Budget Director Charles Schultze. Once in operation, it will enable us to:

(1)   Identify our national goals with precision and on a continuing basis.

(2)   Choose among those goals the ones that are most urgent.

(3)   Search for alternative means of reaching those goals most effectively at the least cost.

(4)   Inform ourselves not merely on next year's costs, but on the second, and third, and subsequent year's costs of our programs.

(5)   Measure the performance of our programs to insure a dollar's worth of service for each dollar spent.

This system will improve our ability to control our programs and our budgets rather than having them control us. It will operate year round. Studies, goals, program proposals, and reviews will be scheduled throughout the year instead of being crowded into "budget time."

To establish this system and carry out the necessary studies, each of you will need a central staff for program and policy planning accountable directly to you. To make this work will take good people, the best you now have and the best you can find.[54]

Six years later, on June 21, 1971, the Office of Management and Budget, the overseer of governmental PPBS efforts, announced the following:

Agencies are no longer required to submit with their budget submissions the multi-year program and financing plans, program memoranda, and special analytical studies . . . that reconcile information classified according to their program and appropriation structures.[55]

Translated, this meant that PPBS was dead! The bravado that ushered in PPBS just six years earlier was missing, and undoubtedly countless "hoorahs" went up within government circles among those who had come to despise it.

Traditionally, public budgeting in the United States has emphasized incremental modifications of budgetary allotments based upon political values and limited program evaluation. The traditional line-item budget, still widely used, was the basic method of budget presentation. In it, costs were itemized but not grouped into program areas. Thus, line-item budgets failed to serve as a planning instrument.

Performance budgeting, a second popular budgeting strategy, attempted to introduce the concept of program evaluation by encouraging efforts to measure the performance (effectiveness) of budgeted programs. Program budgeting (PPBS), in contrast, attempted to depart radically from these two traditions by introducing comprehensive analysis which, in contrast to limited analysis, attempted to measure the impact of all possible means to achieve a given end in as perfect a manner as possible.[56]

The reasons for the failure of PPBS at the federal level are important to our understanding of the frailties inherent in machine bureaucracy. PPBS was dedicated to the "machine" premise that rationality was possible automatically with the administration of public programs if only we applied the correct principles at the right time through the proper administrative framework. But PPBS demonstrated that efforts at inducing rationality in organizational matters may create the reverse of rationality. Armed by the belief that public expenditures could be better predicted if one applied the analytical tools of PPBS, the special studies that accompanied PPBS materials inundated decision makers with so much analysis, much of it irrelevant, that rational choices could still not be guaranteed.

Under PPBS, agencies were directed to define their goals, define their subgoals, demonstrate how these goals interrelated to national goals, and demonstrate which programs could best achieve these goals. Volume after volume of program memoranda were submitted to the Office of Management and Budget, replete with cost-benefit analyses, performance measurement tests, and an array of other impressive technical procedures. PPBS became its own hangman by its fixation on routinized and proceduralized analysis: the process itself became irrational. Only the most rigorous sort of analysis, which would "prove" or "definitely disprove" the effectiveness of a certain government expenditure, was acceptable, since no program could be launched, no money spent, until effectiveness was proven. Agencies became so obsessed with the *process* of goal stating that the substance of the goals themselves often left much to be desired. Much time, money, personal enthusiasm, and other resources were expended, but the results were often not a detailed description of what an agency should do but instead a justification for requesting additional money.

But one cannot ascertain effectiveness before program implementation and neither can one develop a budgeting tool through which only "right" budgetary decisions are made. PPBS would probably have been far more successful at the federal level if it had been used as an ad hoc tool for analysis rather than as a central mechanism for determining agency expenditures. The real irrationality of PPBS was that it led individuals in government to believe that analysis is a *static* element and not an ongoing process. When do we know we have applied enough analysis or even the right kind of analysis? Many government programs, particularly experimental ones (for the poor, the elderly, the handicapped, and others) would never have become policy if we had to prove their viability theoretically and in advance.

Evaluation is ongoing; budgets are, as has long been contended, based on experience and incremental additions.[57] If there were a management and machine bureaucracy tool that would guarantee "right" decisions and "right" choices in advance, then all of us would support its use. But we need to recognize the fallibility of using only scientific, machine approaches — and balance them with humane and political approaches.

When asked by a congressional committee about the utility of exhaustive analysis in policy making, James Schlesinger, then Director of Strategies Studies at the RAND Corporation, responded:

> *An acquaintance, who has been deeply involved in analytic activities in one of the departments, recently commented to me on his experiences. Analysis, he felt, had been relevant in only a small proportion of the decisions. Half the time a decision had been foreclosed by high-level political involvement: a call from the White House, interest expressed by key congressmen or committees. In an additional 30 percent of the cases, the careers of immediate supervisors were involved. Analysis could not influence the recommendations; it could serve only as an irritant. But, he argued, in something like 20 percent of the issues, analysis was unfettered and contributed to much improved overall results.*[58]

PPBS was not intended to be effective only 20 percent of the time. It had failed. Too close to the process itself, its supporters saw not its limitations but sung only to its virtues. In that blindness, they undermined the potential usefulness of PPBS, which as one of several budgetary and machine tools really can be useful in certain settings.

Fixation on tools, strategies, styles, and structures is a common characteristic of machine bureaucracy. It is the rigidity of belief that reflects the weaknesses of machine bureaucracy. We can be no more governed by the application of ritualistic principles than we can be educated by rote memorization. "True believers" abound in all walks of life — those who believe that they hold the key to untapped wisdom or that they have found the only right course of action to take. The true believers in the absoluteness of maxims of efficiency and effectiveness, of the simple application of skills and principles of management to government will always exist.

The improvement of public bureaucracy requires not that we silence these forces but that we balance them against the values of political and humane bureaucracy. The public does have a right to expect efficiency, measurement, analysis, and capable managerial direction within its bureaucracy. In today's era of budgetary limitations and complex social problems, "machine" values remain a crucial component of contemporary public bureaucracy.

NOTES

1. See, for example, the material in chapter 2.
2. An interesting biography of this important man is Reinhard Bendix, *Max Weber: An Intellectual Portrait* (New York: Doubleday Anchor, 1960).
3. For an example of his statement on bureaucracy see H. Gerth and C. Wright Mills, eds., *From Max Weber* (New York: Oxford University Press, 1946), pp. 196 - 244.
4. Ibid., p. 228.
5. Ibid., p. 229.
6. Woodrow Wilson, "The Study of Administration," *Political Science Quarterly* 2 (1887): 197 - 222.
7. Frederick Winslow Taylor, *The Principles of Scientific Management* (New York: W. W. Norton, 1911).
8. Ibid., p. 39.
9. Luther Gulick, "Notes on the Theory of Organization," Luther Gulick and L. Urwick, eds., *Papers on the Science of Administration* (New York: Institute of Public Administration, 1937), p. 7.
10. Major criticisms of the "principles" approach to administrative functions can be found in James G. March and Herbert A. Simon, *Organizations* (New York: Wiley & Sons, 1958), pp. 12 - 33, and Charles McKinley, "Some 'Principles' of Organization," *Public Administration Review* 12 (Summer 1952): pp. 157 - 165.
11. As cited in L. Urwick, "The Functions of Administrations: With Special Reference to the Work of Henri Fayol," Gulick and Urwick, *Papers,* p. 126.
12. The existence of "true believers" — recognizable by their emotionalism and obsession with certain values or ideas — seems to explain some of the dominant moods in public administration. The sociology of the "true believer" is explored in the classic work on the subject, Eric Hoffer, *The True Believer: Thoughts on the Nature of Mass Movements* (New York: Harper & Row, 1951).
13. See, for example, the records of the hearings held prior to the establishment of the Postal Service: U.S. Senate, Committee on Post Office and Civil Service, *Hearings: Postal Modernization,* 91st Cong., 1st sess., 1969.
14. Blue Ribbon Defense Panel, *Report to the President and the Secretary of Defense on the Department of Defense,* July 1, 1970 (Washington, D.C.: U.S. Government Printing Office, 1970).

15. Ibid., p. 23. Emphasis added.

16. For a review of some of the findings and problems of these presidential reorganization commissions see Harvey C. Mansfield, "Federal Executive Reorganization: Thirty Years of Experience," *Public Administration Review* 29 (July - August 1969): 332 - 345, and Peri E. Arnold, "Reorganization and Politics: A Reflection on the Adequacy of Administrative Theory," *Public Administration Review* 34 (May-June 1974): 205 - 211. The possibility of a forthcoming Hoover-type commission is discussed in U.S. Congress, Senate, Committee on Government Operations, Subcommittee on Executive Reorganization, *Hearings: Establish a Commission on the Organization and Management of the Executive Branch,* 90th Cong., 2nd sess., 1968.

17. See U.S. Senate, Committee on Government Operations, *Hearing: Reorganization of Executive Departments,* 92nd Cong., 1st sess., 1971. But also see Douglas M. Fox, "The President's Proposals for Executive Reorganization: A Critique," *Public Administration Review* 33 (September-October 1973): 401 - 406.

18. For a discussion of state government reorganization, see Council of State Governments, *Book of the States: 1974 - 1975* (Lexington, Kentucky: Council of State Governments, 1974).

19. Consult U.S. Department of Health, Education, and Welfare, Division of Grants Administration Policy, *A Program for Improving the Quality of Grantee Management* (Washington, D.C.: U.S. Department of Health, Education, and Welfare, 1970).

20. See, for example, "Environment Protection Agency Preparation of Environmental Impact Statements, Notice of Proposed Rulemaking," *Federal Register* 39: 138 (July 17, 1974), pp. 26254 - 26269.

21. American Bar Association, *Report of the ABA Commission to Study the Federal Trade Commission* (Chicago: American Bar Association, 1969), pp. 13 - 15.

22. See General Accounting Office, *Problems in Obtaining and Enforcing Compliance with Good Manufacturing Practices for Drugs* (Washington, D.C.: March 29, 1973).

23. U.S. Department of Health, Education, and Welfare, *Final Report of the Tuskeegee Syphilis Study Ad Hoc Advisory Panel* (Washington, D.C.: April 28, 1973).

24. The increasing role of the General Accounting Office in conducting program evaluation is an important recent development. See U.S. Comptroller General, *Standards for Audit of Governmental Organization, Programs, Activities and Functions* (Washington, D.C.: General Accounting Office, 1974). See also, Elmer B. Staats, "GAO Audit Standards: Development and Implementation," *Public Management* 56 (February 1974): 5 - 7.

25. See Frank L. Lewis and Frank G. Zarb, "Federal Program Evaluation from the OMB Perspective," *Public Administration Review* (July-August 1974): 308 - 317.

26. Paul E. Mott, *The Characteristics of Effective Organizations* (New York: Harper & Row, 1972), p. 20.

27. Joseph S. Wholey, John W. Scanlon, Hugh G. Duffy, James S. Fukumato, and Leona M. Vogt, *Federal Evaluation Policy: Analyzing the Effects of Public Programs* (Washington, D.C.: The Urban Institute, 1973), p. 16.

28. Consult U.S. Congress, Joint Economic Committee, Subcommittee on Economy in Government, *Hearings: Economic Analysis and the Efficiency of Government*, Parts 1-5, 91st Cong., 1st sess., 1969, and U.S. Congress, Joint Economic Committee, Subcommittee on Priorities and Economy in Government, *Committee Print: Benefit-Cost Analyses of Federal Programs*, 92nd Cong., 2nd sess., January 2, 1974.

29. See, for example, National Commission on Productivity, *Productivity in State and Local Government* (Washington, D.C.: National Commission on Productivity, 1973); National Commission on Productivity, *Improving Management Productivity: The Detroit Refuse Collection Incentive Plan* (Washington, D.C.: National Commission on Productivity, 1974); National Commission on Productivity, *Opportunities for Improving Productivity in Police Services* (Washington, D.C.: National Commission on Productivity, 1973).

30. John P. Ross and Jesse Burkhead, *Productivity in the Local Government Sector* (Lexington, Mass.: D. C. Heath, 1974), p. 11.

31. National Commission on Productivity, *Opportunities for Improving Productivity in Police Services,* p. 3.

32. U.S. Civil Service Commission, General Accounting Office, and Office of Management and Budget, *Measuring and Enhancing Productivity in the Federal Sector: A Study Prepared for the Joint Economic Committee of the U.S. Congress*, Committee Print, 92nd Cong., 2nd sess., August 4, 1972, p. 32.

33. General Accounting Office, U.S. Civil Service Commission, and Office of Management and Budget, Joint Financial Management Improvement Program, *Report on Federal Productivity*, 2 vols. (Washington, D.C.: General Accounting Office, 1974).

34. National Commission on Productivity, *Productivity in State and Local Government: The Wingspread Conference* (Washington, D.C.: National Commission on Productivity, 1973).

35. U.S. General Accounting Office, et al., *Report on Federal Productivity,* vol. 1, p. 62.

36. Ibid.

37. As cited in National Commission on Productivity, *Improving Productivity and Productivity Measurement in Local Government* (Washington, D.C.: National Commission on Productivity, 1971), p. 19.

38. This challenge is made by Frederick C. Thayer, "Productivity and Taylorism Revisited," *Public Administration Review* 32 (November-December 1972): 833 - 840.

39. National Commission on Productivity, *Improving Management Productivity: The Detroit Refuse Collection Incentive Plan.*

40. National Commission on Productivity and Work Quality, *So, Mr. Mayor, You Want to Improve Productivity . . .* (Washington, D.C.: National Commission on Productivity and Work Quality, 1974).

41. For a description of urban computer models, see Jay W. Forrester, *Urban Dynamics* (Cambridge, Mass.: MIT Press, 1969). See, for example, pp. 65 - 70.

42. Many of these are discussed by Leonard W. Hein, *The Quantitative Approach to Managerial Decisions* (Englewood Cliffs, N.J.: Prentice Hall, 1967).

43. Anthony Downs, "Some Aspects of the Proper Use of Economic Analyses in Federal Urban Programs," U.S. Congress, Joint Economic Committee, Subcommittee on Economy in Government, *Hearings: Economic Analyses and the Efficiency of Government,* Part 2, 91st Cong., 1st sess., 1969, p. 280.

44. See, for example, Robert H. Haverman, *Water Resource Investment and the Public Interest: An Analysis of Federal Expenditures in Ten Southern States* (Nashville, Tenn.: Vanderbilt University Press, 1965).

45. See R. Tannenbaum and H. W. Schmidt, "How to Choose a Leadership Pattern," *Harvard Business Review* (March-April 1958).

46. Rensis Likert, *The Human Organization* (New York: McGraw-Hill, 1967).

47. Robert R. Blake and Jane Syrgley Mouton, *The Managerial Grid* (Houston: Gulf, 1964).

48. Ibid., p. 71.

49. See, for example, Robert Presthus, *The Organizational Society* (New York: Knopf, 1962), and Charles Perrow, *Organizational Analysis: A Sociological View* (Belmont, Calif.: Wadsworth, 1970).

50. Office of the President, "Memorandum," April 18, 1973.

51. Cited in Joel Havemann, "OMB's Management-by-Objective Produces Goals of Uneven Quality," *National Journal Reports* 5 (August 18, 1973): 1203.

52. See Robert C. Casselman, "Massachusetts Revisited: Chronology of a Failure," *Public Administration Review* 32 (March-April 1974): 129 - 135.

53. For a basic manual on MMP, see Marvin E. Mundel, *Toward the Improvement of Government* (Silver Spring, Md.: M. E. Mundell & Associates, 1970).

54. Cited in U.S. Senate, Committee on Government Operations, Subcommittee on National Security and International Operations, *Inquiry: Planning, Programming, Budgeting* (Washington, D.C.: U.S. Government Printing Office, 1970), p. 503.

55. Cited in Allen Schick, "A Death in the Bureaucracy: The Demise of Federal PPB," *Public Administration Review* 33 (March-April 1973): 146.

56. A good source book about current budget theory and practice is Robert T. Golembiewski and Jack Rabin, *Public Budgeting and Finance: Readings in Theory and Practice,* 2nd ed. (Itasca, Ill.: Peacock, 1975).

57. The classic account of the limits of rational budget formulation can be found in Aaron Wildovsky, *The Politics of the Budgetary Process,* 2nd ed. (Boston: Little, Brown, 1964, 1971). An analysis that emphasizes the economic shortcomings of PPBS is Leonard Merewitz and Stephen H. Sosnick, *The Budget's New Clothes: A Critique of Planning-Programming Budgeting and Cost-Benefit Analysis* (Chicago: Rand McNally, 1971). The decline of PPBS is discussed by Schick, "A Death in the Bureaucracy."

58. Cited in U.S. Senate, Committee on Government Operations, Subcommittee on National Security and International Operations, *Planning, Programming, Budgeting,* 90th Cong., 1st sess., 1970, p. 127 - 28.

Humane
Bureaucracy

4

In the preceding chapter, we discussed the importance of technical devices and structures capable of achieving public goals and delivering public services. Administrative science has made positive contributions in this area, although we noted that excessive concern with process and procedure may also impede effectiveness, efficiency, and overall responsiveness.

There is another crucial problem with the "machine" approach: it sometimes assumes that human beings are mere cogs in gigantic administrative apparatuses spewing out various public services. Even the emphasis upon styles of leadership in the last chapter contained a quite manipulative notion. Their main purpose was higher productivity and efficiency, not the welfare of employees. We shall now consider various "humane" factors, those dealing with the worth and welfare of individual human beings.

One of our concerns will be the degree of democracy *within* public organizations. For example, do goals of "self-actualization" and personal fulfillment require that people have a greater say in what happens to them as members of organizations? If so, are radical modifications needed in the hierarchical structure of bureaucracy? Or, conversely, should government workers modify their expectations of gaining self-fulfillment from their organizational experience? As members of a political system espousing democratic values, we must consider the degree to which organizations prevent or encourage the achievement of values such as equality of opportunity and meaningful work. Thus, it is important to analyze the philosophical relationship of public organizations to the individual.

At a more practical level there are other significant aspects of the interconnection between individuals and organizations. Public agencies cannot effectively achieve public goals without committed employees. Their commitment comes not only from technical skills and knowledge but also from adequate rewards — material and psychological — that may encourage the individual contributions needed to sustain organizational life and effectiveness. The psychological attitudes of employees are an important dimension of organizational life and constitute a crucial link between public bureaucracy and society at large. Employees' sense of public duty and justice can affect the lives of countless citizens. Yet we shall see that these issues are complex.

The human aspects of organizations are also important because of *largest* the great numbers of individuals engaged in public-service occupations. *er in* As the largest single employer, government can be an important in- *Canada.* fluence in improving the lot of ethnic minorities and other disadvantaged segments of the population, such as women. Government hiring and promotion practices help compensate for injustices in the private sector. Such procedures, therefore, have a profound bearing on the degree of social democracy in America. However, they also have costs.

In this chapter, we shall review the links between individuals and organizations, and the problems and opportunities that arise from this relationship. We shall be especially concerned with the problem of making bureaucracy more "humane" to its membership and shall ask whether or not the "humanely" treated employees will in turn serve the public more effectively. We consider the public bureaucracy - employee interaction from three perspectives: the idea of meaningful work, the quest for equitable treatment, and the quest for individuality. We conclude by discussing an approach to organizational renewal called "organizational development," which is concerned with both humane values and the effectiveness and efficiency of public service.

THE MEANINGFULNESS OF WORK

The impact of organizations on their employees has been much studied recently. Increasingly, a person's job is seen as affecting the quality of his life. Medical evidence, for example, shows that many mental and physical ailments are associated with occupational stress. In contrast, a study of the process of aging showed that the main predictor of longevity was job satisfaction.[1] As people obtain increased professional capacities, they usually acquire higher expectations for job opportunities. This educational factor is supplemented by the contemporary emphasis on quality of life. Writings that advocate greater concern for the worker as a person place increased pressure on employers to facilitate individual development and to encourage job satisfaction. The traditional "Protestant work ethic," which maintained that work itself is inherently desirable, has given way to a more challenging view that stresses not so much the need for work but the kind of conditions under which work takes place.[2]

The dimensions of discontent with work are broad, although there is little clear and unchallenged evidence on the severity of this disenchantment. For example, public opinion polls and other sources indicate that in general Americans are satisfied with their work.[3] But often this satisfaction seems to result from a resignation to the need for employment rather than from finding work fulfilling or rewarding. Research evidence indicates that people with professional jobs tend to be more satisfied with work than individuals without such jobs. Yet even among middle and upper job levels, attitudes toward work are changing. As a Department of Health, Education, and Welfare study noted:

> *Why should there be job dissatisfaction among people who earn twenty thousand dollars a year? Some trained observers say that the new values of the counter-culture have had a noticeable effect even on these workers who clearly espoused mainstream views. As evidence it is claimed that where it used to be considered a sign of dedication and admirable ambition for a manager to be seen carrying home a full attache case, today it is seen only as compulsive behavior or evidence of "workaholism."*[4]

Much blue-collar discontent results from the depersonalization of assembly-line work. Yet many white-collar jobs also involve repetitious and monotonous tasks. The unionization movement among white-collar employees and their increasing tendency to change professions in mid-career are signs of their discontent with their status.[5]

A study by sociologist Daniel Yankelovich of college youth indicates widespread questioning of the traditional authority patterns found in organizations and a commitment on the part of the younger generation to find "rewarding" and "meaningful" employment. Interestingly, America's youth remains ambitious, but the emphasis is upon "doing one's own thing" rather than being an undifferentiated part of a hierarchically structured "machine" bureaucracy.[6] Selfhood and personal dignity have become values that stimulate contemporary concern for work with meaning.

We have been looking at work values for American society as a whole. For the public service, however, the following questions are especially significant: Can a public organization be responsive to its external environment if it fails to provide an optimum working situation, in which dignity, fulfillment, and job satisfaction are encouraged for its employees? Can an employee who feels locked into an "organizational rut" approach public business with enthusiasm and creativity? We shall see that the answers to these questions are complex and that other values compete with worker satisfaction and fulfillment. Before discussing strategies for improving the human condition in public organizations, however, we must analyze more specifically work attitudes in the public sector.

A 1969 Brookings Institution survey demonstrated that a majority of the people queried were willing to stereotype public servants. On the positive side, they were seen as honest and conscientious. But government employees came under fire for lacking drive and being excessively security conscious. For example, a worker in an iron plant described public employees in these terms: "I think they believe they have a job with security . . . that the government will always be here while a company could shut down." A medical worker offered another telling observation: "it would be just like the mailman — a job as long as he lives and he can retire on it."[7]

These popular assumptions are largely sustained by the observations of government employees themselves. For example, in the same study, low-level federal workers were asked to indicate the reasons they had become civil servants. The conclusions are disenchanting to those who assume that the primary motivation should be a desire to "serve the public," as table 4.1 demonstrates.

TABLE 4.1 Reasons for Becoming a Civil Servant (federal employee response)

security and fringe benefits	76%
good financial reward	16%
specific job opportunities	13%
self-advancement/desires success	10%
unable to work or succeed elsewhere	10%
physical environment/working conditions	9%
interest in work	8%
opportunity to be of service	8%

Source: Franklin P. Kilpatrick, et al., *The Image of the Federal Service.* © 1964 by the Brookings Institution, Washington, D.C., p. 231.

At higher levels of government, service and achievement are prime motivations. The importance of the job surpasses security and material incentives, as shown in a 1969 Civil Service Commission survey of federal executives in high-level positions (grades GS 15 through GS 18). Thirty percent of the executives queried said they had entered government because it provided "the best opportunity to follow a chosen occupation." Twenty-five percent asserted that government service offered "an interesting and challenging assignment." Others claimed they entered government service because "it was the best offer I had," because "I felt I could be useful in emergency or special missions" or because they "wanted to work where important decisions were made."[8]

The Brookings survey, however, highlighted certain areas of work dissatisfaction even among these high-level employees. While they looked upon security and financial reward as positive aspects of public employment, they disliked red tape and the restraints inherent in a hierarchical chain of command. Also, many higher-level employees did not feel personally fulfilled in their work.[9]

What does all of this tell us about employee desires? First, for many public employees, government work is viewed primarily as a "job" rather than as an opportunity to be of service. Public employees tend to be self-oriented rather than clientele- or public-oriented. There are, of course, many service-oriented employees at all levels of government, but the pervasive pattern is one of self-interest. This predominantly self-centered employee orientation should caution us against devising better strategies for such purposes as increased productivity, output, and goal maximization. Too single-minded a reliance on efficiency norms and practices could induce greater worker alienation and aggravate the self-preservation and survival values, which would further decrease worker identification with organizational goals and the external public.

The meshing of individual values and organizational goals cannot be done by indoctrination. Nor is improving the "humaneness" of organizations achieved by any single program or strategy. Since it is extremely unrealistic to think that government employees will ever renounce their self-interest, the values of public service and worker identification with organizational goals must therefore seek to supplement self-centered considerations.

Although some of the claims of the adherents of "self-actualization" may be overstated, there is certainly validity to the increasing desire for more "meaningful" work.[10] Undoubtedly, many government jobs could be broadened to give workers greater responsibility and opportunities to exercise independent judgment. It can be argued that this should be done in some situations even at the cost of some reduced efficiency, to make the work setting less destructive to individual growth and fulfillment. But there are, of course, competing values. The elected officials whose duty it is to oversee the operations of bureaucracies must use tax dollars wisely, so the need for a certain level of efficiency narrows the opportunities for making jobs meaningful. And there are some jobs, such as janitorial and sanitation chores, that inevitably remain routine. It must not be forgotten that the primary —though not sole — concern of government should be its contribution to society and the needs of its citizens.

Work and Motivation

In the previous chapter we pointed out that traditional management theory assumed that certain organizational principles determined efficiency and effectiveness. While structure and process provide the formal setting of organizational activities, we now can see that many of the "machine" aspects of bureaucracy may actually be counterproductive, for they treat the individual as a technical cog in the organizational machine.

The central premise of the "humane" approach is that the individual and not necessarily the structure defines organizational capacities.[11] People are seen not as passive instruments but as social beings who have basic needs and desires that must be dealt with before the organization's goals can be met. The motivation of employees to perform well is viewed from a psychological rather than a structural perspective. Self-satisfied employees may be more responsive and productive, although research findings on this point are still not clear.

Much of modern motivation theory is based upon the work of several psychologists, among them Abraham Maslow, who theorized that there exists a hierarchy of human needs. As each level of the hierarchy is satisfied, the next one asserts itself. First come physical needs, such as shelter and food, followed by safety needs, such as freedom from physical attack. At a higher level, there is a need to belong and to be loved by a family or peer group, followed by needs for self-confidence, status, and other forms of esteem. At the highest level is the need for "self-actualization," doing and creating in accordance with one's talents and desires. Thus, the pursuit of self-actualization is seen as a basic human psychological need.[12]

Similarly, the late Douglas McGregor asserted that "man is a wanting animal — as soon as one of his needs is satisfied, another appears in its place."[13] According to him, these needs fall into four basic categories, including psychological and safety needs, social needs (such as acceptance by others), ego needs (the enhancement of one's self-esteem or reputation), and self-fulfillment needs. This last in the hierarchy of needs McGregor defined as "the need for realizing one's own potentialities, for continued self-development, for being creative in the broadest sense of that term."[14] Organizations, McGregor argued, have been derelict in recognizing these basic needs of individual personalities and have been especially deficient in recognizing the ego and self-fulfillment needs.

Labeling "Theory X" the traditional organizational theory as developed by Weber and Taylor, which emphasized control and supervision, he argued for the development of a more psychologically meaningful approach, which he called "Theory Y." Within the Theory Y framework, McGregor called for a new integration of the individual with the organization, an approach to management suggesting that management *guide* not control, *direct* not command, *encourage* creativity not force subservience:

> *The motivation, the potential for development, the capacity for assuming responsibility, the readiness to direct behavior toward organizational goals are all present in people. Management does not put them there. It is the responsibility of management to make it possible for people to recognize and develop these human characteristics for themselves. The essential task of management is to arrange organizational conditions and methods of operation so that people can achieve their own goals best by directing their own efforts toward organizational objectives.* [15]

Related to the views of McGregor are those of psychologist Chris Argyris, who sees a fundamental "incongruency" between the needs of a healthy individual and the requirements of formal organizations. He argues that the traditional view of organizations stresses task specialization, subordination, and control. Within this framework individuals are "provided minimal control over their work-a-day world."[16] Organizational constraints force them to be "passive, dependent, subordinate."[17] They are expected to have a "short time perspective," and, because of the need for specialized skills, "to perfect and value the frequent use of a few superficial abilities."[18] Finally, because of all of the preceding conditions, "they are expected to produce under conditions leading to psychological fatigue."[19] Argyris believes that these requirements run counter to the needs of mature personalities, who prize self-control and development. The resultant effect is a disequilibrium between the individual and the organization, with the individual forced to make the adjustment rather than the organization adjusting to human needs. He notes:

> *All of these characteristics are incongruent to the ones healthy human beings are postulated to desire. They are much more congruent with the needs of infants in our culture. In effect, therefore, formal organizations are willing to pay high wages and provide adequate seniority if mature adults will, for eight hours a day, behave in a less mature manner.* [20]

Frederick Herzberg's "motivation-hygiene" view of work has also received great attention. According to him, the factors leading to job satisfaction are different from those leading to job dissatisfaction. The principal causes ("motivations") of job satisfaction are achievement, recognition, responsibility, and meaningful work. As opportunities for these values increase, job satisfaction increases. But their absence does not create job dissatisfaction; rather, it lowers the motivation to perform well. "Hygiene" factors, on the other hand, such as working conditions, company policy and administration, salary, interpersonal relations, and style of supervision, can produce dissatisfaction, but do not motivate.

Thus, an organization may provide opportunities for individual growth yet be unable to reduce job dissatisfaction. Likewise, a raise in pay, being a "hygienic" factor, will not in itself increase job satisfaction. In Herzberg's framework, personal needs constitute two distinct sets. "Thus, the opposite of job satisfaction would not be job dissatisfaction, but rather *no* job satisfaction; similarly, the opposite of job dissatisfaction is *no* job dissatisfaction, not satisfaction with one's job."[21] The practical as well as theoretical implications of Herzberg's work are apparent: the development of productive, self-satisfied, and responsive employees is much more complex than has often been assumed and requires an awareness of the distinction between "motivational" and "hygienic" factors.

Motivational theory probably *has* had an effect on the way bureaucratic organizations treat their employees, but several points must be borne in mind. One is that goals such as self-actualization seem to be more important to managers and professionals than to people further down the bureaucratic ladder. From a value perspective, moreover, it is by no means clear that a person is juvenile and immature who views a job principally as a source of income and who welcomes nonhostile supervision that clarifies tasks. Also, certain social changes are already compelling less authoritarian supervision in most public settings and providing greater opportunities for employees to control their own work environment. Workers are more educated and more aware of their rights. Increasingly, they have unions to protect them from supervisory abuse, and civil service regulations have long been a source of protection. The civil rights and women's rights movements have brought important procedural changes. These changes are improvements, but they are occurring within the context of the traditional hierarchical framework of bureaucratic organization and not necessarily along the lines suggested by motivation theorists.[22]

A major difficulty with some motivation theory concerns its foundation in a belief in the absolute worth of "self-fulfillment." Perhaps it is more a fault of the followers than of the developers of the creed. In any event, some advocates fail to realize that many employees may not have strong "self-fulfillment" needs. As we noted in chapter 2, the variety of psychological predispositions in organizations should indicate that not everyone can or wants to be fulfilled in the same manner. Research has shown that some workers intentionally choose not to find fulfillment in their work. As one study noted: "By rejecting involvement in their work, *which simply cannot be fulfilling,* workers save their sanity."[23] For some, dependency and subordination are adequate fulfillment of their "psychological contract," or their commitment to providing their services and talents to their organization in return for material and spiritual benefits. Chris Argyris, in fact, has recently amended his theory to indicate that adult wants are less of an absolute than many had originally thought, but vary from personality to personality as well as over time in the same person.[24] Consider, for example, figure 4.1:

Infants begin as	Adults strive toward
(1) being dependent on and submissive to parents (or other significant adults)	(1) relative independence, autonomy, relative control over their immediate world ⟶
(2) having few abilities	(2) developing many abilities ⟶
(3) having skin-surfaced or shallow abilities	(3) developing a few abilities in depth ⟶
(4) having a short time perspective	(4) developing a longer time perspective ⟶

Source: Chris Argyris, "Personality and Organization Theory Revisited," *Administrative Science Quarterly* 18 (June 1973):142

FIGURE 4.1

If one tried to foster fulfillment in an organization by presuming that all individuals reflected "adult" needs as represented at the right of the continuum, one would hamper needs that may be midway along the continuum or still at the left side of the continuum. The desire for self-fulfillment *is* important, but it must be recognized that it is a variable, at one point dominant and at another nonexistent. To superimpose organizational remedies on such shifting sands is to do injustice to the theory and the personalities involved. Furthermore, it is now recognized that "self-fulfillment" is not necessarily a universal human need, but possibly the product of uniquely American or even elitist academic values. Many cultures emphasize collectivist norms, not individualistic self-fulfillment.

Additionally, several researchers have overlooked the fact that job satisfaction varies according to occupational position, with some employees having primary concern for lower-order needs (money, security) rather than the higher-order needs postulated by Maslow and McGregor.[25] Even within a single professional class of managers, job satisfaction is not related to any uniform desire for self-actualization, but to personality, achievement expectations, and other diverse values,[26] illustrating the point that there may be more need to fit unique psychological predispositions to the task than to redesign tasks on the assumption that all workers need to be "self-actualized."

One interesting study indicates that organizations employing McGregor's "Theory Y" (self-actualization structures) do not automatically achieve high worker motivation and, conversely, organizations that operate under "Theory X" do not always induce low motivation.[27] While arguing that people have a basic need to achieve satisfaction, the researchers noted that some individuals can achieve it under Theory Y *or* Theory X. What is needed to achieve worker satisfaction, they argue, is not any broad-scale implementation of Theory Y designs but a "fit" between an individual's motivation and an organizational task. And, even assuming that self-actualization leads to higher morale, research by no means clearly indicates that higher morale leads to greater productivity or effectiveness.

In any case, public organizations are not created for the sole purpose of producing "happy" bureaucrats. If that is achieved, so much the better, but their cardinal goal is to serve an external, not internal, clientele. The motivation model does not concern itself with the "morality" of what bureaucrats do, but with the bureaucrats' self-fulfillment. If self-fulfillment in an organization can be achieved only by turning every specialist into a generalist a problem arises, for other goals conflict: most particularly, the efficient and effective accomplishment of public services and democratic control of the activities of public employees. Which value should win out? If everyone in a bureaucracy were given new responsibilities in line with their constantly evolving and changing interpretation of their self-fulfillment needs, would not the new fulfillment activities become repetitive and monotonous over time or cause the organization to be in a state of constant flux? In brief, self-actualization may be an important goal, but it is only one goal and not necessarily the most vital one. Emmette Redford, for example, emphasizes that the quality of service to the public must remain a fundamental value: "the prime purpose of public organizations is to serve external interests . . . and workers must accept this as fact."[28]

If the public is better served by worker self-fulfillment, decentralization of power, and the weakening of the hierarchy in certain agencies or for certain projects, then so be it. But if in the quest for the self-fulfilled bureaucrat we witness less effective public service or even domination by more remote elites, then the choice between the two values is obvious. While we do not suggest a return to Taylorism, we want to emphasize the need to balance self-actualization and motivation values and programs with the equally important requirements of machine and political bureaucracy.

The main conclusion of much of the motivation research is that human needs are complex and heterogeneous. The stereotyped concept of "organization man" is mythical in the sense that uniform wants and aspirations do not seem to exist. While dissatisfaction with work may be a plight of many in today's society, that dissatisfaction most likely has multiple causes, and no one cure will suffice.

Enlargement and Enrichment

One of the traditional responses to the problem of monotony was to expand the work employees were asked to undertake. Tasks were "enlarged" to accommodate a variety of assignments. Enlargement, however, was often viewed with suspicion by workers and union leaders, who saw it as a device for increasing workloads through the guise of providing more creative and stimulating work. Enlargement in a sense did not mean *better* work opportunities, but *more* work.

The emphasis in current occupational theory and behavioral motivation research goes one step further by suggesting that rather than job enlargement, one should encourage "job enrichment." Briefly, job enrichment refers to strategies for improving the meaning of work tasks, to make them more rewarding and more compatible with self-fulfillment expectations.[29] Primarily based upon the factors of motivation recognized by Herzberg (such as self-esteem, advancement, and responsibility within the work setting), job enrichment programs entail developing systems in which task assignments clearly relate individual effort to organizational goals. Herzberg has identified eight characteristics of the "enriched" job:

(1)   *Feedback.* Individuals are provided with an opportunity to know the results or impact of their action or performance. This feedback is nonevaluative and is intended to provide the employee with the opportunity to learn the consequences of his action.

(2)   *Client Contact.* Individuals have an awareness of serving a clientele or customer, rather than serving a superior within the organizational hierarchy.

(3)   *Opportunity for Learning.* Individuals are afforded new opportunities for psychological and professional development. Jobs therefore become growth opportunities.

(4)   *Freedom in Scheduling.* Individuals are given the responsibility to schedule their activities in the manner they feel is most con-

ducive to responsible task accomplishment. Individuals establish their own pace within the defined deadlines.

(5)   *Developing Unique Expertise.* Individuals are given the opportunity to make their own unique contributions to problem solving, by being provided the chance to apply their creativity to organizational problems that may not be directly related to their primary task.

(6)   *Resource Control.* Individuals appreciate the costs involved in conducting organizational operations and are given responsibility to maximize the impact of limited resources by having a measure of control or oversight over their utilization.

(7)   *Facilitation of Communication.* Individuals are encouraged to engage in direct communication with those with whom the task at hand may occasion communication without necessary obedience to the hierarchical communication pattern.

(8)   *Personal Accountability.* Individuals welcome the opportunity to be held accountable for their activities and reflect an increased sensitivity to the attainment of the mission of the organization.[30]

Thus, job enrichment substitutes notions of autonomy, responsibility, and creativity for the often irrational constraints of hierarchy, constant supervision, and fractionated work.

While supporters of job enrichment point to several successful efforts within private industry, there is among some experts a sobering awareness that not all jobs can be enriched.[31] Even in companies such as Texas Instruments, which have initiated serious and comprehensive efforts to enrich jobs, the effort often includes only a fraction of the work force.[32] Job enrichment is probably viable only for certain tasks and will be successful only with those individuals whose self-actualization needs are compatible with the enrichment model. Research has indicated that the sense of autonomy that enrichment provides is met with some anxiety by those who question their ability to succeed in such an environment of freedom. In addition, organizational conservatism often works against the development of an employee psychology conducive to autonomy, freedom, and the risk and uncertainty implicit in the enrichment model.[33] Further, a well-meaning public administrator who initiates an enrichment program usually has to sell it not only to the employees but also to a rigid civil service system replete with ponderous job descriptions and regulations as well as to inquiring legislators and elected executives. Of course, the limitations of job enrichment do not preclude it from making some important contributions. As long as individuals are not forced to become "enriched" because of some abstract model, enrichment efforts may improve motivation and facilitate employee identification with organizational goals.

But not everyone seeks enriched jobs. In their study of employee values, Flowers and Hughes found that while many seek creative and self-fulfilling opportunities, equal numbers of others associate with an organization because of the ease of the work, salary level, and job security.[34] Thus, organizations may have to provide a mix of incentives, ranging from the fulfillment of enrichment needs to basic "hygienic" needs.

In addition to the enrichment program discussed above, there are other strategies. The Scanlon plan, for example, is a device by means of which employees help define the conditions of work, identify and isolate problems, and help shape the compensation schedule. In addition, employees are rewarded for contributing ideas that can be used to eliminate waste or inefficiency. Another useful practice is the attendance of employees at brainstorming sessions where new ideas for problem solving can be raised. Although retiring and taciturn individuals may feel threatened by the high value attached to participation in such efforts, brainstorming is a useful method of soliciting a wide variety of ideas.[35]

Job enrichment may also be facilitated by developing team approaches to task accomplishment. Volvo, for example, replaced some car production assembly lines with teams that produced an entire car, providing employees the opportunity to utilize multiple skills. The "family approach" created by team efforts is one means of dissipating the alienation and discontent created by assembly lines. This approach requires that team personality and skill resources be complementary and not produce excessive conflict.

Enrichment also implies that organizations be able to fit the needs of the individual to the tasks available. Thus, more conscientious efforts to achieve a "goodness of fit" between the individual and the organizational task may be necessary. This may necessitate providing more opportunities for employees to define their own role and the time framework in which it will be undertaken.[36] Current job descriptions and recruitment procedures tend not to match individual needs with organizational opportunities, not to provide the flexibility of working conditions often required. Instead, they often match limited and narrow skills with limited and narrow organizational niches.

If enrichment is to be successfully employed where appropriate in the public sector, more flexible civil service laws permitting task creativity and worker autonomy may have to emerge. Further, public-sector recruiters might examine the degree to which they oversell the self-fulfillment opportunities available within their organizations. The quickest way to guarantee personnel disenchantment is to have high expectations met with unanticipated boredom. Perhaps a more candid psychology of recruitment, in which one admits that certain kinds of self-actualization may not be possible, will help recruit individuals who have a reasonable level of work expectations.

Salary

Although the evidence is mixed, Herzberg may be right in viewing financial reward as a "hygienic" factor and hence not directly contributing to worker job satisfaction. Nevertheless, most personnel experts see adequate pay and benefits as a means of reducing worker dissatisfaction. By and large, the government approach has aimed at "parity," that is, compensating public employees at a level equivalent to their counterparts in private industry. Through parity, the government hopes to compete successfully with private industry for the best employees.

Since 1945 there have been nineteen salary increments for federal government employees, eleven occurring since 1960, often at the instigation of the unions. Though several of these increments have been very large, most noticeably the 16 percent average increase of 1945, pay raises have generally averaged about 6 percent a year. Given the size and classification schedules of federal employees, this amounts to about 1.9 billion dollars yearly, a sizable chunk of the federal budget.[37] Even allowing for inflation, the results are impressive. For example, in June of 1966, the average annual salary for individuals within the "general schedule" classification (the most widely used salary classification system) was $7898 per year. By 1970, that figure had increased to slightly over $11,000,[38] thereby maintaining parity with private-sector salaries.

The complex relationship between the attitudes of workers and bureaucratic performance is revealed in salary compensation as it is in other areas. Adequate compensation may be a way of decreasing employee dissatisfaction but it might also further isolate public administrators. At the top levels, salaries and benefits are relatively attractive, placing these public managers in a comparatively high income group. Unfortunately, this risks producing elitist sentiments and limiting the ability of administrators to relate to the needs of middle- and low-income groups. It can also detract from managers' willingness to grant access to average citizens. Moreover, growing government expenditures on salaries and benefits produce inflationary pressures on the economy and add to mounting financial difficulties in the public sector. We agree that humane treatment of employees requires adequate compensation for work and that such compensation may often enhance job satisfaction. But it does not automatically follow that better public administration will result. Rather, it is probably a case in which the positive consequences of change outweigh the negative, and in which the negative consequences should be offset by other strategies.

Training and Development

While research findings indicate that salary compensation alone may not be an adequate motivational force for many individuals in public employment, there seems to be agreement that employees who have a sense of *competence* and are given the opportunity to utilize their skills feel a stronger sense of identification and commitment to the organization. Thus, the development of skills in an organization may not only provide the dividend of improved expertise but also enhance the positive sentiments of employees for the organization and its goals.

Governmentally sponsored training programs have been a major method of upgrading the skills and effectiveness of public employees. Courses ranging from basic accounting and computer operations to managerial decision making and collective bargaining now train approximately one-third of all federal public servants in any given year, and surveys completed by the Civil Service Commission show that agencies are increasing opportunities for continuing education.[39]

Although the bulk of the courses given by the government are in the "how-to-do-it" category of technical skills, there are also courses for professional workers (lawyers, physicians, engineers) as well as managers. In fact, so great has been the concern of the national government to develop the skills of its employees that it established in 1968 the Federal Executive Institute as a "staff college" for improving managerial skills. Located in Charlottesville, Virginia, the FEI is designed to help improve the managerial capacities of senior-level civil servants, particularly the "supergrade" incumbents, such as grades 16, 17, and 18. Courses are conducted on campus and typically comprise seven or eight weeks of intensive study. A primary purpose of the institute is to generate competency in three areas: knowledge of the social, economic, political, and organizational environment of administration; the management systems, strategies and processes that can increase program effectiveness; and the strategies of interpersonal and personal dynamics that affect organizational performance.[40]

Training for the public service also has been broadened by two major personnel acts. Under the terms of the Intergovernmental Cooperation Act of 1968, the federal government has committed itself to aiding state and local governments train and develop their personnel. Under the law, the national government is reimbursed for its efforts, but the program operates in such a manner that many free services are actually provided. And through the Intergovernmental Personnel Act of 1970, a more broadbased effort was launched to improve the competence of state and local government employees by means of a grant process.

Of course, such training ultimately involves further professionalization and, as we have seen, professionalism has costs as well as benefits.

Professional training in such sensitive areas as police work can avoid a narrowing effect if it includes humanistically oriented material. Here, university education may be of great benefit, especially if sociological, psychological, political, and ethical material is part of the curriculum. As Frederick Mosher points out, "our dependence upon professionals is now so great that the orientations, value systems, and ethics which they bring to their work and which they enforce on one another are a matter of prime concern to those who would strengthen the democratic system."[41] He goes on to say that professionals increasingly determine public policy and even personnel decisions. Since the inward-looking, self-righteous value systems of many professionals make them resistant to political control or meddling by lay citizens, the problem of broader, interdisciplinary training becomes all the more critical.[42]

REPRESENTATIVE BUREAUCRACY

The term "representative bureaucracy" refers to the degree to which public agencies incorporate members of diverse social groups and backgrounds (race, religion, region, sex, class, etc.) into their employment rosters at all levels of the organizational hierarchy.[43] It has sometimes been argued that by this process values and beliefs from the general public become diffused through public organizations and serve to enhance the representative character of public policy making.

Some scholars have emphasized the point that public agencies in the United States are in their composition far more representative of the American electorate than the formal branches of government.[44] Despite gains by blacks and women, for example, Congress has remained dominated by white Protestant males with higher educations and past incomes than the public as a whole; indeed, the majority are lawyers. Public bureaucracies, by contrast, have always been much more representative of the multiple social sectors of the United States. Virtually every occupational skill, region, religion, and ethnic group in the country finds expression in the many departments, agencies, and commissions comprising the public administrative system. Moreover, the class background (based on father's occupation) of federal employees tends to parallel that of the population.[45]

Two important issues merit attention. First, some argue that to the extent the interests of different sectors of our society find expression in government agencies, access to and influence on policy making may increase. Second, as the largest single employer, the government offers employment opportunities to a broad range of citizens.

During the early history of the United States, the spoils system largely determined public employment, not only at the state and local but also at the national level. Under the spoils system politicians used government jobs as a means of rewarding party workers, obtaining campaign funds ("donations" from government workers), and buying votes. After the Pendleton Act of 1883, however, many federal appointments became divorced from politics, and public workers could not be fired for political reasons nor forced to work in or pay for political campaigns. More important, government employees were selected and promoted largely on the basis of competitive criteria, not because of political influence. The Civil Service Commission became the federal government's guardian of the merit principle of employment.

The merit system gradually incorporated the vast majority of federal workers, and many state and local governments adopted it, too, due to federal insistence that programs funded by the national government but administered by the states be operated on a merit principle. Most states and cities, but not counties, now have merit programs, although the spoils system has not been totally eradicated.[46]

Regrettably, the merit system proved to be no guarantee of bureaucrat representation. Blacks and women were excluded from many government positions, at the national as well as the state and local level. Though some governments employed them in large numbers, they typically held menial jobs such as typists, clerks, and janitors. Various strategies and rules, such as allowing preference to be given to veterans (a disadvantage for women), the rule of three (allowing administrators to take their choice from the three top scorers on exams), and outright discrimination perpetuated the exclusion. A major problem has been civil service testing procedures that place minorities at a disadvantage.

Since the 1950s, however, the civil rights and women's liberation movements, the Civil Rights Act of 1964, the Equal Employment Opportunity Act of 1972, and other laws, as well as various court decisions, have radically reduced such discrimination at all levels of government. The federal government, for example, is now comprised of a higher percentage of black workers than their percentage of the population would indicate.[47] Moreover, because the federal government is a major customer of private industry, and a major financial contributor to such nongovernment organizations as private universities, it is in a position to stimulate greater equality in the private sector by threatening to withdraw its business or its grants if discriminatory practices are not ended.

A number of specific programs contribute to the trend toward greater equality and thus greater representation of previously unrepresented groups. Affirmative action is one of the most important. This program involves more than legal nondiscrimination, which has existed for years with comparatively little impact. It involves instead taking positive steps at the national, state, and local levels toward the recruitment of women and minority citizens, including more active publishing of job vacancies and notification of women's and minority organizations of job openings. In short, affirmative action involves a process of searching for qualified minorities. It also requires that job descriptions and classification schemes not discriminate. Examples of these principles include prohibitions against women being asked questions not asked of men regarding marital status and against arrest records being used to automatically disqualify an applicant when such records are not related to the job and may be a result of a poverty background.[48]

A complementary strategy to affirmative action involves the concept of upward mobility. For although blacks and women have become increasingly prevalent in government, they still fill mostly low-level, non-policy-making positions. Thus, at the top levels, American bureaucracy is not really representative but is still strongly skewed in favor of white, middle-class males. So upward mobility involves an active effort by government to train lower-level personnel for positions of greater responsibility and to ensure that job specifications do not present needless obstacles to their advancement. The ultimate goal of upward mobility programs is to ensure that minority citizens, women, and other disadvantaged groups work their way into high-level positions as fast as their formal administrative skills will make possible.

A final goal of affirmative action programs is continuous evaluation to ensure that effective action continues. Among the many potential obstacles to be guarded against are tokenism, or appointing minority members to high-level positions with no real policy-making powers. Other problems include ensuring equal interagency and intergovernmental mobility and attempting to achieve more equitable assignments, that is, correcting the tendency for some agencies to remain unrepresentative. Since major decisions are made by specific agencies and bureaus, not by public bureaucracy as a whole, the ultimate goal is to enable previously excluded groups to acquire not only equal job opportunities but also a meaningful voice in agencies and policy areas that most directly affect their interests.[49] It should be emphasized that affirmatively seeking qualified minorities does not necessarily mean that such persons will be found. Past discrimination or personal choice may make such candidates unavailable.

Two of the most frequently voiced criticisms of representative bureaucracy concern efficiency and fairness. It is often argued that these programs as practiced reduce the quality of government service by lowering the standards of appointment and promotion. Others charge that the more skilled persons are unfairly denied employment or promotion in order to meet the requirements of programs that go beyond affirmative action guidelines by hiring less qualified minorities. If blacks are favored because of their race, then why not have quotas for Irish-Americans, Italian-Americans, and so on? The answers to these criticisms are complex. Briefly, however, it is apparent that white males have not been subject to the sustained, conscious discrimination suffered by blacks and other groups, such as Mexican-Americans, Indians, and women. Furthermore, the examination process for recruitment and promotion has often discriminated unconsciously as well as consciously against these disadvantaged groups. Blacks, for instance, have somewhat different language patterns, hence white, middle-class language and cultural material on exams preclude an even chance for them. A clear example of the problem concerns Spanish-speaking groups, who are often at a disadvantage when they confront tests given in English. Some courts have ruled, in fact, that entrance exams be given in both English and Spanish. Also, many examination questions, as well as formal education requirements, have not been relevant to the skills needed for specialized job assignments. In this respect, requirements might be altered without impeding administrative efficiency or effectiveness.

Additionally, it could be argued that effectiveness and efficiency may be increased through greater representation of minorities. Representatives of ethnic minorities can often communicate more clearly with members of their subculture and probably elicit greater cooperation. Women may be more sensitive to the problems of women. Broader representation might help provide insight and information, which can facilitate the making of good administrative decisions. The major point made by its proponents is that representative bureaucracy can help make the administrative system more responsive to the needs of previously excluded groups through policy decisions made by more representative administrators.

Yet serious problems remain. Affirmative action and quota systems are interpreted by many as reverse discrimination and may produce alienation among qualified white males. To the extent that such programs go further than seeking qualified candidates, less skilled personnel may sometimes be hired or promoted — a difficulty that can be mitigated by effective training programs. Also, we have seen that at its highest levels public bureaucracy is in fact unrepresentative. Moreover, creating representation on the basis of background does not guarantee representation of diverse interests and values. Public workers of whatever background tend to acquire middle-class values and the organizational orientations noted in chapter 2. Also, high-level administrators from whatever background tend to be upwardly mobile, not always willing to remember from whence they came. Also, as we have seen, many decisions at all levels are made principally out of concern for the self-interest of the individual administrator or the organization. Therefore, we cannot assume that bureaucratic representativeness automatically results in greater policy inputs for a broader section of the American public, although it does seem reasonable to conclude that as higher levels of government bureaucracy become more representative, there will be at least some impact upon policy. In any event, public bureaucracy will never be fully representative because of such factors as personal interests (many people do not want to be government employees) and the skill requirements that inevitably mean staffing by middle-class citizens of whatever group.[50]

The ultimate administrative problem of representation is the equitable treatment of the poor and disadvantaged by bureaucrats and policy makers.[51] Allowing their voices to be heard requires a personal value system on the part of government employees that makes them sensitive to the uneducated, the handicapped, the retarded, ex-convicts, children, and all other disadvantaged citizens. But the personal attitudes of bureaucrats can solve only part of this problem. A more equitable administrative system ultimately rests on the structure of laws, including taxation and funding, established by elected representatives.

INDIVIDUALITY

In the democratic underpinnings of the American political system individuality has an important place. The Declaration of Independence proclaims inalienable personal rights to life, liberty, and the pursuit of happiness. The Constitution provides numerous procedural safeguards intended to protect political freedoms. The first article of the Bill of Rights, for example, prohibits Congress from passing laws that interfere with freedom of speech or religion. There exists in American ideology both a concern for the psychological and social autonomy of individual Americans and a pledge to uphold the right of free choice, concerns that can conflict with the principles of bureaucratic organization.

Modern bureaucracies threaten individuality by erecting numerous barriers. In the extreme, employees may be required by formal or informal rules to follow dress codes and to spend off-duty hours on social, civic, or business activity deemed necessary by the organization. Government employees may also be prohibited from exercising some forms of political expression. Naturally, modern bureaucratic society encourages certain facets of individuality by providing a greater range of career options and a degree of anonymity lacking in smaller, less complex communities. But organizational life can hinder personal flexibility.

Unlike the concepts of self-fulfillment and self-actualization discussed earlier, our use of the term "individuality" does not address itself to the meaning of work. Nor does it imply the frontier spirit of enthusiasm or adventure envisioned by some when they employ the concept of "individualism" in its broader sense. Rather, "individuality" as we use it refers to a citizen's right to autonomy concerning his or her life not connected with organizational duties. It implies the right to preserve one's identity free from organizational sanctions and encroachments and to pursue legitimate political activity without penalties. Our concern with individuality thus focuses on two dimensions. First, there is the right to be "let alone" by the organization, with certain facets of one's life and psychological makeup not part of the contractual agreement between worker and employer. Second, there is the right of the individual employee to be involved in political affairs or social causes without retribution by his or her employer.

The Right to Autonomy

While it is obviously necessary that persons in government jobs perform certain tasks and work productively it does not follow that their private lives are the legitimate concern of management. Yet it is common for overzealous managers to require excessive commitment to the organization and its goals. A supervisor, for example, might urge participation in a government savings bond program and attribute to those who do not participate a lack of teamwork and commitment to the organization — judgments that may affect an employee's promotional chances. A concerned supervisor might also urge employees to participate in "sensitivity training" sessions sponsored by the government, even though such training might require divulging private thoughts and feelings or produce anxiety. Another illustration of the potential for abuse is the forcing of employees to take psychological tests designed to measure their levels of anxiety or their personality, or to agree to other invasions of privacy as a prerequisite for job retention or advancement. Similarly, the private lives of employees may sometimes become the basis of decisions affecting their careers.

Employees at all levels of government are often urged to support political candidates or parties, in clear violation of laws that prohibit forced political participation. This concern over organizational infringements on individual autonomy was reflected in considerable support for a "bill of rights" for government employees considered by the 93rd Congress. Recommended by the Senate Subcommittee on Constitutional Rights, the purpose of the suggested legislation was to:

> . . . *prohibit indiscriminate executive branch requirements that employees and, in certain instances, applicants for Government employment disclose their race, religion, or national origin; attend Government-sponsored meetings and lectures or participate in outside activities or undertakings unrelated to their*

work; submit to questioning about their religion, personal relationships or sexual attitudes through interviews, psychological tests, or polygraphs [lie detectors]; support political candidates or attend political meetings. The bill would make it illegal to coerce an employee to buy bonds or make charitable contributions. It prohibits officials from requiring him to disclose his own personal assets, liabilities, or expenditures, or those of any member of his family unless, in the case of certain specified employees, such items would tend to show a conflict of interest. It would provide a right to have a counsel or other person present, if the employee wishes, at an interview which may lead to disciplinary proceedings. It would accord the right to a civil action in a Federal court for violation or threatened violation of the act, and it would establish a Board on Employees' Rights to receive and conduct hearings on complaints of violation of the act and to determine and administer remedies and penalties.[52]

This legislation, interestingly enough, was opposed by the Civil Service Commission on the grounds that it would impose restraints on the management of organizations. While the commission did not advocate practices counter to the principle of individuality, it maintained that any restraining legislation would have the effect of discouraging efforts to direct and channel employees' activities in positive directions. The opposition of the Civil Service Commission illustrates the point that even individuality must confront competing values. Though part of the opposition to the measure may have resulted from a self-serving desire to retain supervisory prerogatives, there is a quite legitimate concern that public managers be able to direct the activities of subordinates toward the accomplishment of public goals. It is also apparent that some jobs might legitimately require the use of psychological testing or even the use of polygraphs (e.g., intelligence officers). But such procedures should not be used indiscriminately. Most government jobs do not seem to require such techniques, and in no event does their use for generating information unrelated to work performance seem warranted.

The Right to Be Involved

The right of public employees to participate in the political process constitutes one of the most problematic aspects of humane bureaucracy. While political participation is a basic democratic right, there are competing values. The most important of these is the need for impartiality. It is true that whatever public administrators do tends to benefit some interests over others, but it is also clear that public agencies should not be allowed to serve as vote-getting machines for particular politicians, factions, or parties. Public agencies also ought not be a means of dispensing benefits to political supporters of elected officials. There is an important distinction between an agency modifying policy alternatives at the direction of political leaders and that same agency dispensing indiscriminate benefits and privileges to particular persons or groups.

Laws that prohibit public employees from contributing to the electoral campaigns of political superiors and that prevent them from serving as campaign workers, then, are valid and valuable. In fact, as has already been suggested, the chances for infringements upon individuality are great without such measures. By the same token, the restrictions on political participation now so broadly and vaguely stated by the Hatch Act should be clarified. Although the act was intended to resolve a key problem facing public bureaucracy, its uneven application by the Civil Service Commission has had a "chilling effect" on constructive forms of political participation.[53]

It is also apparent that public administrators ought not to participate in affairs that might involve a conflict of interest, or even the appearance of a conflict of interest. A hearing examiner for the National Labor Relations Board, for instance, has no business participating in efforts to organize workers into unions. Similarly, public administrators must take care where appropriate to ensure that their audience knows when they are speaking as a private citizen rather than as a government official. Moreover, certain positions are so extraordinarily sensitive that the very survival of democracy may depend upon prohibiting certain public officials from all but the most basic forms of participation, such as voting. The military, intelligence, and certain law-enforcement agencies are obvious examples.

With these limitations in mind, there is still substantial opportunity for participation. It seems reasonable, for example, that federal employees be able to run for part-time elected office in state and local government. The need to prevent partisan bureaucracy while improving First Amendment guarantees is reflected in the recent passage of a resolution by the American Society for Public Administration, the main professional organization of public administrators, which included the following points:

(1)   There is a need to protect the civil service merit system and impartial government and at the same time permit public employees to participate in the political process as fully as possible. . . .

(2)   Federal employees should be permitted to be candidates for, or to serve as, delegates, alternates, or proxies in a political convention, subject to strict avoidance of any appearance of conflict of interest, or the statement of official, as opposed to personal positions. However, federal employees should not be permitted to

serve as officers or employees of political conventions, even when such an employee would be on leave without pay.

(3)   Federal employees in duty status should not be authorized to become candidates for nomination or election to any national office or to any full-time state, county, or municipal office.

(4)   Federal employees should be allowed to seek part-time state, county, or municipal offices which, although necessarily having a partisan designation, actually involve societal duties of citizenship, such as city and county councils, boards of education, boards of tax appeal, zoning boards or such purely local part-time offices as justice of the peace, constable, or registrar of voters.

(5)   The Civil Service Commission should be required to maintain at all times an investigative capacity for enforcing the provisions of the political activities laws.

(6)   There should be established an independent federal office to which employee complaints of coercive actions and violations of law could be submitted, investigated, and prosecuted.

(7)   A criminal penalty should be established for those persons who knowingly attempt to influence a civil servant to contribute to a political candidate or party or participate in a campaign of a political candidate or party.[54]

It may also be reasonable to allow employees to state publicly their opposition to policies of the government agencies for which they work. Employees occasionally feel sufficiently aroused to picket, petition, or otherwise oppose agency actions and perhaps even these activities should be tolerated, except perhaps for such obviously sensitive positions as certain intelligence personnel. Might not a housing department employee who feels that his or her agency is derelict in pursuing public goals be allowed off the job to organize citizen activities challenging administrative inertia? Might not welfare workers be permitted on off-duty hours to promote activism by welfare recipients, who are typically unorganized and without political resources? Of course, if liberal or radical welfare workers are allowed such rights, ought not conservative or reactionary welfare workers have the same freedoms? Obviously, an off-duty worker participating in a John Birch Society program that seeks to halt expansion of welfare activities has the same constitutional rights as his or her colleagues who hold differing views.

Employees who oppose their agency's policies run considerable risks, and there should be prohibitions against firing employees exercising their freedom of expression. The complexity created by competing values, however, suggests that blanket freedom of speech is not possible, particularly where sensitive personal or classified information is concerned. Some may argue, for instance, that Daniel Ellsberg served as a vehicle for greater government responsiveness in releasing the Pentagon Papers in 1971, and there seems little denying that many leaks to the press have augmented bureaucratic accountability. But the dangers of releasing unauthorized information are also apparent and include jeopardizing the rights of government employees, impairing national security, and breeding excessive conservatism among administrators. Explicit guidelines on these matters are likely to emerge only through statutory law amplified by judicial decisions.

The advantages of greater freedom of expression seem to outweigh the disadvantages. Realistically, few employees are likely to risk alienating their superiors by publicly disagreeing with them. Even if they need not fear losing their job, they are unlikely to be recommended strongly for promotion. Moreover, research on participation indicates that few Americans are activists or joiners of political and social causes.[55] The vast majority of employees will remain passive even with greater freedom for political expression.

More important, these freedoms can help stimulate greater responsiveness and sensitivity to a broader public constituency. From a "machine" perspective, more information on opinions and values can increase the capacity for effective decision making. Thus, government employees as well as the administrative and political systems stand to benefit from a greater tolerance for this facet of individuality. While the very notions of country, society, and organization imply a significant degree of collectivism, the philosophical values espoused by the United States seem to compel an unflagging concern for the individuality of government workers.

ORGANIZATIONAL DEVELOPMENT: AN INTEGRATIVE APPROACH

Organizational development (OD) is a systematic process involving the discovery and resolution of issues detrimental to organizational effectiveness. It is a relatively new concept, designed to facilitate the creation of an open problem-solving environment. Whereas traditional approaches to solving organizational problems were based upon the application of some management principle, often suggested by an external consultant, organizational development views the resolution of organizational conflict as possible through the interaction of all relevant parties. This includes subordinates as well as managers.

As a problem-solving device, organizational development concentrates primarily on the "human" aspects of organizations: interpersonal rivalry, management-subordinate difficulties, skill inadequacy, and the like. While it may deal with the more overt aspects of an organization, such as its structure, its goals, and its financial resources, it can also deal with the more hidden part of the "organizational iceberg": attitudes, feelings, group norms, and informal organizational elements.[56] Robert Golembiewski, a public administration scholar, has identified several goals of the OD approach, including (1) the development of an "open, problem-solving climate throughout the organization," (2) the development of trust between individuals and groups within the organization, (3) the readjustment of faulty decision-making processes, (4) the harnessing of dysfunctional organizational competition, (5) the development of a meaningful reward system, and (6) increasing the potential for more sensitive public managers.[57]

An analysis by the late scholar, Kurt Lewin helps us understand the actual processes of organizational development. Lewin saw three key phases: unfreezing, changing, and refreezing. The "unfreezing" aspect involves an examination of the undesirable present situation by participants, generally through some form of group interaction. It entails a catharsis, or purging, in which values, behavior, and perhaps expectations are unearthed and examined in terms of their organizational impact. The purpose of the unfreezing is to achieve a "clean slate," to examine one's "ingrained habits of feeling, thought and action."[58] The "change" process involves, first, a search for solutions to problems; it may include managers changing distorted views of their organization or it could aim to improve mechanisms for communicating organizational goals so that employees might find greater rationality and meaning in them and develop a more positive set of attitudes. There might also be a broad-based design to improve organizational health through a series of training programs and upward-mobility incentive systems. The third and critical step is the need to "refreeze" or capture this action-oriented energy, this newfound dynamism, and maintain it at the desired level. Maintenance of the desired state must involve a conscious effort on the part of all participants lest the organization revert to its old traits. Because of an organization's tendency to return to its previous pattern of behavior, this process of unfreezing, change, and refreezing may result in a continuous and ongoing process, one that is easier stated than accomplished.[59]

Up to this point, organizational development may seem to focus only on broad administrative problems. Specific areas can be targeted for improvement, however, through "intervention strategies" designed to solve the problem. French and Bell provide a particularly useful and succinct list:

(1) Interventions directed toward improving individual effectiveness. Included as strategies in this process could be sensitivity sessions, "life and career planning activities" (which are concerned with measuring and evaluating an individual's assessment of career mobility and success), role playing, and problem-solving exercises.

(2) Interventions directed toward improving the effectiveness of two or three member groups (dyads or triads). Tools of intervention in such cases could include the utilization of a third-party "peacemaker," or process consultation (the utilization of a consultant in examining difficulties in a particular organization process such as communication, cooperation, leadership).

(3) Interventions directed toward the effectiveness of teams or groups. Intervention strategies could team task executions, survey mechanisms, role analysis, and sensitivity training.

(4) Interventions directed toward improving intergroup relations. Intervention strategies could include "organizational mirroring" (meetings in which three or more groups engage in joint activities as a group), survey feedback analysis, or group experimentation and analysis of new structural devices that may be used within the system.

(5) Interventions directed toward enhancing the effectiveness of the whole organization. These may include survey feedback strategies, confrontation sessions, or multiyear organizational development programs.[60]

Despite the potential of organizational development, several limitations need to be considered. First, OD may create internal problems. Designs that attempt to "unfreeze" the organizational status quo may produce anxiety in some employees, thus reducing their effectiveness. Golembiewski has observed: "The T group experience induces a heightened awareness of Self, one of whose threatening implications is that the individual may discover something about himself which is unacceptable to others and perhaps even to himself."[61] Furthermore, organizational development interventions often revolve around group problem solving, in which the role of authority is lessened. The group may be encouraged to develop new task patterns liberated from dependency upon authority figures, which, while they may prove creative in the experimental OD laboratory setting, may also produce "sufficient antiauthoritarian leadership attitudes to reduce their contributions to the organization at times when such directive leadership is required."[62] Finally, some researchers have noted that the group approach to problem solving may cause monopolization by more vocal elements and consequently hinder the involvement of the more reticent. This could reinforce the exuberance for problem solving for those already so inclined and reinforce further the noninvolvement of others. In short, such decentralization may impede innovation and reduce cooperation.[63]

Second, there is a danger of overemphasis on organizational development. If OD becomes an end in itself, then its potential contribution to public responsiveness is undermined. As with other concepts in administration, OD must be continuously linked with goals. If it is reduced to little more than sensitivity sessions, or in-house surveys of employee attitudes, it will have failed in making a meaningful contribution to the achievement of bureaucratic responsiveness. This is a real danger, for there is much within public administration that takes on the characteristics of "trendy" phenomena, of which PPBS and OD are only two examples.

Third, public administration is different from private enterprise, where organizational development strategies have been more widely used. In the public sector, civil service job protection is a prime value and there is often little support for experimentation, which inevitably involves uncertainty and risk. Likewise, public bureaucracies are not merely impartial or self-serving organizations. What they may do under the guise of organizational development strategies could have a significant impact on the political units that are linked to them. A personnel director in an agency may think that sensitivity training is desirable, but a legislative subcommittee or clientele interest group may be opposed to such innovations because they may change the expected pattern of organizational behavior. An "innovation" that makes an organization less responsible to traditional political or clientele centers is not viewed favorably by those parties. In the public sector one cannot initiate experiments such as OD without casting a questioning eye at those other groups and forces concerned with the activities of the agency, although the search for more broadly based responsiveness may require that an agency vigorously argue for such innovations, since the legislative subcommittees and present clientele may reflect very narrow social interests.

In any case, public bureaucracy's foundation in law may seriously limit possible change. Consider this hypothetical setting: Employees in the Internal Revenue Service might decide through an OD program that their job descriptions are "dysfunctional" and inhibit the growth of a healthy organizational spirit. They may decide through team problem solving to rewrite the descriptions. While this solution may be possible in a liberal private-sector organization, it is hardly compatible with the legally binding administrative regulations and related position classifications and job descriptions of public bureaucracy. The laws, principles, regulations, and multiple social and political ramifications of public agencies may preclude OD interventions on any large scale.

Nevertheless, the quest for a more humane bureaucracy will inevitably continue by means of small changes in most agencies, with perhaps a few major innovations in a few. An organization that has benefited from organizational development does not automatically become an effective or responsive bureaucracy, but an organization that is in need of some internal examination and fails to undertake steps toward it cannot hope to prove a responsive instrument for policy implementation.

THE PRESENT AND THE FUTURE

We have noted that attitudes toward work are currently evolving. There is an undeniable movement away from the simple logic of "machine" bureaucracy and a concern that its benefits be coupled with a realistic appraisal of individual needs and expectations. Rising professionalization and growing emphasis on the autonomy and worth of each worker have the net effect of increasing the emphasis on the more "humane" aspects of bureaucracy.

Yet, humane bureaucracy can contribute to public administration only if public goals and objectives are maintained. An organizational development effort that does not tie the resolution of a problem to the goals or objectives of the organization is but an example of isolated and random activity. So is an affirmative action program based solely on numbers, and not on the objectives of the organization. Any effort to improve the health of a more humane bureaucracy not integrated with critical values of machine and political bureaucracy serves no long-range purpose. Also, the achievement of more humane conditions for workers ought to be linked, where possible, to the goal of a more humanitarian approach to citizens. We are not interested solely in producing happy bureaucrats; we must also be concerned with the development of professional civil servants who find meaning and dignity on the job and couple this with an understanding of "machine" values and political accountability. To ensure that "machine" and "political" goals are pursued while strengthening "humane" values is a major task for contemporary public administration.

NOTES

1. Erdman Palmore, "Predicting Longevity: A Follow-Up Controlling for Age," *Gerontology* (1969). See also his "Physical, Mental and Social Factors in Predicting Longevity," *Gerontology* (1969).

2. See, for example, James O'Toole, ed., *Work and the Quality of Life: Resource Papers for Work in America* (Cambridge, Mass.: MIT Press, 1974).

3. For data on different aspects of work satisfaction, see Robert L. Kahn, "The Work Module," in O'Toole, ibid.

4. Special Task Force to the Secretary of Health, Education, and Welfare, *Work in America* (Cambridge, Mass.: MIT Press, 1973), p. 40.

5. Ibid.

6. Daniel Yankelovich, *The Changing Values on Campus* (New York: Washington Square Press, 1972).

7. Franklin P. Kilpatrick, et al., *The Image of the Federal Service* (Washington, D.C.: The Brookings Institution, 1969).

8. Bureau of Executive Manpower, U.S. Civil Service Commission, *Characteristics of the Federal Executive* (Washington, D.C.: U.S. Civil Service Commission, November 1969), p. 11.

9. Kilpatrick, et al., p. 134 - 39.

10. See *Work in America* for a general review of this theme.

11. For examples of the early literature of the human relations school see F. J. Roethlisberger and W. J. Dickenson, *Management and the Worker* (Cambridge, Mass.: Harvard University Press, 1947), and Elton Mayo, *The Social Problems of an Industrial Civilization* (Cambridge, Mass.: Harvard University Press, 1945).

12. See Abraham Maslow, *Eupsychian Management* (Homewood, Ill.: Dow Jones-Irwin, 1973) and *Toward a Psychology of Being*, 2nd ed. (New York: Van Nostrand Reinhold, 1968).

13. Douglas McGregor, "The Human Side of Enterprise," Warren G. Bennis and Edgar H. Schein, eds., *Leadership and Motivation* (Cambridge, Mass.: MIT Press, 1966), p. 8.

14. Ibid., p. 11.

15. Ibid., p. 15.

16. Chris Argyris, "The Individual and Organizations: Some Problems of Mutual Adjustment," *Administrative Science Quarterly* 2 (June 1957). See also his *Interpersonal Competence and Organizational Effectiveness* (Homewood, Ill.: Dorsey Press, 1962), *Personality and Organization* (New York: Harper & Row, 1970), and *Integrating the Individual and the Organization* (New York: Wiley & Sons, 1964).

17. Argyris, "The Individual and Organizations," p. 18.

18. Ibid.

19. Ibid.

20. Ibid.

21. Frederick Herzberg, *Work and the Nature of Man* (New York: World, 1966), pp. 75 - 76.

22. See Charles Perrow, *Complex Organizations: A Critical Essay* (Glenview, Ill.: Scott, Foresman, 1972), pp. 106 - 115.

23. Mitchell Fein, *Approaches to Motivation* (Hillsdale, N.J.: Mitchell Fein, 1970), p. 31. Emphasis added.

24. Chris Argyris, "Personality and Organization Theory Revisited," *Administrative Science Quarterly* 18 (June 1973): 142.

25. See David G. Kuhn, John W. Slocum, Jr., and Richard B. Chase, "Does Job Performance Affect Employee Satisfaction?" *Personnel Journal* 50 (June 1971): 455 - 459, 485.

26. See Larry L. Cummings and Aly E. Elsalmi, "The Impact of Role Diversity, Job Level, and Organizational Size on Managerial Satisfaction," *Administrative Science Quarterly* 15 (March 1970): 1 - 10.

27. See John J. Morse and Jay W. Lorsch, "Beyond Theory Y," *Harvard Business Review* 48 (May-June 1970): 61 - 68. For another criticism of the sweeping claims of Theory Y, see J. M. Colin, "After X and Y Comes Z," *Personnel Journal* 50 (January 1971): 56 - 59.

28. Emmette S. Redford, *Democracy in the Administrative State* (New York: Oxford University Press, 1969), p. 173.

29. For a basic review, see John R. Maher, ed., *New Perspectives in Job Enrichment* (New York: Van Nostrand Reinhold, 1971).

30. See Frederick Herzberg, "The Wise Old Turk," *Harvard Business Review* (September-October 1974): 70 - 80.

31. David A. Whitsett, "Where are Your Enriched Jobs?," *Harvard Business Review* (January-February 1975): 74 - 80.

32. Fein, *Approaches,* p. 20.

33. A good treatment of the limitations of enrichment can be found in William E. Reiff and Fred Luthans, "Does Job Enrichment Really Pay Off?," Keith Davis, *Organizational Behavior: A Book of Readings* (New York: McGraw Hill, 1974), pp. 96 - 109.

34. Vincent S. Flowers and Charles L. Hughes, "Why Employees Stay," *Harvard Business Review* (July-August 1973): 49 - 60.

35. See Thomas J. Bouchard, Jr., and Melana Hare, "Size, Performance, and Potential in Brainstorming Groups," *Journal of Applied Psychology* 54 (February 1970): 51 - 55.

36. See Kahn, "The Work Module."

37. Based on 1974 figures that indicate that 32 billion dollars were spent on federal civilian personnel. See *Special Analyses: Budget of the United States Government* (Washington, D.C.: U.S. Government Printing Office, 1975), p. 134.

38. For a summary, see U.S. Civil Service Commission, *Pay Structure of the Federal Civil Service* (Washington, D.C.: U.S. Civil Service Commission, 1970), p. 30.

39. U.S. Civil Service Commission, *Employee Training in the Civil Service,* Pamphlet T-7 (Washington, D.C.: U.S. Civil Service Commission, 1970).

40. An analytical portrait of the FEI is found in Paul C. Buchanan, ed., *An Approach to Executive Development in Government: The Federal Executive Institute Experience* (Washington, D.C.: National Academy of Public Administration, 1972).

41. Frederick Mosher, *Democracy and the Public Service* (New York: Oxford University Press, 1968), p. 10.

42. Ibid., pp. 124 - 215.

43. See Samuel Krislov, *Representative Bureaucracy* (Englewood Cliffs, N.J.: Prentice Hall, 1974), p. 5.

44. Norton Long, "Bureaucracy and Constitutionalism," *American Political Science Review* 46 (September 1952): 808 - 818.

45. See, for example, W. Lloyd Warner, et al., *The American Federal Executive* (New Haven: Yale University Press, 1963), and U.S. Civil Service Commission, Bureau of Executive Manpower, *Characteristics of the Federal Executive* (Washington, D.C.: U.S. Civil Service Commission, November 1969).

46. Martin and Susan Tolchin, *To the Victor: Political Patronage from the Clubhouse to the White House* (New York: Random House, 1971).

47. U.S. Civil Service Commission, *Minority Group Employment in the Federal Government* (Washington, D.C.: U.S. Civil Service Commission, November 30, 1970).

48. For a more extensive treatment see Bureau of Intergovernmental Personnel Programs, U.S. Civil Service Commission, *Equal Employment in State and Local Governments: A Guide for Affirmative Action* (Washington, D.C.: U.S. Government Printing Office, 1972).

49. Further discussion may be found in Lloyd G. Nigro, ed., "A Mini-Symposium: Affirmative Action Public Employment," *Public Administration Review* 34 (May-June 1974): 234 - 246.

50. Krislov, *Representative Bureaucracy,* p. 63.

51. See Gideon Sjoberg, Richard A. Brymer, and Buford Farris, "Bureaucracy and the Lower Class," *Sociology and Social Research* 50. (1966): 325 - 337 for an interesting discussion.

52. U.S. Senate, Committee on the Judiciary Report, *Protecting Privacy and the Rights of Federal Employees,* Report No. 92-554, 92nd Cong., 1st sess., December 6, 1971.

53. See Charles O. Jones, "Re-evaluating the Hatch Act: A Report on the Commission on Political Activity of Government Personnel," *Public Administration Review* 29 (May-June 1969): 249 ff., and the important district court decision: U.S. District Court, District of Columbia, *National Association of Letter Carriers* v. *United States Civil Service Commission* (July 31, 1972), Civil Action No. 577-71.

54. Reproduced in *ASPA News and Views* 25 (May 1975): 14.

55. See, for example, Lester Milbrath, *Political Participation: How and Why Do People Get Involved in Politics?* (Chicago: Rand McNally, 1965).

56. For an explanation of organizational development, see Wendell L. French and Cecil H. Bell, Jr., *Organization Development: Behavioral Science Interventions for Organization Improvement* (Englewood Cliffs, N.J.: Prentice Hall, 1973), and Richard Beckhard, *Organization Development: Strategies and Models* (Reading, Mass.: Addison Wesley, 1969).

57. Robert T. Golembiewski, *Renewing Organizations: The Lab-*

oratory Approach to Planned Changes, (Itasca, Ill.: Peacock, 1972), pp. 128 - 129.

58. See Kurt Lewin, "Studies in Group Decision," Dorwin P. Cartwright and Alvin Zander, eds., *Group Dynamics: Research and Theory* (New York: Harper & Row, 1953), pp. 287 - 301. Comments in quotes are the thoughts of Rolf P. Lynton and Udai Pareek, *Training for Development* (Homewood, Ill.: Dorsey Press, 1967), p. 37.

59. See Gordon L. Lippitt, *Organizational Renewal,* (New York: Appleton-Century-Crofts, 1969).

60. French and Bell, *Organization Development,* p. 107. See also Warren Bennis, *Organization Development: Its Nature, Origins and Prospects,* (Reading, Mass.: Addison Wesley, 1969), esp. pp. 37 - 39.

61. Golembiewski, *Renewing Organizations,* p. 231.

62. Bernard M. Bass, "The Anarchist Movement and the T-Group," *Journal of Applied Behavioral Sciences* 3 (April 1967): 216.

63. See Bouchard and Hare, "Size, Performance and Potential in Brainstorming Groups." For a more extensive review of OD limitations, see Robert T. Golembiewski, "Organization Development in Public Agencies: Perspectives on Theory and Practice," *Public Administration Review* 29 (July-August 1969): 367 - 377.

Political
Bureaucracy

Machine bureaucracy centers on the need to make public organizations efficient, rational, and capable of responding in a technological or professional manner to specific problems and tasks. Machine bureaucracy is problem-solving bureaucracy, removed from political demands. It is purposeful bureaucracy, dedicated to the objective application of skills. Humane bureaucracy focuses on the need to make public organizations responsive to the needs of the worker by, among other things, granting equal employment and promotion opportunities and providing for participation and involvement in organizational matters that traditionally were the purview of a managerial elite. Implicit in this perspective is the notion that responsiveness to the citizenry will be enhanced by a heightened concern for individual and professional needs.

Although both machine and humane bureaucracy are based upon different premises and values, we have suggested that the maximization of one should not come at the exclusion of the other. On the contrary, we have argued that effective and responsive bureaucracy can be achieved only by the development of organizational capacities that allow for a variety of values and techniques.

Yet we have also noted that machine and humane principles alone do not provide adequate guidelines for public bureaucracy. Both focus primarily on values that effect the internal characteristics of the bureaucracy. While internal improvement can and does produce external benefits, it can also lessen the capacity of government organizations to meet public needs and to serve equitably all citizens if applied in a vacuum, removed from system values and expectations. It is, therefore, essential to complete the three-dimensional framework by linking bureaucracy to the expectations and ideals of the American political system.

How can the logic of machine bureaucracy and the spirit of humane bureaucracy be related to the political system? It should be recalled first that certain aspects of both humane and machine bureaucracy do help foster responsiveness to political values and institutions. For example, management by objectives can serve as an important organizational guide for the achievement of politically determined goals. Also, efforts to improve the representative character of bureaucracy may help infuse government organizations with important values that were once excluded and can help improve the life chances of millions of citizens. Likewise, efforts to liberalize the amount of political freedom afforded to public servants may help democratize access by outside ideas and interests. Nevertheless, these are indirect potentials, and the political responsiveness of bureaucracy must be encouraged through more direct means.

"Political" bureaucracy refers to the capacity for responsive interaction between public organizations and private citizens, groups, political associations, and the formal structures of government — the executive, legislative and judicial branches. Thus, political bureaucracy deals with the relations between public bureaucracy and the rest of the political system. Ultimately, we are concerned with the problem of how public organizations can become more responsive to the demands and values of that system.

"Political bureaucracy," however, must not be confused with "partisan bureaucracy," which acts to support the interests or values of one dominant group. Political bureaucracy is sensitive to political values and political leaders because of their legitimacy, regardless of their party affiliation. Improving the political responsiveness of bureaucracy is one of the most serious challenges facing American democracy, for, as we have seen, virtually every facet of life is subject to government bureaucratic activities and influence.[1] We noted in chapter 1 that by virtue of its function, public bureaucracy is inherently political. It makes choices. It exerts influence and indicates policy preferences. Yet, public administrators are not elected, and government bureaucracy has become a quasi-autonomous entity within the political system. So, we must concern ourselves with ensuring that the role of public bureaucracy in the political process remains compatible with democratic values, sensitive to citizen needs, and subject to political accountability and control. While formal political controls, such as legislative and executive review, are important cornerstones for sustaining political bureaucracy, other complimentary mechanisms are also critical to the attainment of responsive public bureaucracy. Before reviewing the formal political controls, we will discuss four contemporary dimensions of political bureaucracy that are especially important: 1) accessibility to organizations and their information; 2) accountability of public bureaucracy to citizens; 3) decentralization of policy development and implementation; and 4) participation by citizens.

DIMENSIONS OF POLITICAL BUREAUCRACY

Accessibility by Citizens
and the Press

Generally, Americans are socialized into the belief that their government is an open one, in which citizens can gain access to their leaders and institutions.[2] This traditional presumption of governmental openness, however, is not always validated by experience in the administrative world. While the theory of democracy suggests comparatively open exchange between citizens and their public servants in government institutions, the reality often indicates a different pattern.

Restrictions imposed on public access to agency actions and materials have been grounded on two principles. The first is called the "need to know." By it, the distribution of some government documents and data is limited by such labels as "eyes only," "confidential," and "top secret" to those people who are judged by classification standards used by governmental administrators to have a legitimate reason to see them: a "need" to know. Of course, some information, such as data on the construction of nuclear weapons, should have limited circulation, but there has been a tendency in recent years on the part of government authorities to overclassify documents, thus limiting their dissemination even within the official bureaucracy as well as to Congress.

Excessive use of this principle prevents citizens from access to vital knowledge and, even more seriously, often withholds information from elected political representatives. While the public's need or right to know is not an absolute, the decisions concerning the release of material have too often been based upon partisan or self-serving calculations. The Pentagon papers are a case in point. This history of the United States' role in Indochina was classified top secret (though it contained no current information) to guard facts and opinions that were often at variance with the information released to the public during the years of American involvement in Vietnam, facts and opinions that might well have altered public thought in a way elected leaders in the late 1960s did not want. It took a Supreme Court decision in 1971 to allow the press to continue their publication of the papers, in spite of government protests that national security was endangered.

The second restriction on access is based upon "convenience," the assertion that people would overwhelm the government with requests for information if access were made too easy, thereby wasting valuable time and compromising agency activities in other areas. Both of these principles were invoked by President Ford in his veto of the Freedom of Information Act amendments on October 17, 1974.

But these principals are being challenged. Many state governments are beginning to establish — or have already established — mechanisms whereby citizens can obtain information on government programs and policies formerly removed from public view. As instances of bureaucratic abuse of citizens' rights to privacy and access become more publicized, individuals tend to become more aggressive in seeking information. This new mood can be seen in changing attitudes toward the Internal Revenue Service and the Federal Bureau of Investigation, two agencies that have tended by the nature of their mission to discourage accessibility to their data. For example, within the past few years the IRS has been met with a number of legal challenges over the secrecy it attaches to some of its procedures. These challenges, generally raised by individuals who believe they have been the subject of an unfair tax decision compounded by what may be perceived as arbitrary administrative standards, have had the broader impact of focusing more continuous attention and pressure on the comparatively closed bureaucratic systems that affect citizens. And the FBI is now required by law to divulge upon request the contents of files it holds on the individual making the request.

Access to governmental information is a critical element in maintaining control. Without access, agencies cannot be effectively challenged to defend the basis of their actions, nor is the accuracy of the data upon which they base decisions subject to scrutiny. Although there are instruments for achieving access other than direct citizen inquiry — such as through investigative reporting by journalists and legislative fact finding — citizen access requires an agency to think of policy in citizen-impact terms. For a unit of government whose rituals and procedures often produce an insulated environment, this forced awareness can help produce greater concern for the treatment of individual citizens.

The recalcitrance evidenced by public bureaucracy in allowing open inspection of its activities led in the 1960s to a major political challenge to bureaucratic secrecy. The passage of the Freedom of Information Act in 1967 created for the first time a comprehensive federal program to facilitate access to agency documents, data, or other materials not expressly excluded by the legislation. It allowed anyone to obtain documents "without having to state a reason for wanting the information," with the "burden of proving withholding to be necessary placed on the federal agency."[3] The legislation provided for nine exempt categories of information, including:

(1)   Material specifically excluded by executive order in the interest of national defense or foreign policy.

(2)   Material dealing solely with internal personnel rules of the agency.

(3)   Materials specifically exempted by statute.

(4)   Trade secrets or commercial information considered privileged.

(5)   Interagency or intraagency memoranda or letters that would not be available by law to a party other than an agency in litigation with the agency.

(6)   Personnel and medical files and similar files the disclosure of which would constitute a clearly unwanted invasion of personal privacy.

(7)   Investigatory files compiled for law enforcement purposes except to the extent available by law to a party other than an agency.

The legislation required that agencies establish guidelines and regulations consistent with the new requirements and publicize them adequately so that the public might take advantage of the opportunities provided. Although the Freedom of Information Act has encouraged some citizens to seek information that for years had been forbidden to them, most observers recognized that due to bureaucratic foot dragging it was not the effective instrument originally envisioned. Ralph Nader's 1974 survey of the act, for example, noted that the success of the legislation was "not attributable to the good-will of the agencies but to the obstinacy of a few citizens who have fought vigorously to obtain materials through the legislation."[4] Earlier, in 1972, the House Committee on Government Operations had castigated the bureaucracy's penchant for secrecy and for failing to live up to the spirit of the legislation: "The efficient operation of the Freedom of Information Act has been hindered by 5 years of foot-dragging by the federal bureaucracy. The widespread reluctance of the bureaucracy to honor the public's legal right to know has been obvious in parts of two administrations."[5] While the committee did note many of the progressive efforts of a few agencies in implementing the legislation, its report stressed the serious defects of the 1967 law:

1.   *Inadequate procedures* to ensure that all requests were handled with timeliness. A survey by the Congressional Research Service of the Library of Congress indicated that the average number of days for an agency to respond to a request for information was 33. For the 27 agencies examined, the range was between 8 days for the Small Business Administration and 69 days for the Federal Trade Commission.[6]

2.   *Requiring excessive specificity* of the materials requested. For example, many agency guidelines required individuals to specify exactly the materials they needed and others often required *total* detail of the document desired.

3.   *Inequitable fee schedules* for information searching. These fee schedules were not uniform, and since a citizen had no idea how long an agency would take to locate the material, the specter of a sizeable bill

often discouraged him or her from seeking wanted information. Some search fees, for example, exceeded three dollars an hour.

4. *Lack of seriousness of purpose in implementation.* Many agencies viewed the legislation as a requirement placed upon agencies other than themselves. A case in point is the battle of the Philip Long family of Seattle to obtain information from the Internal Revenue Service on the standards used to determine the need for an audit of income tax returns. The IRS refused to provide the information, claiming that the data sought was related solely to the internal operations of the agency and therefore exempt from release, a claim difficult to contest by an outsider. (In 1974 the IRS made public most of the guidelines used to determine whether or not to audit.)

The weakness of the original Freedom of Information Act led to congressional efforts to add amendments, which culminated in the passage of legislation in November 1974 that corrected many of the abuses and deficiencies of the original. President Ford vetoed the bill, but his veto was overridden by both houses. The amendments required agencies to establish uniform fee structures and to provide information to individuals upon "reasonable" rather than "specific" description of the desired materials. It also broadened the authority of the courts to require agencies to release materials and allowed them to consider cases concerning release of information on a priority basis, so plaintiffs would not suffer lengthy delays as the court dealt with a backlog of other cases. The courts were also given the authority to determine whether government officials were arbitrary or capricious in withholding information, thereby making them subject to Civil Service Commission investigation and disciplinary action. Thus, where it may have been compatible with the civil servants' survival instincts under the original legislation *not* to provide individuals with requested information, it may now be in their best interest to provide the information.

There will undoubtedly remain, however, a rather natural reluctance by public employees to divulge information that might be an embarrassment, such as data reflecting errors in judgment, or that might make an agency's officials vulnerable to criticism. Thus, the openness of the bureaucracy will continue to be enhanced by the vigor with which the press pursues bureaucratic activities. Newspapers, journals and the electronic media have a natural interest in uncovering imcompetence and abuse, since such stories may contribute to their commercial success. Also, the professional ethics of good media personnel demands that they seek the truth. Greater access to government, of course, strengthens the media's role as a democratic control over the public bureaucracy.

The Freedom of Information Act will be a crucial test of the degree to which openness and effective bureaucracy can be made to coincide. As we noted, bureaucracies often fear and oppose any form of public inspection of their activities. This reluctance has led to individual foot dragging and institutional negligency in providing access to information about governmental policies.

We should also note that the existence of both the Freedom of Information Act and the Privacy Act, also passed in 1974, illustrates the competing forces that buffet public organizations. While the Freedom of Information Act seeks to guarantee access to information, the Privacy Act attempts to prevent bureaucracies from divulging information that invades personal privacy. Yet in most cases the quest for freedom of information and for the protection of privacy are compatible.

Accountability to Citizens

In addition to encouraging the openness of government administration, political bureaucracy values suggest that actions by the bureaucracy be subject to redress and review by independent and impartial authorities. This requirement implies that there be mechanisms to challenge and perhaps reverse agency policies. There are several ways in which this can be facilitated. As we noted earlier, the concept of "rule of law" as applied through the courts provides an important check on bureaucratic actions. However, as we have also noted, the legal process tends to be slow and time consuming, as well as inherently conservative. Moreover, most people cannot afford expensive court action. The personal anxiety that may ensue also deters them from seeking direct accountability of public bureaucracies through the courts. Above all, the courts often refuse to consider challenges on the substantive issues of cases, concerning themselves instead with procedural matters.

Other elements of the political process help protect the individual from bureaucratic abuse. Congressional committees, for example, are an important source for uncovering agency maladministration. Inquiries on behalf of constituents by legislators also encourage bureaucratic response to citizen complaints. The utility of congressional inquiries, however, depends on the agency concerned as well as the influence of the particular legislator. Also, such intervention is sometimes politically motivated and may more greatly benefit the affluent and highly educated citizen.

For over a decade there has persisted the argument that "ombudsmen" could serve to check public bureaucracy. An ombudsman is an individual empowered by law to investigate citizen complaints about bureaucratic actions (or inaction). The ombudsman's primary tool is publicity, a potent weapon since bureaucratic officials are eager to avoid a negative image with legislatures, elected executives, and the press, and many genuinely want to redress errors once they are pointed out. The ombudsman idea, which originated in Sweden, has grown in popularity in Europe as the scope of modern government bureaucracies has increased. In the United States there are already several ombudsman offices: Hawaii has established one as have King County in Washington and Nassau County in New York, among other places.

Ombudsmen can be made as powerful as legislative assemblies want to make them, but a conflict arises here, for ombudsmen can become competitors to legislators, one of whose main roles is to investigate citizen complaints about public bureaucracies. This role is a primary device by which legislators seek to retain favor with their constituents. If ombudsmen are given this function, an important political service of legislative bodies and a mechanism through which legislators often sustain themselves could be weakened. It is unlikely that legislative bodies in the United States will vote themselves out of an important and visible service area. It is precisely for this reason that the Hawaiian ombudsman has been required to channel citizen complaints through the legislators office representing the person filing a complaint.[7]

In addition, there are other reservations raised about the desirability of ombudsmen. The chief benefit attributable to the role of ombudsman is that it should be a small enterprise capable of decisive and prompt intervention. While this system might work at the state or local level, a national ombudsman, like any other national effort, might increase in size and responsibilities to the point of reducing its speed and potential effectiveness. This danger could be circumvented by limiting the size of the ombudsman office. Donald Rowat, a supporter of the ombudsman idea, has suggested, for example, that a national ombudsman office need not be larger than a hundred persons.[8]

One could also attempt to reorient the values of existing agencies, making them more sensitive to citizen complaints. The development of an ombudsman capacity within each agency could help resolve the problem of responsiveness by particular agencies. There is, of course, the danger that such units might become little more than public relations offices, trying to mollify complaints without rectifying injustices for fear of alienating senior agency administrators. But the development of this capacity would relieve some of the burden on ombudsmen and provide one more channel of access.

The key point about ombudsmen and consumer protection agencies is that they represent either individual citizens or unorganized groups of citizens as a whole. In a sense, one could argue that such organizations are more representative of the community (at the state, local, or national level) than are the other agencies of government. As we have seen, most administrative departments represent particular groups. The Department of Agriculture, for instance, tends to support the interests of farmers, especially the larger, more powerful farmers' groups. The individual citizen, consumers, or the public at large are relatively unorganized or apathetic, and usually have less influence than more powerful and better organized interests. Not only can ombudsmen or consumer officials help speak for the unorganized, they can also facilitate the hearings and appeals processes that citizens may initiate against bureaucracy, thus minimizing the need to resort to expensive lawyers.

One overriding problem remains, however. Any public "watchdog" system may — intentionally or unintentionally — perpetuate the biases of the majority in the system. We have been talking about "individual citizens" and the "public" as if they were monolithic categories, yet despite some recent progress, certain sectors of society — blacks, the poor, the handicapped — are still often ignored and have comparatively little access to government through elected officials, the courts or even consumer agencies, which can become oriented mainly to the interests of the middle class. What can be done to alter these "institutionalized" patterns of injustice? Conceivably, ombudsmen could help ferret out patterns of discrimination. The point is that ombudsmen and consumer agencies should specifically and consciously incorporate methods to ensure equal concern for the needs of all citizens.

Decentralization

One of the major contemporary strategies for enhancing the political values is decentralization, the transferring of political or administrative authority from a central jurisdiction to other political or administrative units that are more geographically proximate to the area being served. Its goal is to ensure that the formulation and/or implementation of public policy occurs at the closest level of impact, thereby permitting greater attention to individual and local needs and enhancing the opportunity for access to government.

Decentralization as a solution to the negative aspects of contemporary bureaucracy received its principal impetus during the 1960s, when it became an alternative method of providing much-needed urban services, such as education, housing, and health programs.

In the aftermath of the urban disorders of the 1960s, for example, many large city school systems were criticized for being unresponsive to the needs of the community. Indeed, school boards, often chosen through at-large elections, tended to represent the interests of the white middle or working classes, but not sizable numbers of minority citizens. Decentralization was viewed by reformers as a mechanism to provide more representative and responsive school administration through challenging the domination of education policy making by a remote bureaucracy and redistributing policy making to neighborhood boards.

Efforts to decentralize the school systems have had limited success nationally, partially because of the opposition by professional educators as well as union leaders and members, who argued that decentralization would produce inferior schools and who were concerned that decentralization might threaten their jobs or influence. In Detroit and New York

City, however, the issue was joined and at least partially won by the advocates of decentralization. The attempt at decentralization of school administration in these two cities demonstrates the entrenched power of organized groups and bureaucracies in forming public policy and the difficulty of removing their control.

The forces in the school decentralization controversy in New York in 1966 were many and complex. The major cause of demands for decentralization was the slowness of the board of education's integration program. Activist residents of minority neighborhoods argued that they should have the power and responsibility to ensure quality, integrated education and that they should participate in shaping educational programs. Faced with continuing pressures from neighborhood civil rights and parents' associations, the board in 1967 created on an experimental basis three project school districts. These projects, supported in part by the Ford Foundation, were granted generally autonomous power to establish their own educational programs.

But the experiment in decentralization became embroiled in controversy and turbulence almost immediately. In September 1967, one of the districts, Ocean Hill - Brownsville, replaced retiring principals with people who were not on the "approved" civil service list. This action antagonized the education professionals, who viewed the list as the only suitable basis for determining eligibility for movement up the career ladder. It also angered the unions, primarily the United Federation of Teachers (UFT) with over 40,000 members in New York City, which felt that the action violated standard hiring procedure and professional requirements. In short, the unions and the professionals opposed decentralization partly because they had been excluded.

To demonstrate its hostility to the Ocean Hill - Brownsville action, the UFT called a citywide strike, one of the many that were to plague the city from September 1967 to November 1968. During the strike, union hostilities were aggravated by the efforts of Mayor John Lindsay, who attempted to convince the state legislature that New York should be required to develop a decentralization plan for the entire city.

In this already tense situation, McGeorge Bundy of the Ford Foundation released a committee report on decentralization in November 1967. This plan called for the creation of thirty to sixty rather autonomous urban school districts for the city, each governed by a board of eleven members, five of whom were to be appointed by the mayor and six elected by parents in the established district. The unions, school officials, and many professionals in the education community, who had so vehemently opposed the actions of the Ocean Hill - Brownsville experimental district, now combined their energies to attack the Bundy proposal, charging that citywide decentralization would produce a chaotic and balkanized educational program and would increase the danger of political patronage by undermining collective bargaining standards.

In May 1968 the Ocean Hill - Brownsville district administration "transferred" ten teachers and nine administrators, some of whom were opponents of decentralization. The unions perceived these as firings and struck again, continuing their battle of trying to convince the state legislature not to mandate any citywide decentralization program. The persistence of Ocean Hill - Brownsville district officials is reflected by the fact that they did not reverse their position even after a court judge ruled that they had exceeded their power.

The opposition of the professional education lobby, the unions, and the city educational bureaucracy forced the state legislature to water down the decentralization proposals, which they did by passing in 1970 a structure that "balanced" centralized educational administration with a measure of decentralization. Under the plan, each decentralized school district was to be governed by a nonsalaried board elected on a proportional representation basis. Although the boards were to have responsibilities in such areas as curriculum development and personnel hiring, their responsibilities were severely limited by the authority of the city board of education to intervene and reverse their decisions. Critics of the legislation viewed the measures as tokenistic, providing little autonomous control for the neighborhoods: "The New York Law gave the semblance of decentralizing education decision making, but essentially preserved the status quo. It denied local boards any substantial authority over personnel, budget, and educational programs."[9]

The issue of decentralization is important in urban politics, for it has come to mean an opportunity for groups and interests previously excluded from policy making to wield power and challenge the status quo. But there is a certain irony in the call for decentralization. We must recognize that one reason for the greater centralization at all levels of government was the failure of earlier localized administration. Centralized school boards, for example, were created partly in reaction to the often corrupt politics of many wards, precincts, and independent school systems. Centralized school boards and centralized bureaucracies were the result of reform movements!

The general interest in decentralization is also reflected in the efforts to decentralize city halls by providing multiservice centers throughout urban areas as a way of facilitating citizen access to public programs. The efforts to decentralize the city bureaucracy through the establishment of "little city halls" are prime examples of attempts to bring government closer to the citizen. Little city halls were established in the late 1960s in such cities as Boston and New York as a means of making city government more responsive to the needs of the heterogeneous neighborhoods within the community. They have been concerned principally with maintaining and improving police and fire protection, sanitation services, and heating facilities in apartment buildings. For the most part, little city halls have served as a referral service, resolving citizen complaints about public agencies as best they can, in a low-keyed manner.[10]

Seldom have little city halls been aggressive spokesmen for the community or challenged the city bureaucracy, for to do such would require little city hall directors to challenge their boss, the mayor, who has the power of appointment and removal. Political realities typically preclude the establishment of localized power centers, so the presence of little city halls within the community is often mainly symbolic, representing the nearness of government to the citizen. Little city halls do not decentralize political power, but they do serve to decentralize the administration and speed resolution of citizen complaints. It is in the facilitation of such services that they have provided for greater responsiveness.[11] They also offer an important feedback mechanism for public officials, who can then be more attuned to the voices of dissent within the neighborhoods.

Efforts at decentralization are also taking place at the national level. This is manifested in efforts to transfer or share program responsibility in many areas from the federal to state and local governments or for the federal government itself to delegate program responsibility from its central offices to its ten federal regional offices. Many of these decentralization efforts were collectively symbolic of the "New Federalism" concept which came into vogue in the late 1960s.[12] The creation of federal regional councils, composed of agency representatives from each of the ten regions into which the country is divided, provides an opportunity for evaluating national policy from a regional perspective. Although these councils do not have any binding power over the collective council, their meetings (held sporadically) can help facilitate policies that are better coordinated with related federal agencies and sensitive to regional needs.

In addition, the federal government is moving away from a categorical grant-in-aid project approach to funding, which provides funds in separate areas of activity, to a more liberalized block-grant approach, which provides lump-sum payments that can be applied to a large number of programs. The 1974 Housing and Community Development Act, for example, eliminated some of the more traditional grant categories, such as urban renewal and historical renovation, and replaced these with a more open, comprehensive, and creative approach, granting comprehensive funding for various urban beautification and community development projects. This approach allows a community to apply for a total package of funded projects rather than applying separately for a host of different programs, thereby avoiding much of the cost and confusion common to grantsmanship.

The strongest effort at fiscal decentralization is revenue sharing, which was initiated in 1972. By means of a complex series of formulas, billions of dollars have been provided to state, county, and local governments on an essentially unrestricted basis — local governments are free to use the money as they wish. Because all political jurisdictions automatically receive money under the formulas, nonprogressive as well as progressive governmental units benefit from the program. As the federal Advisory Commission on Intergovernmental Relations observed, "revenue sharing tends to prop up certain duplicative, obsolete, and/or defunct units of local government."[13] Nevertheless, revenue sharing has attempted to equalize fiscal opportunities for most governmental jurisdictions.

Anxiety over revenue sharing has primarily centered over the uses to which the money is applied. Although there are some restrictions, communities can for all practical purposes, use the money to support any expense by discreetly rechanneling money from programs that can be paid for by revenue-sharing funds into other areas. Through this strategy, communities can avoid using the money in areas that could most benefit from it. A recent survey of revenue-sharing expenditures has borne out this point. It noted, for example, that "health and social service programs normally associated with low-income or socially disadvantaged groups have not received a large proportion of general revenue sharing funds" and that "general revenue sharing funds have gone . . . to support already existing programs and have not been widely used to develop new and innovative programs."[14] Thus, while contributing to fiscal decentralization, revenue sharing may actually impede the achievement of machine and humane values as well as those of a political nature, since the decentralization of fiscal responsibility means that important national goals or programs may be subverted by local strategies and tactics.[15] From the standpoint of practical politics, continued fiscal decentralization through revenue sharing will probably be constrained by national legislators who see it as a means of propping up nonresponsive state or local governments. Many legislators do not want to see an abandonment of federal responsibility in problem areas, particularly if it were to result in newly subsidized support of parochial forces wishing to resist social and political change. It is unlikely that many reform-minded national legislators will sit idly by and watch a federally induced dismantling of national goals and objectives.

Thus, while new federalism can be a means of increasing the effectiveness and efficiency of government as well as a method of generating greater responsiveness to individual citizens and local values, it can also prove to be a tool for uncaring or even corrupt forces within local communities who oppose reform or who seek to subvert democratic participation. A strong national government can force local action in sensitive areas such as race relations, low-income housing, and education. Although the desirability of intervention by the national government can sometimes be open to question, new federalism may provide an escape valve for communities that ignore or abuse legitimate values and interests.

Decentralization does provide some real advantages as a means of encouraging greater responsiveness. The smaller scope of activities may facilitate the identification and accommodation of individual needs. Interests lost in a large, complex milieu may have greater impact at the local level. However, as we noted, the very complexity of interests in larger systems may also help prevent abuse by more homogeneous local majorities. There is no easy rule for determining when decentralization or centralization creates greater responsiveness. A number of conflicting variables and values are involved. Most programs have benefits as well as liabilities. The increasing scope and complexity of government, however, seems to place a premium on decentralization.

Citizen Participation

Generally, decentralization and participation are complimentary values, one often implying the existence of the other. Indeed, the process of decentralization is frequently intended as a means of encouraging the participation of those who have been excluded from policy formulation or evaluation. Although administrative and political decentralization do not automatically increase citizen participation, they may enhance opportunities for individuals and groups to influence the activities of government.

Participation means involvement in the policy-making process of government. Attending a meeting of a public utility commission and listening to deliberations is a kind of participation, but a passive kind, for there is no direct involvement. Being a citizen representative on a local model city agency is also a type of participation, and it is far more direct and influential. So, citizen participation is not an absolute but reflects a continuum of varied behavior and involvement, ranging from the passive and indirect to the active and forceful. Sherry Arnstein has illustrated this continuum by means of a "ladder" reflecting degrees of participation ranging from none to direct control and influence. According to this model, (see figure 5.1) some participation is clearly not participation: some clearly molds and directs involvement for the purpose of an external agent (manipulation), while other presumed participation is little more than an exercise designed to uncover and discuss an individual's weaknesses and deficiencies (therapy). Tokenistic participation does not involve the individual in decision making but serves merely to inform or appease (placation). Real participation, according to Arnstein, involves the evolution of a decision-making role by the individual in policy outcomes. Thus, "partnership," "delegated power," and "citizen control" are the higher rungs on the ladder of citizen participation.

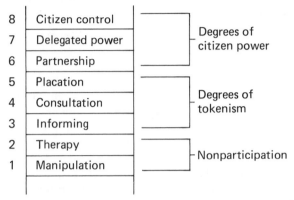

8	Citizen control	
7	Delegated power	Degrees of citizen power
6	Partnership	
5	Placation	
4	Consultation	Degrees of tokenism
3	Informing	
2	Therapy	Nonparticipation
1	Manipulation	

Source: Sherry Arnstein, "Ladder of Citizen Participation." Reprinted by permission of the *Journal of the American Institute of Planners*, Vol. 35, No. 4, July 1969.

FIGURE 5.1

The doctrine of citizen participation implies that responsive policy and administration can be realized only if administrators and politicians are forced to confront the needs, values, and policy demands of citizens and to encourage their full involvement. An extreme view of public participation requires that administrators always guide their actions by the wills and inputs of the "citizen." The model cities program and much of the efforts of community action programs, both of which were designed to rejuvenate central city neighborhoods, tend to follow this approach.[16] Of course, arguments for this kind of participation imply the need to define "citizens" and to develop mechanisms for their selection and involvement, as well as mechanisms to determine their "will."

Unfortunately, the ideal of citizen participation is more easily stated than achieved. Most citizens do not seem eager to participate. Many model cities elections, for example, witnessed only a 5 percent or less turnout of the eligible voters. Rousseau once said that in a perfect democracy everyone flies to the assemblies. Unfortunately, our assemblies are often barren of participants. A vast body of research suggests that active forms of participation, such as committee work, are carried out by a small minority of citizens. Even the simple act of voting often draws less than one-half of the eligible electorate.[17]

Moreover, many efforts at citizen participation, particularly at the local level, have resulted in friction between citizen groups and elected officials. Naturally, such tension can sometimes produce positive results, but too much tension may indicate inappropriate strategies of participation or nonresponsive leaders. In any event, it can weaken the capacity of government bureaucracy to carry out public tasks. Relentless in their belief that they were not elected to abdicate power and responsibility, city officials sometimes prove extremely reluctant to encourage greater citizen involvement. The results are often greater hostility, deterioration of racial relations, and a heightened suspicion of the power holders by the citizens. Yet not all resistance to citizen pressure is undemocratic; a quite respectable viewpoint holds that elected officials are chosen to exercise their judgment, even if it sometimes conflicts with public sentiment.

Despite the frequently disappointing results, there have been important gains in the use of participation that have resulted in more responsive administration. Consider, for instance, the case of the Army Corps of Engineers, which is responsible for protecting the navigable waters of the United States and for undertaking major water resource and flood protection projects. For years it has been a perfect example of bureaucratic insulation, undertaking and recommending projects with little attention to soliciting inputs from those affected by its activities. But in the early 1970s it committed itself to the goal of "participative planning" for the development of water resources,[18] and in 1972 developed regulations to guide agency hearings and investigations to ensure public involvement. Although these regulations do not force the Corps to consider all citizen inputs, they do provide a long-needed opening to a tightly closed agency, showing that even highly technologically oriented bureaucracies can adapt to emerging needs and values.[19]

Continuing pressures by Congress, aimed at improving the responsiveness of bureaucracy, will probably force other federal agencies to give greater opportunity for public involvement in agency policy making.[20] Certainly, the National Environment Policy Act of 1969 provides some important opportunities for citizens to submit comments on agency projects that could have an adverse impact on the environment.[21] Generally, groups and individuals are invited by public notice to make known their views on particular proposals. Thus, conservation groups, lobbyists for construction groups, homeowners' associations, and others are provided with a forum.

The issue of citizen participation, however, must be put into proper perspective. We cannot assume that participation automatically produces desirable public policy. Also, some public participation in policy making is elitist, since not all citizens participate. Notions that participation might be more equitable if reflected through vehicles such as area-wide surveys or opinion polls may prove more viable than developing new quasi-elitist citizen committees. Moreover, the notion of an "attentive" public overstates citizen interest, for only a fraction of the citizenry is concerned on a continuous basis with matters of public policy.[22]

Nor is all policy making that precludes citizen participation evil, capricious, or misdirected. After all, public bureaucracy is an important repository of skills, values, and insights within the political system. It is likely that many of the values and insights that could be brought to bear via the conduit of citizen participation are already present within the bureaucracy. Thus, the problems occasioning the need for citizen participation may be partially resolved by maximizing humane bureaucracy principles of representativeness or machine bureaucracy standards of objective analysis.

In the last analysis, we must keep in mind the distinction between "process" or "product." Certainly, if the *process* of participation becomes an end in itself without having any effect on improving policy, then it is a shallow value. The purpose of public bureaucracy is not to conduct courses in civics. In fact, emphasizing meaningless and ritualistic forms of participation risks alienating citizens and hampering more productive participatory activities, activities that should aim to have significant effect on bureaucratic decisions and actions.[23]

Let us examine, in illustration, the myths that surround the "town meeting," the traditional form of New England government. The image of a typical New England meeting is one of full citizen participation, where the people themselves control the direction of community government. This picture fails to take into account the countless numbers of town meetings that are canceled for want of a quorum, the emotionalism with which issues are often debated, the concern in debate that is generally given to immediate needs rather than long-range problems, and the tendency of special-interest groups to pack meetings to ensure passage of one article on the town warrant and then to leave the meeting when victory has been achieved. And it fails to recognize that town meetings often have an attendance of only 20 to 25 percent, hardly a testimony to participative society.[24]

For those who find citizen apathy a shocking state of affairs in a nation that calls itself democratic, several points should be borne in mind. First, citizen nonparticipation at the individual level may be rational. Most people have responsibilities and burdens that take up virtually all of their energies: studies, jobs, families, friends, and so forth. The reward for becoming involved is often limited. Even with respect to voting, the truth is that one vote seldom determines an election. We are not arguing against participation in principle nor certainly against voting, but merely pointing out certain realities of the political world. Most people probably vote, for example, out of a sense of duty, thus helping the political system to operate. Those who do participate more actively occasionally have some specific reason, such as an issue particularly related to their interests, and some people do so because they enjoy it, have the time, seek power or status, or for some similar reason.[25]

Excessive participation, moreover, could saturate the administrative system and prevent bureaucracies from accomplishing public goals. Constant meetings with clients, handling complaints, or dealing with a fragmented and volatile constituency could prevent an administrator from taking any effective action. Moreover, professional administrators may at times be more responsible than aroused citizens, who can have little regard for the welfare of future generations, the society (city, state, or nation) at large, or competing groups.

Nevertheless, it is clear that political bureaucracy values require the possibility of citizen participation, otherwise the administrative system becomes — indeed, often has become — dominated by professionals who themselves often have limitations, such as excessively narrow points of view and more concern for the stability and smooth operation of the system. In short, there is room for greater participation in our administrative system as it stands today as long as it is balanced by other factors.

Trends toward greater student participation in university administration, for instance, show the need for balance. Unfair evaluation standards, too rigid curricula, and other inequalities can be more easily resolved with direct student input. Yet, one need only look at some Latin American universities (and perhaps a few American ones) to see the dangers of excessive democratization: domination by elitist student members unrepresentative of the student body and an erosion of academic standards, produced by political considerations in assigning grades and in faculty personnel decisions.

So, there must be balance. Political bureaucracy values require opportunities for participation; intelligent and fair administrative decision making requires citizen and group input. But the process must have some policy significance and above all it must become more truly representative.

FORMAL POLITICAL CONTROL

Judicial Supervision

Control by elected leaders as well as the courts is perhaps the most important key to politically responsive bureaucracy. Although the judicial system is slow and lacks the capacity to oversee bureaucratic activity as a whole, the courts can help ensure that bureaucracies follow proper procedures. They can even lead in the quest for justice rather than follow the sometimes undemocratic sentiments of the majority of voters, to whom elected politicians are more responsive. It is no accident that the Supreme Court, under Chief Justice Earl Warren, played a decisive role in the struggle for civil rights. Left to the electorate or to the legislatures, greater rights for black Americans might have been achieved at a much slower pace.

In a few cases the courts have intervened directly in administration. In the Boston struggle over busing and desegregation, for example, a federal judge placed South Boston High School in receivership. Among judicially mandated actions were the appointment of the school's principal, in opposition to the wishes of the elected school board. Federal law enforcement officials were also ordered into the school to help maintain order.

In addition, courts have been particularly influential in expanding citizen access to information as well as in providing opportunities for redress of agency actions that adversely affect them, particularly where procedural violations have been demonstrated. As guardians of the "rule of law" trust, courts can be particularly effective in sustaining the application of new expansions to this concept, such as the Freedom of Information and Privacy Acts. Of course, as we have already noted, legal processes are generally time-consuming and expensive, with little guarantee of a satisfactory outcome. Thus, this control mechanism must be supplemented by the controls imposed by the other branches of government. The ability to achieve political bureaucracy values, therefore, depends in large measure on increased legislative and executive capacities to monitor and direct bureaucratic activities.

Legislative Supervision

If there is one central characteristic of the American political system, it is that the institutions of government are not monolithic enterprises that can either control or be controlled in a single direct way. The bureaucracy is not controllable by any one institution of government because of its size, the complexity of its tasks, and its function within the system as the recipient of multiple demands. Control of such a far-flung, complex enterprise is by nature imperfect. (Some would argue that the elusiveness of bureaucracy and its imperviousness to control help assure that it will not be captured by any single interest or group and is, therefore, an advantage.) Nor is the legislature itself a monolithic control mechanism. Like the bureaucracy, the legislature reflects a multiplicity of values and interests within the society at large. In a sense, there are many legislatures within Congress and within state assemblies. For example, there is the "partisan legislature" that shapes and interprets bureaucratic actions in terms of party issues; there is the "personality legislature," in which actions and influence are sometimes determined by personal desires, needs, and conflicts; there is the "committee legislature," in which issues are viewed through the perspective of committee jurisdiction and competition with other committees for privileges and publicity; further, there is the "executive legislature," or that group within the legislative body concerned with supporting the prerogatives of the executive branch; there is also the "institutional legislature," defining the issues in terms of competing institutional responsibilities and needs, as seen in the rivalry between House and Senate. The legislature in short, has many faces.

These are of course artificial divisions by which we attempt to isolate different kinds of motivation and behavior within legislative assemblies. But the divisions affect legislative review of bureaucratic activity because they reflect a diffused perspective among legislators. A legislator who is a strong believer in the need for the president (or governor or mayor) to establish the tone of public policy may view legislative fact-finding into bureaucratic behavior as a potential source of embarrassment to the executive branch; he or she, therefore, may attempt to counter these control activities. An individual who sees his or her committee assignment as a primary role may be motivated to inquire into every organizational activity that affects policy decisions and performance. Legislators who have aspirations for higher office may zealously pursue investigations of bureaucracy as a means of attracting publicity. While some may wish to pursue and inquire into organizational activities with the intent of limiting agency actions, others may want to investigate bureaucratic action as a means of encouraging the bureaucracy to do more. Because legislators are generally appointed to committees that parallel constituent interests, they typically specialize in following the activities of a limited number of relevant agencies. In this self-feeding relationship between constituents, allied agency, and legislators, there is often an effort not to attack the actions of a bureaucracy that provides constituent services. A congressperson from a district made up of farmers, for instance, may find little motivation to root out waste in the Department of Agriculture lest his or her constituents perceive this as an attack upon the agency that nurtures their interests.

Control and supervision of the bureaucracy, then, is in large measure based upon political calculations and individual perceptions of proper legislative roles. While there are some legislators who make a career out of exercising vigilance over segments of the bureaucracy, there are others who perceive this function as secondary to more creative or even less taxing legislative responsibilities.[26] Legislative efforts to review bureaucratic actions most often occur when (1) partisan advantage may be achieved by embarrassing bureaucratic officials appointed by the opposition party, (2) interest-group or constituent pressures require investigation, and (3) agency action contradicts a legislator's belief about the proper conduct of public affairs.[27] As an aide to a congressman noted in commenting on the calculations — personal, political, and institutional — that determine legislative review of agencies:

> The subjects of congressional investigations are scandals,
> corruption à la Watergate, or executive branch hanky-panky or
> law-twisting. These are the things that bring headlines and turn

on the TV klieg lights and the public. But oversight, unless it turns up a scandal or gross maladministration, is dull and politically dangerous. If effective oversight turns up an ineffective program which results in its proposed elimination, the greatest hue and cry goes up from those with a vested interest in the program, and not from taxpayers overjoyed at the prospect of reduced federal spending.[28]

Although much of the literature about legislative behavior and supervision of the bureaucracy has emphasized national and state activities, there is complementary data indicating that local legislators (city councillors) are also subject to the same mix of motivational forces. Cortus Loehler, for example, has demonstrated that the willingness of city councillors (elected) to monitor the policy-development process of city managers (appointed) is determined primarily by the values of the councillors themselves rather than by formally designed responsibilities.[29] Thus, not all councillors take seriously the notion that one of their major functions should be oversight.

Because of the mixed composition of legislative bodies and the diverse role perceptions of individual legislators, it is important that more institutionalized mechanisms of legislative oversight be developed and strengthened. In the past, legislative supervision of the bureaucracy has been hampered by inadequate resources. Congress has not kept pace with the growth of the very extensive information-generating and storage capacities of bureaucracies and has been forced to rely heavily on information provided by the bureaucracy itself in any attempt to monitor it. And past interaction between Congress and the bureaucracy indicates, as we would expect, that bureaucracies tend to provide self-serving and positive information.

The primary investigative agent of Congress is the General Accounting Office. Although it is one of the most aggressive watchdogs of the public bureaucracy, it is hard pressed to solve all of the investigative needs of Congress. At state government levels, the legislators are even more impoverished in their lack of staff assistance. Bureaucracies, then, often need not fear aggressive challenges of their decisions by elected legislators and their staffs. Indeed, in many states and localities, the press tends to uncover more significant levels of bureaucratic abuse than do the legislative assemblies.

Efforts to facilitate greater legislative supervision have been increased during the past few years. The 1970 Legislative Reorganization Act gave greater responsibilities to the General Accounting Office to undertake systematic studies of the effectiveness of government programs and activities. Under the same legislation, all congressional committees are required to report annually on their oversight efforts. More important, the Congressional Budget and Impoundment Control Act of 1974 attempted to improve oversight capacities by strengthening the role of Congress in the budget process. This legislation created new budget committees with the authority to establish spending policies for government agencies. In addition, it established a budget ceiling, or limit to spending, which may force congresspeople to take a closer look at agency activities (particularly those that serve no personal constituent interest) so that a greater share of the limited budget can go to priority areas.

In the first test of this law, in May 1975, Congress for the first time established an overall budget ceiling to limit the options of congressional committees as they make recommendations. In a way, this innovation is the political response to PPBS which, as discussed in chapter 3, failed largely because it tried to objectify political values and needs. Under the present system, political calculations of the budget will undoubtedly still occur, but they will be bounded by the "rationality" of a ceiling, which provides an agreed-upon closure to expenditures but allows debate within this ceiling.

In addition to the creation of the budget committees and a revised budget process, the act also created a Congressional Budget Office to provide greater staff assistance and give greater support to the General Accounting Office and individual congressional committees undertaking evaluation of agency activities and programs. On the surface, at least, the 1974 legislation provides improved institutional mechanisms for congressional review of the activities of organizations. However, the determining factor of the seriousness with which this review process is undertaken will most likely be based upon congressional perceptions of constituent response to this evolving watchdog role. In the last analysis, effective supervision of government bureaucracy by legislatures may depend more upon citizen and group reinforcement of this role than upon legislative willingness and initiatives.

Executive Supervision

Many of the factors making the bureaucracy impervious to legislative control also contribute to diminishing the effectiveness of executive control. Increasing professionalism, expanding bureaucratic activities, protective civil service status, and agency-clientele relationships all diminish the impact of executive control. Indeed, the very fact that the American political system divides power and responsibilities among three coordinate branches gives bureaucracy a chance to garner autonomy.

Executive efforts to control the bureaucracy are exercised in part through formal control mechanisms. Departmental regulations established by executive appointees set the tone for departmental activities, and nonperforming individuals can generally be transferred if not removed. The increasing role of staff agencies, such as the Office of

Management and Budget, which is responsible for the preparation of the federal executive budget, also helps the executive branch to harness the activities of the far-flung bureaucracy. The establishment within the executive branch of the Domestic Council, designed to provide a mechanism to increase the coordination among and effectiveness of domestic programs, is another example of a response to the need to integrate agency activities.

As many observers of the presidency have indicated, however, power and authority are generally based upon informal mechanisms. Presidential power consists essentially of bargaining and persuasion.[30] Executive control over the bureaucracy, therefore, may be increased more by informal strategies of cooperation and the mutual development of trust and respect than by the creation of ever more government agencies. It can be argued that the effective executive can better control bureaucracy by using formal controls where necessary but informal mechanisms whenever possible, for blatant disregard for the professional administrators may actually make the bureaucracy more defensive and removed from control.

Executives should attempt to exercise necessary control just as administrators should not sacrifice professional ethics or resist legitimate executive directives. The failure of Richard Nixon to control the bureaucracy was not solely a result of the difficulties of achieving political control. It also resulted from a reaction to the manner in which control was attempted. During his administration, many career bureaucrats with long years of government service were given little opportunity to help shape public policy. Their role was largely supplanted by a corps of political appointees who felt inordinate suspicion of and disdain for bureaucrats. President Nixon's frequent reference to public employees as "petty bureaucrats" did little to encourage warm relationships between the executive and the bureaucracy.[31]

One example of presidential miscalculation of bureaucratic independence is not enough to diminish the validity of the value that requires elected political officials to oversee the activities of a nonelected bureaucracy. If failures occur in the pursuit of this principle then we should not dismiss the principle but perhaps elect executives who are better equipped to deal with government bureaucracy. This goal may also require that executive aides be chosen on the basis of relevant merit — not their ability to manage a campaign or their past friendship with a new president, governor, or mayor.[32] The problems generated by the Nixon administration in dealing with the bureaucracy were in large measure the problems created by the overzealous and often abrasive behavior of top-level political appointees interested only in maintaining the power of their boss. The bureaucracy was not reacting negatively to the principle of executive control so much as it was reacting to the strategy of control.

One recommendation for improving executive control advocated the establishment of a federal executive service to increase the available pool of top-level civil servants by drawing skilled administrators from a variety of settings. Another proposal to provide a balance between the need for executive control and the danger of domination of the bureaucracy by an overzealous or incompetent elite of political appointees has been made by a panel of the National Academy of Public Administration: the hiring of people who are not career bureaucrats. Political appointees from the professional, business, and academic worlds can bring fresh insights to government bureaucracy, provided they are selected for merit and not primarily for political reward. Naturally, most elected leaders are not so foolish as to knowingly appoint incompetent people to sensitive positions, but they often compromise their standards on the lesser but still important posts.

To avoid the tensions that can arise between the career and noncareer officers of government, the panel described an alternate strategy for selecting and limiting the noncareer officers by suggesting that:

> *The number of posts in the subcategory of personal and confidential advisors to the President and to the heads of the departments and agencies under him be strictly limited by Congress through its authorizations and appropriations, and that persons in these posts be denied the power to exercise Constitutional or statutory powers beyond routine functions.*
>
> *The major party organizations develop and maintain lists of the best qualified persons for possible political appointment.*
>
> *The President maintain an assistant on personnel, with adequate staff, who would, among other duties, develop and maintain a continuing roster of the best qualified possible appointees to executive and judicial offices.*
>
> *The primary authority and responsibility for political appointments be vested in the heads of departments and agencies who would work with the assistance of the Presidential staff suggested above, and whose choices would be subject to Presidential veto.*
>
> *The Senate and its committees be more careful and thorough in their review of the nominated heads and subheads of agencies than they have been in the past; this would include nominees' attitudes toward the prrograms of those agencies.*
>
> *Proposed appointees to the more specialized political posts be reviewed and approved or vetoed prior to their appointment by nonpartisan panels of experts in their fields.*
>
> *New political appointees be encouraged or even required to attend educational briefing sessions concerning their responsibilities and particularly their relations with career personnel.*[33]

These recommendations are, of course, not an automatic solution to the problems of executive relationships with the bureaucracy. Nor do they deal with the all-too-frequently narrow mentalities of some administrators, who view political control as illegitimate rather than as a vital part of the democratic process. But they do increase the chances for obtaining qualified, responsible administrators.

Responsible control of bureaucracy requires that the executive's use of oversight be coupled with a willingness to respect the professional capabilities of the career bureaucrat. Ultimately, however, elected officials should have the last word. Providing that ethical considerations are not involved and acknowledging that career bureaucrats have an obligation to argue strongly for their professional judgments, resolution of disagreements between administrators and elected legislators and executives ought to be in favor of the elected officials. If the elected officials are wrong, the electoral process, however imperfectly, exists as a check on their actions. If they are undemocratic in their policies, as happens sometimes even with electoral support, the courts constitute an additional check. Though elections are no guarantee of responsive political bureaucracy, and constitute only one device for its attainment, they do represent the single most important control over public bureaucracy.

DEMOCRATIC BUREAUCRACY

Political bureaucracy values have a crucial place in public administration. Bureaucratic officials cannot and should not be relied upon exclusively for the establishment and implementation of public policy. Though essential and legitimate, machine and humane values alone also exclude the notion of the supremacy of the public. In the final analysis, democratic bureaucracy requires that political controls have a primary place in the structure and operation of the administrative system.

It is true that the goals of political bureaucracy often result in slower decision making and a more limited ability to plan for the future. It is also true that many democratic political controls are seriously lacking in America today. Unfortunate examples, such as the CIA's role in Chile — and in the United States, for that matter — continue to surface. One of the most serious impediments to democratic political control is the imperfection of the structure and operation of the electoral system at all levels of government, which allows unequal access by some citizens and groups. But there are structural changes that could help democratize electoral influence. Further reforms in financing, for example, could help equalize influence and strengthen public control of government. Yet so vast is the influence of public bureaucracy today that traditional electoral and political controls are inadequate. Hence, the other strategies discussed in this chapter assume great significance. Implicit in the preceding analysis is the notion that public administrators ought to view political values as legitimate. Public access, control by elected officials, and citizen participation constitute values that ought to be an integral part of guidelines that also include efficiency, effectiveness, and humane treatment of employees.

NOTES

1. For a useful discussion of certain aspects of political bureaucracy see Lewis Mainzer, *Political Bureaucracy* (Glenview, Ill.: Scott, Foresman, 1973).
2. U.S. Senate, Committee on Government Operations, Subcommittee on Intergovernmental Relations, *Confidence and Concern: Citizens View American Government,* 93rd Cong., 1st sess., December 3, 1973.
3. U.S. Congress, Committee on Government Operations, *Administration of the Freedom of Information Act,* 92nd Cong., 2nd sess., September 20, 1972, p. 3.
4. James R. Michael, ed., *Working on the System: A Comprehensive Manual for Citizen Access to Federal Agencies* (New York: Basic Books, 1974), pp. 45 - 46.
5. *Administration of the Freedom of Information Act,* p. 8.
6. Ibid., pp. 16 - 17.
7. See Stanley V. Anderson and John E. Moore, eds., *Establishing Ombudsman Offices: Recent Experiences in the United States* (Berkeley, Calif.: Institute of Government Studies, 1972). See also, Walter Gellhorn, *Ombudsman and Others: Citizens' Protectors in Nine Countries* (Cambridge, Mass.: Harvard University Press, 1966).
8. Donald C. Rowat, "Ombudsman for North America," U.S. Senate, Subcommittee on Administrative Practice and Procedure, *Hearing: Ombudsman,* 89th Cong., 2nd sess., 1966, p. 327.
9. Marilyn Gittell, "Decentralization and Citizen Participation in Education," *Public Administration Review, Special Issue: Curriculum Essays on Citizens' Politics and Administration in Urban Neighborhoods* 32 (October 1972): 678. For other commentaries on the decentralization controversy in New York City, see Philip Mersanto, *School Politics in the Metropolis* (Columbus, O.: Merrill, 1970); Joseph F. Zimmerman, "Neighborhoods and Citizen Involvement," *Public Administration Review* 32 (May-June 1972): 201 - 209; and Mario Fantani and Marilyn Gittell, *Decentralization: Achieving Reform* (New York: Praeger, 1973).
10. For a good discussion of the role and challenge of little city halls, see Eric A. Nordlinger, *Decentralizing the City: A Study of*

Boston's Little City Halls (Boston: Boston Urban Observatory, 1972).

11. See Advisory Commission on Intergovernmental Relations, *The New Grass Roots Government? Decentralization and Citizen Participation in Urban Areas* (Washington, D.C.: Advisory Commission on Intergovernmental Relations, January 1972).

12. For a review of the concept of new federalism see American Society for Public Administration, Special Publication: "The Administration of the New Federalism: Objectives and Issues," *Public Administration Review* (September 1973).

13. Advisory Commission on Intergovernmental Relations, *General Revenue Sharing: An ACIR Evaluation* (Washington, D.C.: Advisory Commission on Intergovernmental Relations, 1974), p. 12.

14. David Caputo and Richard L. Cole, "General Revenue Sharing Expenditure Decisions in Cities over 50,000," *Public Administration Review* 35 (March 1975): 141. See also their *Urban Politics and Decentralization* (Lexington, Mass.: D. C. Heath, 1974).

15. Michael D. Reagan, *The New Federalism* (New York: Oxford University Press, 1972).

16. For a review of some of the problems that plagued model cities programs see Daniel P. Moynihan, *Maximum Feasible Misunderstanding* (New York: Free Press, 1969).

17. Lester Milbrath, *Political Participation: How and Why Do People Get Involved in Politics?* (Chicago: Rand McNally, 1965).

18. U.S. Army Corps of Engineers, *Public Participation in Water Resources Planning* (Alexandria, Va.: U.S. Army Corps of Engineers Institute for Water Resources, 1970).

19. Daniel A. Mazmanian and Mordecai Lee, "Tradition Be Damned! The Army Corps of Engineers Is Changing," *Public Administration Review* 35 (March 1975): 166 - 172.

20. See, for example, U.S. Senate, Committee on the Judiciary, Subcommittee on Administrative Practice and Procedure, *Response to Questionnaire on Citizen Involvement and Responsive Agency Decision-Making*, 92nd Cong., 1st sess. 1971.

21. See U.S. House, Committee on Merchant Marine and Fisheries *Hearings: Environmental Citizen Action*, 92nd Cong., 2nd sess., 1972.

22. See Donald J. Devine, *The Attentive Public: Polyarchical Democracy* (New York: Rand McNally, 1970).

23. See George Frederickson, ed., *Neighborhood Control in the 1970's: Politics, Administration and Citizen Participation* (New York: Chandler, 1973).

24. These figures are from Massachusetts town meetings statistics compiled by Commonwealth of Massachusetts, Legislative Research Council, *Report Relative to the Form of Government in Large Towns*, No. 5302, March 16, 1971, p. 155.

25. See Sidney Verba and Norman H. Nie, *Participation in America* (New York: Harper & Row, 1972).

26. See Malcolm E. Jewell and Samuel C. Patterson, *The Legislative*

Process in the United States (New York: Random House, 1966).

27. Seymour Scher, "Conditions for Legislative Control," *Journal of Politics* 25 (1963): 526 - 551.

28. Cited in *Congressional Quarterly Weekly Report* (March 22, 1975), p. 595.

29. Cortus T. Loehler, "Policy Development and Legislature Oversight in Council Manager Cities: An Information and Communication Analysis," *Public Administration Review* 33 (September-October 1973): 433 - 442.

30. Richard Neustadt, *Presidential Power* (New York: Wiley & Sons, 1960).

31. See his speech of March 20, 1972, when he signed the Drug Abuse Office and Treatment Act. Also, see Richard P. Nathan, *The Plot that Failed* (New York: Wiley & Sons, 1975).

32. See David T. Stanley, ed., "Symposium on the Merit Principle Today," *Public Administration Review* 34 (September-October 1974): 425 - 451.

33. Frederick C. Mosher, et al., *Watergate: Implications for Responsible Government* (New York: Basic Books, 1974), pp. 68 - 69.

The Integration of Machine, Humane, and Political Values

THE STATUS OF PUBLIC BUREAUCRACY

As we look at public bureaucracy in the United States over the years, two points stand out. First, the institution has been in a state of flux, buffeted by new demands, changing values, and evolving technology. Affirmative action, organizational development, management by objectives, new federalism, freedom of information, and other concepts represent current concerns for making the administration of bureaucracy responsive to today's values and beliefs. The quest for improved public bureaucracy is not new, but new problems and demands have emerged with the growth of the country, the advances in knowledge, and the increased complexity and specialization of the administrative system. Moreover, the heightened awareness of and concern for the individual that are part of today's ethos are causing important changes in America's political culture, changes that have an inevitable effect upon public administration.

Even when change occurs, however, it is not necessarily system-wide. The diversity of demands upon public bureaucracies, the relative uniqueness of their individual environments, and the heterogeneous motivations that inspire or delay action make it impossible to consider bureaucracy a monolithic force. And certain key problems persist. Despite the changes we may witness, despite the vitality that sometimes appears, there are still traits that often make public bureaucracy the drag anchor of the American political system. Proceduralism, employee conservatism, fragmentation, inertia, and self-interest weaken the ability of organizations to serve the public. These factors, coupled with a political system that itself is highly fragmented, pluralistic, and often incapable of decisive leadership, produce a maze of institutions unresponsive to many important demands and values.

The convergence of these two traits — change and persistence — produces a blurred portrait of the bureaucratic system: public bureaucracy in the United States is both dynamic and dull, representative and elitist, progressive and conservative, broadly responsive and narrowly responsive. There is room for optimism, but there is even greater reason for a measure of sobriety as we move toward the future. Criticisms of an agency that lead to corrective changes may become irrelevant within the span of a year, but maintaining these changes over extended periods of time may prove enormously difficult. The tendency of solutions to lapse into their former problem state is perhaps one of the main reasons for the persistence of bureaucratic failings. An effective innovation in public administration is not a guarantee of continuing results or a signal to relax vigilance. Changes become outdated, and the reforms of today are often tomorrow's abuses. We have to understand the evolutionary nature of values and needs and the impossibility of institutionalizing mechanisms that will guarantee only positive results.

THE THREE-PART FRAMEWORK

In chapter 1 we noted that successful and democratic bureaucracy requires a multidimensional approach, emphasizing "machine," "humane," and "political" values. As we have discussed, each avenue alone leaves key dimensions of the administrative system untouched and often generates its own problems. An understanding of the dynamics of bureaucracy demands attention to each area, while a strategy for improved public administration requires inclusion of all three.

The Machine Approach

To perform adequately requires capability. Hence, government agencies need effective administrative techniques as well as viable structures. For this reason, "machine" traits are vital components of public administration. In fact, given the enormous problems and plethora of tasks confronting modern government, it is not an overstatement to claim that appropriate structures, usually but not always of the hierarchical bureaucratic variety, are basic not only to sound administration but to the survival of the political system. Government must be able to deliver certain key goods and services.

"Machine" techniques promote efficiency and effectiveness, for no matter how representative or democratically responsive the government personnel, they cannot function well with structural roadblocks such as inadequate liaison with central offices, deficient communications structures, or excessive numbers of reports to complete. Machine approaches prove especially useful in structuring office designs for maximum work efficiency, in teaching managers skills that increase their effectiveness, and in maintaining information flow. They also contribute to more rational decision making through such devices as cost-benefit analysis and computer simulations. Sound structures and innovative technologies have contributed more than anything else to the skill and productivity of public agencies.

Given the increasingly scarce resources of societies and governments, efficiency in the achievement of tasks constitutes a necessary component of effective action. Money saved by means of increased efficiency means more money available for other services or for reduced taxes.

The Humane Approach

Similarly, we have seen that human-resource strategies serve not only democratic and individualistic ideals but may also improve the productivity and efficiency of public bureaucracy. Because so many citizens work for the government, their treatment as employees contributes to social opportunities for personal growth and freedom. Greater employee participation in decision making can help rationalize the administrative process by providing more realistic information to top-level administrators. To the extent that public employees help determine their working conditions through participative mechanisms, abusive and inhumane treatment can be diminished.

Effective educational opportunities may engender attitudes that stimulate more equitable treatment of citizens and foster a greater sense of public service, especially when combined with supportive work environments. Technical training contributes to greater productivity and efficiency and thus is a necessary corollary of "machine" values. Although increased professionalism may imperil responsiveness by causing nongovernment professional associations to dominate public policy and by encouraging narrow, self-righteous attitudes, the technical complexity of contemporary society demands expertise. The negative aspects of professionalism must be controlled by techniques other than a rejection of competence.

Bureaucratic representation is very important. Without the participation of minorities, women, and the disadvantaged, it is unlikely that government agencies can adequately represent their interests. Though minority or female bureaucrats do not necessarily serve as advocates for their own groups, their chances of doing so seem greater than if positions are held exclusively by white males. Furthermore, bureaucratic representation facilitates communication and helps overcome cultural barriers. It also may provide more valid information to decision makers. In a society that continues to discriminate against minorities and women in spite of significant improvements, public employment also provides opportunities for jobs and for social and economic advancement. Greater tolerance for individuality in political freedoms as well as organizational development strategies can also improve public bureaucracy's capacity to meet employee and external citizen needs.

The Political Approach

Political control constitutes the most fundamental safeguard against arbitrary and capricious bureaucracy. However imperfectly, the electoral process places ultimate control of public policy in the hands of legislators and executives. Judges, whether appointed or elected, are another institutional mechanism for the maintenance and enhancement of administrative responsibility to democratic values. Bureaucratic accountability to Congress, the president, and state and local officials contributes to financial control as well as policy guidance. Although administrators determine much public policy, their actions are bounded by laws and administrative structures sanctioned by politicians and judges. It is the political structures that can demand more open administration and procedural safeguards for employees and citizens. And it is the political institutions that can restructure administrative and political processes through decentralization and other mechanisms that can improve opportunities for meaningful participation.

THE NEED FOR INTEGRATION

Machine, humane, and political values should be viewed as interdependent, complimenting or restraining the others. "Machine" values of efficiency and "machine" tools such as cost-benefit analysis, for example, can limit the tendency of politicians to award contracts and other benefits on the basis of power and influence. Similarly, "humane" values can minimize the arbitrary and harsh treatment of human beings who work for government and who are served by it. Yet public bureaucracy must be ultimately responsive to democratic political institutions and values if it is to serve rather than dominate. If these three approaches to understanding and improving bureaucracy are interactive and interdependent, why are they not more often pursued with greater sensitivity to their interdependence? The answers to this question revolve around the problems of unidirectionalism and intensity.

Positive, well-intentioned efforts at administrative change tend to be unidirectional, that is, they attempt to resolve a particular problem by the application of a single strategy or skill. Thus, if an organization is beset by charges of inefficiency, it may institute "machine" methods, although in fact part of the problem may reside in humane or political bureaucracy insensitivities or incapacities. On the other hand, if an organization is confronted by motivation problems, human relations experts called in to assist may be oblivious to machine and political values. The consumer advocates in an organization, sensitive to political values and protective of their vision of the public interest, may deny the need for evaluative tools or fail to see their personal impact on other employees in the agency because of excessive commitment to their own viewpoint.

In public administration there is much action designed specifically to improve performance, but it often fails because it attempts to resolve complex and interdependent phenomena with a masterful but single sweep of the brush. The pitfalls of unidirectionalism are compounded further by intensity. Supporters of change sometimes manifest an obsession with their vision and often attempt to overapply their solutions. Thus, a tool, concept, or belief with an important but limited capability may be transformed into a major program or policy. For example, a human relations program in an organization may become so overbearing that it tends to demotivate or bore those individuals who participate in it. The goal of citizen participation can produce an obsession with process rather than product; quite frequently, the more participation that is encouraged the less becomes the capability to elicit effective participation. Such important strategies for control and supervision as management by objectives may become overproceduralized and so obtuse that they lead to a massive paperwork process, further confusing the statement and attainment of objectives. One of the real difficulties that beset PPBS was that agency officials who became involved with the tool unwittingly helped contribute to conflict between the employees who had PPBS-oriented skills and those who did not, causing destructive intraorganizational conflict.

The consequences of this form of obsession should be obvious. Pursuing with single-minded intensity important machine, humane, or political values leads to a disproportionate amount of organizational energy and resources being targeted for one goal. There is a sad paradox in all of this. It is because we often become obsessed with the need to solve problems that we are blinded to their multifaceted components, and hence plunge into a course of action doomed to provide only marginal results. In this pursuit, other goals become displaced and the real contribution that could have been achieved is lost in a maze of recrimination, cynicism, and hindsight speculation.

We argue, however, for more than Aristotle's golden mean, in which moderation is prized as a virtue above all else, for the improvement of public bureaucracy sometimes requires immoderate action. What is fundamentally required is the generation of organizational mechanisms that can serve as links between machine, humane, and political approaches. Rather than becoming simplified, bureaucracy may have to develop more complex strategies to maximize the interdependence and interaction of these three important facets. Perhaps the keys to this synthesis will be (1) the manner in which we train individuals for the public service, and (2) the internal mechanisms we generate within organizations to foster cooperation in thought and action.

Professional Training

Public administration as a formal field of study is relatively youthful. The American Society for Public Administration, the main professional society of public administrators, has been in existence only since 1939. The oldest public administration degree-granting program is at the Maxwell School of Syracuse University, Syracuse, New York, which recently celebrated its fiftieth anniversary. Only within the past few years has there been a dramatic rise in the number of universities and colleges offering advanced degrees in public administration.

This rise is due partly to pressures upon universities to seek out added attractions in the face of declining enrollments. But it is also the result of a recognition of the importance of academic training for the public service and of the legitimate career development needs of those who wish to enter public employment. The increased emphasis upon training for public servants is an important bridge between the world of ideas and the world of application. However, for this training to achieve its full promise, academic programs must be eclectic, offering a broad range of skills and insights.

We have argued that public bureaucracy requires a collection of skills and behaviors reflecting machine, humane, and political values. It follows that the training and recruitment process for public servants — and the career development opportunities within bureaucracy — must provide for education in all three values. An example of this comprehensive, multifaceted approach to public administration training is reflected in the guidelines generated by the National Association of Schools of Public Affairs and Administration (NASPAA), which has been concerned that public administration training ranges from the excessively narrow to the unnecessarily abstract.[1] The guidelines stress the *knowledge, skills, public interest values,* and *behavior* needed in critical areas affecting public management and suggest questions that reflect desired traits in public managers.

(1)   Does the public administrator have a knowledge of the political, social, and economic values of the system, and can he ana-

lyze the implications of these? Does the administrator have a commitment to democratic values and beliefs, and understand the need for group access to the decision-making centers of government?

(2)   Can the public administrator apply both qualitative and quantitative skills to the solution of public problems? [Are] objectivity and impartial inquiry reflected in [his or her] behavior?

(3)   Does the public administrator understand the complexities of individual, group, and organizational interactions? Does [he or she] have a knowledge of individual motivational needs and group attributes that affect organizational behavior? Can [he or she] act to reconcile private interests and public needs?

(4)   Does the administrator have a knowledge of administrative and analytical tools to apply to policy analysis? Does the administrator reflect the behavior and public interest values necessary for application of policy analysis skills?

(5)   Does the public administrator have knowledge of management concepts and tools such as planning, organizational design, personnel administration, and budgeting? And are these skills and behavior complemented by public interest values of openness, high standards of performance, and citizen accountability?[2]

These areas cover the machine, humane, and political aspects of bureaucracy and comprise a model of public service training for both university and perhaps some in-house professional education.

Organizational Design

While eclectic education for the public service can make an important contribution, it must be matched by organizational frameworks that facilitate the interaction of machine, humane, and political techniques while minimizing the negative consequences of each. The classical division of organizations into units and subunits defined by specialization of tasks often may have to be modified to permit increased cross-fertilization of techniques, values, and processes.

Within traditional bureaucratic organizations protecting one's turf becomes an important and self-serving goal, while a broadened interpretation of the public interest takes a distant second place. The establishment of interdivisional task teams is just one of several supplements to traditional organizational designs. Comprised of individuals from different offices or agencies, and including various types of experts, these teams provide broader skills as well as less narrowly defined organizational interests. The effectiveness of team strategies, however, may depend on a modification of reward patterns. Individuals could be evaluated partly according to their team input rather than solely according to their individualized behavior. But for this to work the foundation of the personnel system — position classifications and job descriptions — must be modified from a narrow framework to a more flexible and comprehensive one.

The effective interaction of machine, humane, and political values sometimes requires systems of organization that help offset bureaucracy's tendency toward excessive specialization and isolation. Machine techniques must be constantly checked for usefulness. Humane values must demonstrate their contribution to improved public service. And political controls must be vigorously guarded and improved where necessary. This process cannot be achieved in an organization that affords inadequate structural opportunities for exchange. In brief, the flexibility, comprehensiveness, and capability that should be nurtured in our public servants through training must also be developed within organizational structures and, conversely, efforts to develop flexible organizational structures must be met by efforts to train individuals to operate effectively within them.

CONCLUSION

Problems confronting American society make vital the incorporation of machine, humane, and political values. The need for effective and efficient use of public resources, for example, comes not only from national economic problems but also from long-term international stresses as well. We live in an increasingly interdependent world. In illustration, the rise of the third world nations has produced higher domestic costs for products such as oil and stimulated various budgetary pressures.

Similarly, the continuing impact of civil rights and liberation movements here and abroad has made the demands for equality and individual rights permanent pressures upon public bureaucracy. Research findings, moreover, have demonstrated the significance of the human element in organizations from the standpoint of both productivity and responsiveness to democratic political values. Humane strategies, therefore, serve not only to improve the quality of life for government employees but also may serve to promote machine values and perhaps to increase responsiveness to legitimate political controls.

The size and complexity of modern government have made political bureaucracy values a central problem for the maintenance and enhancement of political democracy. The paramount role of public bureaucracy in the formulation and implementation of government policy affecting all facets of our society illustrates the point that the very possibility for continuing political democracy depends in large measure on effective multiple controls upon bureaucratic activities.

Yet these problems may be viewed not merely as threats but also as opportunities. The pressures to increase machine capabilities can improve the performance of public bureaucracy in such important areas as public health, education, and law enforcement. Demands for more humane administrative structures have the similar benefit of improving the quality of life for large numbers of citizens, and, if properly developed, for increasing the productive capacity of public organizations. Finally, the compelling need for achieving political bureaucracy goals provides the opportunity for change that can elevate responsiveness to needs external to the interests of bureaucracies and their employees, while fostering greater support for political institutions that have suffered a serious decline in public support.

In sum, economic constraints and political demands could make necessary change a difficult, tension-ridden process. Scarcer resources will require greater efficiency. Previously excluded groups and individuals will demand quicker action and greater involvement. And the complexity and size and role of public bureaucracy will compel greater accountability and control. The success of public bureaucracy in meeting these demands may well determine the future of the American political system.

NOTES

1. National Association of Schools of Public Affairs and Administration, *Guidelines and Standards for Professional Master's Degree Programs in Public Affairs/Public Administration.* (Washington, D.C.: National Association of Schools of Public Affairs and Administration, 1974).
2. Ibid.

For Further Reading

Altshuler, Alan A. *The Politics of the Federal Bureaucracy*. New York: Dodd, Mead, 1968.

Argyris, Chris. *Integrating the Individual and the Organization*. New York: Wiley, 1964.

Blau, Peter M., and Meyer, Marshall W. *Bureaucracy in Modern Society*. 2nd ed. New York: Random House, 1971.

Burch, John G. Jr., and Strater, Felix R., Jr. *Information Systems: Theory and Practice*. Santa Barbara, Calif.: Hamilton, 1974.

Dahl, Robert A., and Tufte, Edward F. *Size and Democracy*. Stanford: Stanford University Press, 1973.

Downs, Anthony. *Inside Bureaucracy*. Boston: Little, Brown, 1967.

Ellul, Jacques. *The Technological Society*. Trans. John Wilkenson. New York: Knopf, 1964.

Frederickson, George, ed. *Neighborhood Control in the 1970's: Politics, Administration and Citizen Participation*. New York: Chandler, 1973.

French, Wendell L., and Bell, Cecil H., Jr. *Organization Development: Behavioral Science for Organization Improvement*. Englewood Cliffs, N.J.: Prentice-Hall, 1973.

Gellhorn, Walter. *Ombudsmen and Others: Citizen's Protectors in Nine Countries*. Cambridge, Mass.: Harvard University Press, 1966.

Gerth, Han H., and Mills, C. Wright, trans. *From Max Weber: Essays in Sociology*. New York: Oxford University Press, 1946.

Gulick, Luther, and Urwick, L., eds. *Papers on the Science of Administration*. New York: Institute of Public Administration, 1937.

Herzberg, Frederick. *Work and the Nature of Man*. New York: World Publishing, 1966.

Huff, Darrell. *How to Lie with Statistics*. New York: Norton, 1954.

Katz, Daniel, and Kahn, Robert. *The Social Psychology of Organizations*. New York: Wiley, 1966.

Krislov, Samuel. *Representative Bureaucracy*. Englewood Cliffs, N.J.: Prentice-Hall, 1974.

Likert, Rensis. *The Human Organization.* New York: McGraw-Hill, 1967.

McGregor, Douglas. *The Human Side of Enterprise.* New York: McGraw-Hill, 1960.

Mainzer, Lewis C. *Political Bureaucracy.* Glenview, Ill.: Scott, Foresman, 1973

Mansfield, Harvey C. "Federal Executive Reorganization: Thirty Years of Experience." *Public Administration Review* 29 (July-August 1969): 332 - 345.

March, James G., and Simon, Herbert A. *Organizations.* New York: Wiley, 1958.

Michael, James R., ed. *Working on the System: A Comprehensive Manual for Citizen Access to Federal Agencies.* New York: Basic Books, 1974.

Milgram, Stanley. *Obedience to Authority: An Experimental View.* New York: Harper & Row, 1974.

Mosher, Frederick C. *Democracy and the Public Service.* New York: Oxford University Press, 1968.

National Commission on Productivity. *Productivity in State and Local Government.* Washington, D.C.: National Commission on Productivity, 1973.

Newland, Chester A., ed. "A Symposium: Productivity in Government." *Public Administration Review* 32 (November-December 1972): 739 - 750.

Perrow, Charles. *Complex Organizations: A Critical Essay.* Glenview, Ill.: Scott, Foresman, 1972.

Raiffa, Howard. *Decision Analysis: Introductory Lectures on Choices Under Uncertainty.* Reading, Mass.: Addison-Wesley, 1968.

Rawls, John. *A Theory of Justice.* Cambridge, Mass: Harvard University Press, 1971.

Redford, Emmette S. *Democracy in the Administrative State.* New York: Oxford University Press, 1969.

Redman, Eric. *The Dance of Legislation.* New York: Simon & Schuster, 1973.

Rivlin, Alice M. *Systematic Thinking for Social Action.* Washington, D.C.: Brookings Institution, 1971.

Rogers, Rolf. *Organizational Theory.* Boston: Allyn & Bacon, 1975.

Rourke, Francis E. *Bureaucracy, Politics, and Public Policy.* Boston: Little, Brown, 1969.

Schein, Edgar H. *Organizational Psychology.* Englewood Cliffs, N.J.: Prentice-Hall, 1971.

Simon, Herbert A. *Administrative Behavior: A Study of Decision-Making Processes in Administrative Organizations.* 2nd ed. New York: Free Press, 1966.

Stanley, David T., ed. "Symposium on the Merit Principle Today." *Public Administration Review* 34 (September-October 1974): 425 - 452.

Weiss, Carol H. *Evaluation Research: Methods for Assessing Program Effectiveness.* Englewood Cliffs, N.J.: Prentice-Hall, 1972.

Wildavsky, Aaron. *The Politics of the Budgetary Process.* 2nd ed. Boston: Little, Brown, 1971.

Yates, Douglas. *Neighborhood Democracy: The Politics and Impacts of Decentralization.* Lexington, Mass.: D. C. Heath, 1973.

Index